WALKING THE WORLDS

Volume 2 | Number 2 | Summer 2016

PHILOSOPHY AND POLYTHEISM

Walking the Worlds is a serious, peer-reviewed journal devoted to the exploration of spiritwork and polytheism from a broad spectrum of perspectives, traditions and disciplines. It is published twice a year on the solstices.

Managing Editor: Galina Krasskova
Editor-in-Chief: H. Jeremiah Lewis
Editorial Board: Edward Butler, Ph.D., P. Sufenas Virius Lupus, Ph.D.
Designer: Sarah Kate Istra Winter

Each issue of *Walking the Worlds* focuses on a different theme; please keep these in mind when submitting essays (poetry and fiction are not currently being accepted). The deadline for the Winter issue is October 1, and for the Summer issue it is May 1. Accepted submissions receive set monetary compensation, all rights reverting back to the author after six months. Essays should run approximately 2500-7000 words, excluding notes, and be accompanied by a brief biography and abstract. Illustrations and artwork may be accepted on a case-by-case basis. Please visit our website for full submission guidelines.

Upcoming Themes
Winter 2016: Ecstatic Practices
Summer 2017: Divination
Winter 2017: Text and Tradition

Single issues are available for $20, and a full year subscription (two issues) for $30. Back issues are also available. Orders can be placed online. Appropriate advertisements may be accepted, with rates being $25 for a quarter-page, $45 for a half-page, and $75 for a full page. Specifications can be found on our website.

For more information, visit **WalkingTheWorlds.com**.

Published by:
Walking the Worlds
P.O. Box 228
Beacon, New York 12508

CONTENTS

Introduction

EDWARD P. BUTLER

Philosophy was born not in one place or historical moment alone, but independently in multiple sites, even if we keep ourselves to a restrictive definition. Should we broaden our notion of what constitutes philosophical inquiry, then it is to be found everywhere there are wisdom traditions that articulate a set of concepts or categories applicable to Being as such, and these are virtually ubiquitous. Clearly, therefore, philosophy emerged in polytheistic civilizations, since polytheism was the default mode of religious life for all but a relatively brief time and in a circumscribed territory. For too long, however, philosophy in the West—which has, of course, promoted itself aggressively as the home of philosophy in the strictest sense—due to its long alliance with Christian monotheism, and the luxury afforded Christian philosophers for centuries of conceiving their religious Other purely in terms of other monotheisms, has regarded the polytheistic conditions of its emergence as at best accidental. Or, worse, philosophy has seen something of its essence to lie in its successful overcoming of polytheism, and its historical alliance with monotheisms as a matter predestined. This is not the place to restate the many confusions and untruths embodied in this view. Let it suffice, rather, to say that the circumstance of a revival of polytheism in the West affords the opportunity for comprehensive reexamination of the role of philosophy both in relation to historical polytheisms and in the lives of contemporary polytheists. As a practicing polytheist for my entire adult life, and a philosopher by vocation, let me say that this project is close to my own heart, and that it has barely begun.

The contributions to this issue come both from within and from outside the polytheist community. Some of them do the work of philosophy directly, while others intervene in the history of philosophy or the history of ideas more broadly, to reshape these narratives, or to intervene in contemporary debates, whether those concerning religion, which are virtually always conducted in ignorance of the polytheistic position, or in other matters of concern to contemporary thought, and which can be informed by the novel perspective polytheism offers. Some of them, though not strictly philosophical in topic or method, offer us a glimpse into the processes internal to religious experience by virtue of which philosophy may be thought to have emerged, in response to the conceptualization of theophanic experience.

Theophany inspires in its reception both a practical and a theoretical response. Philosophy begins, Aristotle says, from awe, and there can have been, and still can be no more awesome experience than the encounter of living Gods. The results of this experience have never been limited to the institution of cults, but have always also brought in their wake conceptual determinations of the cosmos, of the social space, and of the psyche. These concepts, given the social space to develop, eventually acquire a degree of autonomy from particularly religious concerns that make it seem as though they can be separated entirely from their religious roots. For that matter, the same processes allow these concepts eventually to be considered in separation from virtually *all* the cultural circumstances of their emergence. Hence these concepts and categories can be translated into foreign languages, patient intellectual consideration coaxing their cultural dependences to yield up their intelligible content and make it available to grasp by 'outsiders.' But the future of philosophy does not lie solely in this project and the denuded concepts resulting from it, any more than it lies in the refusal of translation and the insulation of traditions from one another. It cannot, because neither of these will satisfy the imperatives of thought, which can neither be restrained from seeking out and exploring the Other, nor be contented with any solution to the question of its origins so shallow as the narrative of emancipation, either from theophany as an existential determinant of human life, or from the cultural difference of which polytheism is at once the frankest, and the purest expression.

This issue's exceptionally diverse articles highlight many different ways in which philosophy and polytheism can inform one another. Neve Antheus' "The God of Queer Theory: A Dionysian Exegesis" looks at the history of a particular branch of contemporary philosophy through a new lens, seeing in the emergence of queer theory the sign of the resurgence of the God Dionysos in the world. Virginia Carper's "Romans, Gods, Politics, and Bathrooms" thinks about how devotion might constructively inform political activism, treating the successful campaign to eliminate pay toilets in the U.S. as manifesting the values of the Gods of the Capitoline and Aventine Triads, while "Hearing the Roar of Godzilla: Looking for the Gods in Pop Culture" draws on her personal cultic experience in the effort to articulate categories by which entities presencing through popular culture may be integrated into theocentric practice. Steven Dillon's "An Ontological Argument for Polytheism" presents an innovative polytheistic reformulation of one of the most debated arguments in the last millennium of Western philosophy. Paul T.M. Jackson's "The Polytheism of the Epicureans" is a groundbreaking investigation of Epicurean theology, arguing that Epicureans were not only sincere theists, but that the reality of the Gods and the experience of them plays a crucial role in the Epicurean project of *ataraxia*. Galina Krasskova's "The Paradoxical Ambivalence of Giving: Seneca and the Virtue of Clemency" examines the asymmetrical relationship inherent in *clementia*, an asymmetry that also pervades the relationship between mortals and the Gods. Dagulf Loptson's "Iðunn: Goddess of the Heart" is a paradigm of the mythological exegesis that was, and is, a taproot for philosophical thought, in addition to its specific concern with the heart/mind, the instrument of philosophy. P. Sufenas Virius Lupus' "'Would the Real Philosopher-King Please Stand Up?': Hadrian and the Philosophers" makes a case for the philosophical engagement of this most pious of emperors, and presents a translation of an eclectic philosophical text featuring Hadrian as interlocutor. Ludwig Maisel's "Presocratic Theology and the Great Tablet of Thurii" works toward freeing the Presocratic philosophers from the monotheizing/atheizing preconceptions of modern scholars and argues for the relevance of strains of Presocratic philosophical thought to a Bacchic eschatological text, illustrating the porous boundaries between philosophy and theology in a polytheistic context. Julie McCord's "Cheaper by the Dozen: On Swinburne's Argument Against Polytheism" defends Hume's ironic inference of polytheism from Christian teleological arguments against Swinburne's criticisms. Erik Meganck's "Theisms" explores the significance of the very notion of polytheism to the critique of metaphysics, providing an alternative to other approaches to the philosophical revaluation of polytheism on display in this issue, which involve the embrace of classical metaphysics. Wayland Skallagrimsson's "The Dawkins Delusion" critiques the New Skeptics, whose arguments play an outsized role in a cultural moment polarized between dogmatic monotheisms and naïve scientism. Finally, my own contribution to this issue, "Polytheism and the *Euthyphro*," argues that Plato's dialogue, generally treated today as a radical critique of Hellenic polytheism would have been, and still can be, read quite differently without the prejudices the modern reader unthinkingly brings to it.

Edward P. Butler
Associate Editor
June 20, 2016

The God of Queer Theory: A Dionysian Exegesis

NEVE ANTHEUS

Since its beginning, with the publication of *Epistemology of the Closet*, Dionysos can be found just below the surface of the modern philosophical discipline of queer theory. A certain current of Dionysian influence spans generations and culminates in queer theory as one of its many expressions. By looking at its relationship to figures including Friedrich Nietzsche, Gilles Deleuze, Guy Hocquenghem, Eve Sedgwick and others, we can begin to trace the labyrinthine dance of queer theory and the God. The myths and mysteries of Dionysos could perhaps be used to examine and even answer the questions posed by contemporary queer theorists.

While one can justifiably and quite fruitfully engage with the question at hand—polytheism and philosophy—by analyzing the polytheistic worldview and practices of the philosophers of antiquity, or or by looking to what contemporary polytheists in enduring or revived traditions are doing in the field, I'm interested here in a different sort of inquiry. Taking for granted that the Gods have an existence independent of human conception of them, and also that for their own reasons they have an interest in our activity (even if we cannot always perceive or comprehend those reasons) it follows that the relationship of the Gods to philosophy is not limited to those bookend periods where 'out' polytheists have openly philosophized. My wager here is that an inquiry into those opaque periods, the intermediary times between late antiquity and the present, might prove particularly meaningful; that the places where the Gods work in secret might yield powerful revelations. I'll go further and say that a polytheist approach to philosophy, if it is to put the Gods first, has a particular need to peel back the mask of supposedly secular philosophy and reveal whatever mystery might be waiting just beneath. My intention presently is to gaze into the hollow eyes of one such mask—queer theory—and look for what (or Who) might be returning my gaze.

* * * * * * *

In 1990, an English professor named Eve Kosofsky Sedgwick published a book entitled *Epistemology of the Closet*, and in doing so helped to found the discipline of queer theory. A full treatment of Sedgwick's dense and groundbreaking book is beyond the scope of these pages, but it is worth at least noting that *Epistemology* attempted a vicious critique of all that which until then was held as axiomatic within philosophy and left uncriticized in critical theory. In particular, Sedgwick aimed to undermine the supposed naturalness and givenness of the heteronormative and binarist foundations of modernity. This skepticism and methodological undermining of axiomatic binaries and self-confirming truisms about gender and sexuality was complemented by the publication of Judith Butler's *Gender Trouble* in the same year. Together these books tore a hole in the prevailing discourses surrounding the study of gender and sexuality through which they were able to pull queer theory into the world. From those early days onward, queer theory would aim to undermine binary thinking wherever it occurred and to pose instead a theory of gender and sexuality as fluid, multiple, paradoxical and and above-all performative.

By now I hope to have caught the attention of Dionysian and pro-Dionysian readers alike. (As a consequence I may have also lost some duotheist readers; sorry duotheists!) Those still following along may notice in these originary blows of the discipline an implication that has led some to declare reading queer theory to be a devotional activity in honor of Dionysos.[1] I said already that Eve Sedgwick came, hammer in hand, to smash binaries. She does this by closely reading a handful of authors: Proust, Wilde and (significantly to the task at hand) Friedrich Nietzsche. My intention here is not to argue for or reiterate the significance of Nietzsche as a sort of 'pagan' philosopher, nor will I attempt to prove Nietzsche's polytheism. These aspects of his thought, and our indebtedness to those aspects, are succinctly elaborated elsewhere.[2] Rather, what I will attempt to reveal is something significant about his Dionysianism and its meaning when invoked here at the origins of queer theory.

In the chapter "Some Binarisms (II): Wilde, Nietzsche, and the Sentimental Relations of the Male Body," Sedgwick uses Nietzsche, often against himself, to illustrate the absurdity and self-defeating logic of many binaries, especially those held up as natural in Nietzsche's thought. It's worth listing them: health/illness, invention/recognition, wholeness/decadence, abstraction/figuration, same/different, homo/hetero, direct/vicarious, art/kitsch, sentimental/anti-senti-mental, and most notably considering the occasion of this text, Greek/Christian. Sedgwick goes after those binaries in Nietzsche specifically by teasing out and illustrating his complicity with and even not-so-veiled desire for those sides of the binary derided in his writing. Nietzsche figures as a sort of fool,

---

[1] See for example "Devotional Activities for Dionysians" in *Ecstatic* by H. Jeremiah Lewis.

[2] For example, by his very inclusion as a Hero in the Starry Bull Tradition, or as articulated in Finnchuill's lovely "Nietzsche & Dionysos," (https://finnchuillsmast.wordpress.com/2015/12/05/nietzsche-dionysos/)

saying one thing while pantomiming its opposite. Singing of health while suffering from illness, decrying decadence while being wholly fixated on it, etc. Sedgwick plays with this to great effect, and with a fair bit of humor. Her funniest moments all amount to a sort of teasing illustration of the homo-eroticism that Nietzsche laces into his words, almost in spite of himself. She jokes that a phrase index to Nietzsche could easily be confused with Proust's *Sodome et Gomorrhe*. She also draws special attention to the pervasive occurrence of the disrobed male body, or the male body in agony/ecstasy. She indicts in his anti-sentimentality a type of sentimentality entirely wrapped up in these homo-erotics:

> Nietzsche's most effective intensities of both life and writing were directed toward other men and toward the male body... Nietzsche offers writing of an open, Whitmanlike seductiveness, some of the loveliest there is, about the joining of men with men, but he does so in the stubborn, perhaps even studied absence of any explicit generalizations, celebrations, analyses, reifications of those bonds as specifically same-sex ones. Accordingly, he has been important for a male-erotic-centered anarchist tradition extending from Adolf Brand and Benedict Friedlander through Gilles Deleuze and Felix Guattari, that has a principled resistance to any minoritizing model of homosexual identity.[3]

Something in reading this seizes me. Well, a few things, some of which I'll return to later. For now, I'm captured by this affect of an overflowing homo-eroticism which resists self-awareness as such. Sedgwick locates this cathexis in Nietzsche first and foremost in his writings about the deity who would prove to be a constant fixation and companion until his end: Dionysos: "Nietzsche instead associates instance after instance of homoerotic desire, although never named as such, with the precious virility of Dionysiac initiates or of ancient warrior classes."[4]

Dionysos' centrality here will be intuitive to those familiar with the God and his mysteries. The erotic figures strongly in his myths, but precisely that aspect of the erotic which draws one into an adventure, which borders on the chthonic, which undermines the boundaries between self and other. Sedgwick demonstrates this paradox of desire by posing Nietzsche's 'Hellenism,' with its sign of the male body, as being also tied up in Nietzsche's attention paid to superfluous Catholic depictions of the body of Christ. She plays against one another his various identifications of himself, at different moments, with

---

[3] Sedgwick, *Epistemology of the Closet*, p. 133.
[4] Ibid, p. 134.

'Dionysos,' but also 'the crucified,' but always with the "unclothed or unclothable male body, often in extremis and/or in ecstasy, prescriptively meant to be gazed at and adored."[5] Sedgwick here deploys a schema where the adoration of the ecstatic body in Nietzsche is able to overcome, explode or subvert otherwise stable dualisms. He is able to experience himself as other. She takes this mode to its conclusion by turning it on itself. She suspends her analysis to momentarily don Nietzsche himself as a mask and to speak through him. She says, paraphrasing and quoting Nietzsche:

> I do not desire, let us say Wagner; I *am* Wagner. In the loving panegyric of *Wagner in Bayreuth,* 'I am the only person referred to—one may ruthlessly insert my name ... wherever the text gives the word 'Wagner' ... 'Supposing I had baptized my Zarathustra with another name, for example with the name Richard Wagner, the perspicuity of two millennia would not have sufficed to divine that the author of *Human, All Too Human* is the visionary of Zarathustra' ... 'I here too avoided the little word "I" ... I do not desire Zarathustra, though 'we celebrate the feast of feasts; friend Zarathustra has come, the guest of guests! Now the world is laughing, the dread curtain is rent, the wedding day has come for light and darkness'—rather at the moments of definitional stress, I *am* Zarathustra. I do not desire Dionysos, for all the gorgeous eroticism...

Here, a close reader can almost feel Eve lose a firm grasp on herself. The Nietzsche she wears as a mask has outgrown its limits. The boundaries that delineate 'I' from 'Nietzsche' from 'Dionysos' grow permeable and an ecstatic quality tinges her words. There are several slippages here: me, citing Sedgwick, performing as Nietzsche, describing Dionysos. She pushes beyond her play-acting to channel Nietzsche in his own words in gorgeous and erotic praise of:

> the great hidden one, the tempter god... whose voice knows how to descend into the underworld of every soul, who says no word and gives no glance in which there lies no touch of enticement... the genius of the heart... who divines the hidden and forgotten treasure, the drop of goodness and sweet spirituality under thick and opaque ice, and is a divining-rod for every grain of gold... the genius of the heart from whose touch everyone goes away... newer to himself than before, broken open, blown upon and sounded out by a thawing wind, more uncertain perhaps, more delicate, more fragile, more broken, but full of hopes that as yet have no names, full of new will and current, full of

---

[5] Ibid, p. 140.

new ill will and counter-current… Dionysos, that great ambiguous and tempter god.[6]

When the mask speaks, it speaks as a void. The increasing difficulty required to separate Nietzsche's words from Sedgwick's, here where words reach a fever pitch, is a testament to the 'blowing open' and 'thawing' that she cites in Nietzsche's recognition of the work of the God. This act of divination, spoken of above, locates that 'hidden and forgotten treasure': ecstatic gnosis, knowledge of a God by way of stepping outside one's self. This openness and receptivity, and the subsequent temporal loss of identity, is precisely what is at stake, for Sedgwick and for Nietzsche, in the great queer work of imploding the boundaries which delineate neat dualisms (self and other, performance and identity, then and now, mask and void). Returning slowly from channeling Nietzsche, Sedgwick continues:

> – no, in the last analysis I *am* Dionysos. (The dedicatory phrases, for instance, that begin the 'Dionysos' section of *The Will to Power,* 'To him that has turned out so well, who does my heart good, carved from wood that is hard, gentle, and fragrant—in whom even the nose takes pleasure,' turn up almost verbatim in the 'Why I am so Wise' section of *Ecce Homo,* with the notation 'I have just described *myself.*') Indeed, 'What is disagreeable and offends my modesty is that at bottom I am every name in history' … Nietzsche as the *contra* Wagner; '*Dionysos against the Crucified*' (the last words of *Ecce Homo*); Nietzsche, in perhaps the most central turn, as the Anti-Christ.[7]

Those fluent in Dionysian myth will surely recognize here a comparison readily presenting itself: that of Nietzsche and Pentheus. Pentheus, as told by Euripides, in his need for order and control, becomes fixated on the imagined outside of that order: Dionysos and his Bacchae. Driven mad with paranoia and an unsatiated lust to witness the darkest corners of his own fantasy world, the young and doomed king of Thebes soon finds himself dressed in the ceremonial garb of the Maenads, caught in a tree, and ritually torn apart. In short, he is initiated into the mysteries that he both would banish but also cannot help being drawn into.[8] Like Pentheus, Nietzsche himself plays the part of the mirror image of his own demons.

In 1886, Nietzsche would revisit *The Birth of Tragedy* in a new introduction wherein he would self-critically describe it as:

---

[6] Ibid, p. 162.

[7] Ibid, pp. 162-163.

[8] For more on Pentheus see: "Pentheus as Hypostasis of Dionysos" by Guy Smoot.

a book for initiates, 'music' for those dedicated to music, those who are closely related to begin with on the basis of common and rare aesthetic experiences... Still the effect of the book proved and proves that it had a new knack for seeking out fellow rhapsodizers and for luring them on to new secret paths, and dancing places. What found expression here was anyways—this was admitted with as much curiosity as antipathy—a *strange* voice, the disciple of a still 'unknown God'... here was a spirit with strange, still nameless needs.[9]

A book for initiates, written by a disciple of an unknown God with nameless needs. How does Nietzsche unearth these names? He does so by gazing into a mirror. "If we have virtues we shall presumably have only such virtues as have learned to get along with our most secret and heartfelt inclinations, with our most fervent needs. Very well, let us look for them within our labyrinths!"[10]

And so in Sedgwick's reading we see several Nietzsches: Nietzsche the fool, Nietzsche in the labyrinth, Nietzsche as Pentheus, Nietzsche the initiate, queer Nietzsche. What's more, in addition to inaugurating queer theory as a discipline, Sedgwick demonstrated what would quickly become its defining methodology: the search for hidden queer content in the literature of 'the closet.' The descent into the labyrinth.

* * * * * * *

Eve gives us a thread to follow. I cited it above, but you may have missed it. There is a whole tradition indebted to Nietzsche: an anarchistic and queer one, motivated by eroticism but also attempting to avoid identification with those erotics. Sedgwick begins this tradition with Adolf Brand, the publisher of *Der Eigene*,[11] published between 1896 and 1932. *Eigene* holds the honor of being the first openly homosexual newspaper in the world. It also, interestingly, is responsible for propagating early on an individualist anarchism inspired by the previously less-known Max Stirner. Sedgwick is undeniably correct in noting Nietzsche's significance to *Eigene* and its milieu, but Nietzsche was not the only influence. Besides Stirner, we could add the early Uranian texts, Shelly and Byron, and a newfound romantic 'Hellenism.'[12] The pagan dimension of this

---

[9] Nietzsche in "Attempt at Self-Criticism," the 1886 introduction to a reissue of *The Birth of Tragedy*, as cited by Sedgwick in *Epistemology of the Closet*, p. 167.

[10] From *Beyond Good and Evil*, as cited in *Epistemology*, p. 170.

[11] For more on *Eigene* see Hubert Kennedy's *Homosexuality and Male Bonding in Pre-Nazi Germany*, 1992.

[12] For an interesting speculative treatment of the potential interplay of these sources, see "Hellenism and Homoeroticism in Shelley and His Circle" by John Lauritsen, *Journal of Homosexuality* 49(3-4): 357-76 (Brooklyn, NY: Autonomedia, 2004), pp. 29-39.

tradition is noticeably omitted by Sedgwick, despite its clear prominence (just look at all the Satyrs dancing across the pages of *der Eigene!*).

Between *Eigene* and Deleuze and Guattari, there are quite a few links in the chain worth naming and putting into dialogue with one another. We might add Edward Carpenter, the prolific poet who wrote many texts include "Civilization: its Cause and Cure," "Pagan and Christian Creeds," and also, interestingly enough, an early monograph on Shelley teasing out the queerness latent in the poet's life and work (a notable early deployment of the method that Sedgwick would cement a century later). Carpenter was an early advocate of free love, a non-binary view of gender, and a return to pre-Christian religious traditions. Though hardly a Nietzschean, the interplay of Nietzsche and Carpenter created a space of intense fecundity. From that space, and drawing heavily from both, we see a branch of this unnamed tradition spanning the better part of the following century. There's Emma Goldman, famed anarcha-feminist and "morning star of sexual anarchy," who toured the U.S. lecturing on reproductive freedom, free love, and Nietzsche. Sadly, all her notes and written materials for the Nietzsche lectures were seized by the police and none now remain. Thus, like a latter day Sappho, we are left to piece those teachings together based on fragments and commentary by those who attended the lectures.[13] From the same intellectual parentage—Carpenter and Nietzsche—we can trace the Order of Woodcraft Chivalry, Walter Otto, Károly Kerényi, Arthur Evans, D.H. Lawrence and many others. What's notable in this motley crew is decisive and recurring emphasis on both the 'Hellenic' and the queer. Many place an emphasis on the sexual and religious practices of ancient Greece, and most pay particular attention to Dionysos.

* * * * * * *

I've traced, if hastily, the threads spun together after Nietzsche in the German and English speaking world, but we haven't yet touched on the French duo who wraps up Sedgwick's neat package. If I could only afford to move through the preceding links in the chain rather quickly, it is worth slowing down here. But before doing so, it is worth noting the events and circumstances of Nietzsche's afterlife in France. In 1945 Georges Bataille wrote *On Nietzsche*, in the final months of the Nazi occupation of France. He published it in an attempt to redeem Nietzsche by debunking the Nazi appropriation of his thought. In doing so, he made it possible for French intellectuals to engage with him once more.[14]

---

[13] Leigh Starcross attempts such a reconstruction in "Reconstructing Emma Goldman's Nietzsche lectures" in *I am not a Man, I am Dynamite!* John Moore (ed.), 2004.

[14] There is obviously much more to say about the relationship of Bataille and Nietzsche, as well as Bataille and Dionysos—for example, his role in founding the secret society *Acephale* which worshiped a syncretic Nietzsche-Dionysos. But that is another paper…

After Bataille we get a whole host of French philosophers and critical theorists now empowered to incorporate Nietzschean thinking into their own and to great effect. Michel Foucault, for example, secures the return and permutation of Nietzsche's method of genealogy. This method, coupled with his own classicism and interest in ancient Greece will lead Foucault to write his *History of Sexuality*, without which it is unlikely we would have the queer theory of the subsequent decades.

Our present inquiry turns, not to Foucault, but rather toward his contemporaries, Deleuze and Guattari. Though most well known for their perverse reading of Marx and Freud, *Capitalism and Schizophrenia,* they are, by their own account, wholly indebted to Nietzsche for the most vital elements of their thinking, first among those elements the concept of 'becoming.' Becoming, in D&G and following Nietzsche, is opposed to static or fixed Being. It is the entrance of change, flux, perversity, multiplicity, recurrence and paradox into Being. It is not an end, but a process. Not an identity but a trajectory. (If this bears a similarity to the project of our queer theorists as discussed above, remind yourself that there are no coincidences in the labyrinth!) Dionysos and his divine love, Ariadne, both figure prominently in Deleuze's book length treatment of Nietzsche, *Nietzsche & Philosophy*. The book is well worth the read, at points ecstatic in its pace,[15] but I want to dwell for a moment longer on Deleuze's reading of Nietzsche in the eponymous chapter found in *Pure Immanence: Essays on a Life*. In *Pure Immanence*, Deleuze begins by teasing out some of the binaries that Sedgwick would return to 25 years later. Regarding sickness/health he says:

---

[15] For example: "The labyrinth designates the eternal return itself: circular, it is not the lost way but the way which leads us back to the same point, to the same instant which is, which was and which will be. But, more profoundly, from the perspective of the constitution of the eternal return, the labyrinth is becoming, the affirmation of becoming. Being comes from becoming, it is affirmed of becoming itself, in as much as the affirmation of becoming is the object of another affirmation (Ariadne's thread). As long as Ariadne remained with Theseus the labyrinth was interpreted the wrong way round, it opened out onto higher values, the thread was the thread of the negative and *ressentiment*, the moral thread. But Dionysos teaches Ariadne his secret: the true labyrinth is Dionysos himself, the true thread is the thread of affirmation. 'I am your Labyrinth.' Dionysos is the labyrinth and the bull, becoming and being, but becoming is only being insofar as its affirmation is itself affirmed. Dionysos not only asks Ariadne to hear but to affirm affirmation: 'You have little ears, you have my ears: put a shrewd word there.' The ear is labyrinthine, the ear is the labyrinth of becoming or the maze of affirmation. The labyrinth is what leads us to being, the only being is that of becoming, the only being is that of the labyrinth itself. But Ariadne has Dionysos' ears: affirmation must itself be affirmed so that it can be the affirmation of being. Ariadne puts a shrewd word in Dionysos' ear. That is to say: having herself heard Dionysian affirmation, she makes it the object of a second affirmation heard by Dionysos."

With Nietzsche, everything is mask. His health was a first mask for his genius; his suffering, a second mask, both for his genius and for his health. Nietzsche didn't believe in the unity of a self and didn't experience it. Subtle relations of power and of evaluation between different 'selves' that conceal but also express other kinds of forces— forces of life, forces of thought—such is Nietzsche's conception, his way of living. Wagner, Schopenhauer, and even Paul Ree were experienced as his own masks. After 1890, his friends sometimes thought his madness was his final mask. He had written: 'And sometimes madness itself is the mask that hides a knowledge that is fatal and too sure.' In fact, it is not. Rather, it marks the moment when the masks, no longer shifting and communicating, merge into a death-like rigidity. Among the strongest moments of Nietzsche's philosophy are the pages where he speaks of the need to be masked, of the virtue and positivity of masks, of their ultimate importance. Nietzsche's own beauty resided in his hands, his ears, his eyes (he compliments himself on his ears; he sees small ears as being labyrinthine secrets that lead to Dionysos).[16]

In his lifelong struggles with illness and madness, Nietzsche experienced a transmutation, an exaltation, a 'strange wellbeing.' "His suffering continued, but it was often dominated by an 'enthusiasm'[17] that affected his very body."[18] It was in this state, while walking along the lake of Silvaplana where Nietzsche was overwhelmed by the revelation of the eternal return and with the inspiration for *Zarathustra*. The remainder of Nietzsche's life would be characterized by a tragic interplay of these forces, this game of masks, culminating in the Turin incident and his ultimate breakdown.

The overall paralysis marks the moment when illness exits from the work, interrupts it, and makes its continuation impossible. Nietzsche's

---

[16] Deleuze, *Pure Immanence*, pp. 59-60.

[17] Enthusiasm: c. 1600, from Middle French *enthousiasme* (16c.) and directly from Late Latin *enthusiasmus*, from Greek *enthousiasmos* "divine inspiration, enthusiasm (produced by certain kinds of music, etc.)," from *enthousiazein* "be inspired or possessed by a god, be rapt, be in ecstasy," from *entheos* "divinely inspired, possessed by a god," from *en* "in" (see **en-** (2)) + *theos* "god" (see **theo-**). Acquired a derogatory sense of "excessive religious emotion through the conceit of special revelation from God" (1650s) under the Puritans; generalized meaning "fervor, zeal" (the main modern sense) is first recorded 1716.

[18] Ibid, p. 60.

last letters[19] testify to this extreme moment, thus they still belong to his work; they are a part of it. As long as Nietzsche could practice the art of shifting perspectives, from health to illness and back, he enjoyed, sick as he may have been, the 'great health' that made his work possible. But when this art failed him, when the masks were conflated into that of a dunce and a buffoon under the effect of some organic process, the illness itself became inseparable from the end of his oeuvre (Nietzsche had spoken of madness as a 'comic solution,' as a final farce).[20]

For Deleuze, Nietzsche's life was inseparable from his philosophy, and it was precisely this space of indistinction and interplay that made Nietzsche so dangerous as a philosopher. The intertwining of life and thought, for Deleuze, is the precondition for becoming. It is also a great peril to the life of the thinker, as evidenced in Nietzsche's final days. It is a dangerous work, and still it figures as a reason for a type of model in Deleuze's mind for the future of philosophy.

> The philosopher of the future is the explorer of ancient worlds, of peaks and caves, who creates only inasmuch as he recalls something that has been essentially forgotten. That something, according to Nietzsche, is the unity of life and thought. It is a complex unity: one step for life, one step for thought. Modes of life inspire ways of thinking; modes of thinking create ways of living. Life *activates* thought, and thought in turn *affirms* life. Of this pre-Socratic unity we no longer have even the slightest idea. We now have only instances where thought bridles and mutilates life, making it sensible, and where life takes revenge and drives thought mad, losing itself along the way. Now we only have the choice between mediocre lives and mad thinkers. Lives that are too docile for thinkers, and thoughts too mad for the living.[21]

Primary in this life-philosophy is Nietzsche's conception of the will. Deleuze takes pains to clarify that the will to power is not the will to dominate, not to covet or to take, but rather to create and to give. "Power, as a will to power, is not that which the will wants, but *that which* wants in the will (Dionysos himself). The will to power is the differential element from which derive the forces at work, as well as their respective quality in a complex whole.

---

[19] These are the letters wherein Nietzsche regularly signs his name "Dionysos," "Dionysos Zagreus," etc.
[20] Ibid, pp. 64-65.
[21] Ibid, pp. 66-67.

Thus it is always given as a mobile, aerial, pluralist element."[22] For Deleuze, Dionysos is not only desire, but desire as an active force, desire armed with will. Desire figures prominently as a force in Deleuze's thought, but few to no readers of D&G acknowledge the fundamentally theistic underpinning of this concept. That desire is a force, but also has desires of its own, "that which wants in the will." He names this desire of desire as Dionysos. Philosophy, especially after Freud, speaks of desire as a vast powerful force, but only as cut off from its own desire. Deleuze is the first to return desire to its agency, to speak not only of it but to it. In doing so, he displaces the humanist trappings which would limit desire as something internal to us, a consequence of human biology. Instead, he paints desire in all its glory: expansive, complex, multiple, itself full of desire and permeating the boundaries that separate us and the world. This plural, mobile nature emphasized by Deleuze resonates with Dionysos' many associations as a wanderer, an outsider, multi-formed, many-named, etc. Behind the subjectivist mask of desire, now fallen aside, we see Dionysos Himself, and he is affirmation, but affirmation of difference.

Deleuze reads the Nietzschean transvaluation of values as an active becoming of forces, a triumph of affirmation in the will to power, Dionysos himself. But affirmation of what? Of Life! Of the Earth! The wild! But, he clarifies, never as monisms, not as the One, but as the multiple, the plural, becoming, multiplicity. "In the affirmation of the multiple lies the practical joy of the diverse. Joy emerges as the sole motive for philosophizing."[23] This joy, and this desire for desire, this double affirmation is realized in Ariadne, whose relationship with Dionysos is described by Deleuze as "a play of mirrors." This doubling, these reflections, again prefigure the sort of mirroring that we read about in Sedgwick. Pentheus recurs. The stable boundaries between self and other are once more subject to Dionysian transmutation in Nietzsche. As Deleuze tells it:

> Dionysos was defined through his opposition to Socrates even more than through his alliance with Apollo; Socrates judged and condemned life in the name of higher values, but Dionysos had the sense that life is not to be judged, that it is just enough, holy enough, in itself. And as Nietzsche progresses further in his work, the real opposition appears to him: no longer Dionysos versus Socrates, but Dionysos versus the Crucified. Their martyrdom seems the same, but the interpretation, the evaluation of it are different: on one side, a testimony against life, a vengeance that consists in denying life; on the other, the affirmation of life, the affirmation of becoming and multiplicity that extends even in

---

[22] Ibid, pp. 73-74.
[23] Ibid, p. 84.

the very laceration and scattered limbs of Dionysos. Dance, lightness, laughter are the properties of Dionysos. As power of affirmation, Dionysos evokes a mirror within his mirror, a ring within his ring: a second affirmation is needed for affirmation to be itself affirmed. Dionysos has a fiancee, Ariadne... Ariadne completes the set of relations that define Dionysos and the Dionysian philosopher.[24]

It is here, more than anywhere else, that the underlying polytheism in Deleuze, by way of Nietzsche, emerges ("Given the preceding terminological precisions, we can avoid reducing Nietzsche's thought to a simple dualism, for, as we shall see, affirmation is itself essentially multiple and pluralist, whereas negation is always one, or heavily monist."[25]). I said polytheist, though I have up until now recited an almost henotheistic line of argument. Dionysos clearly holds a central place within this queer cosmology, but the cosmology itself assumes polytheism. I say polytheism precisely because he exists in a complex web of relationships that always already includes other forces, powers and spirits: Ariadne, Apollo, the Crucified, Zarathustra, Nietzsche. The space opened by Nietzsche, by way of Deleuze and Sedgwick, within queer theory as a single discipline could similarly be opened up in any field where humans attempt to bring our necessarily limited understandings and perceptions to bear on an infinite and mysterious universe. In this vast field of divergent, sovereign, and relational forces, Dionysos is one among many. Deleuze elaborates:

> Multiplicity is no longer answerable to the One, nor is becoming answerable to being... Or, as Nietzsche puts it, the necessity of chance. Dionysos is a player. The real player makes of chance an object of affirmation: he affirms the fragments, the elements of chance; from this affirmation is born the necessary number, which brings back the throw of the dice. We now see what this third figure is: the play of the eternal return. This return is precisely the Being of becoming, the one of multiplicity, the necessity of chance. Thus we must not make of the eternal return a *return of the same*. To do this would be to misunderstand the form of the transmutation and the change in the fundamental relationship, for the same does not preexist the diverse... *It is not the same that comes back*, since the coming back is the original form of the same, which is said only of the diverse, the multiple, the becoming.[26]

Labyrinths, masks, rings, mirrors, dice, dance, laughter, returns: the stuff of Dionysian mystery fills the pages. These symbols, so vital to the various

---

[24] Ibid, pp. 85-86.
[25] Ibid, p. 74.
[26] Ibid, pp. 86-87.

Dionysian mystery cults of antiquity,[27] return here in Nietzsche and Deleuze. This emphasis on chance and fragments and reflections is necessary in a worldview devoid of a single omnipotent and omniscient God. The death of a monotheistic God, as told by Nietzsche, makes space for desire within the divine and thus requires movement of the chaotic cosmos. From affirmation to affirmation, everything dances. Deleuze views this dancing as a wheel:

> The eternal return should be compared to a wheel whose movement is endowed with a centrifugal force that drives out everything negative. Because Being is affirmed of becoming, it expels all that contradicts affirmation, all the forms of nihilism and reaction; bad conscience, resentment...we will see them only once... How can reaction and nihilism, how can negation come back, since the eternal return is the Being that is only said of affirmation, and becoming in action? A centrifugal wheel, 'supreme constellation of Being, that no wish can attain, that no negation can soil.' The eternal return is repetition; but it is the repetition that selects, the repetition that saves. The prodigious secret of a repetition that is liberating and selecting.[28]

This centrifugal purification, this ring between Dionysos and Ariadne, is an initiation, a death and a rebirth, an elevation of that which can be affirmed, a recurrence as a new type of life, a pure immanence, the child of Dionysos and Ariadne.

* * * * * * *

D&G's ideas were undoubtedly disruptive events in critical theory, but their though only truly became a weapon when it fell into the hands of the nascent group of homosexual revolutionaries in Paris calling themselves the *Front homosexuel d'action révolutionnaire* (FHAR). The FHAR was founded in 1971 by queers who were inspired by the utopian impulse within the May 1968 uprisings (especially those elements informed by the Situationist International), but frustrated nonetheless by the lack of space, in the uprising and subsequent movements, to discuss or organize around sexual freedom and gender domination. Though an intergenerational group, FHAR derived much of its energy from the newly radicalized youth within it. One such youth, noteworthy with regard to the influence of Deleuze, was Guy Hocquenghem. Despite the leaderless nature of FHAR, Hocquenghem emerged as a sort of poster boy for the group after his role in editing a notorious special edition of the journal *TOUT* focusing on homosexuality. Hocquenghem also published his own book

---

[27] For more see: *Spirits of Initiation* by H. Jeremiah Lewis.
[28] Ibid, pp. 89-91.

the same year that *Anti-Oedipus* was published, a sort of theoretical manifesto for the nascent gay movement: *Homosexual Desire.*

Beatriz/Paul Preciado, in the introduction to the Spanish translation of the book,[29] said of the relationship between Hocquenghem and D&G: "The Hocquenghem of *Homosexual Desire* is a reader of *Anti-Oedipus*, in the same way that D&G are readers of Foucault and inspired by the student and sexual revolts all over France." Preciado goes on to describe "the appearance of Guy Hocquenghem, accompanied by some members of the FHAR (Rene Scherer and a group of fags, queens and dykes), exclaiming, *Anti-Oedipus* in hand, that he'd found the theory he needed to undertake a critique of the heterosexual regime."[30]

D&G can be said to be as much inspired by the application of their theory to the new sexual liberation struggles as those movements are by D&G. The FHAR would be invited to edit a special edition of Guattari's journal *Recherches.* The result was called "Three Billion Perverts: Grand Encyclopedia of Homosexualities," which was promptly banned, seized, and destroyed by the police. Guattari himself had to defend the publication and the FHAR in court.

In their writings, and especially in Hocquenghem's book,[31] we find a worldview, like in D&G, which places sexuality and desire as the central organizing forces of our world. The homosexual desire of the book's title does not refer exclusively to same-sex desire, but is a synecdoche for a whole range of polymorphous and undefinable desires which Hocquenghem theorized as a will, a force of disintegration and liberation. Alongside D&G, Hocquenghem celebrates the marginal, the 'mad,' the criminal, those who reject bourgeois society, all those outside the dominant social order. He calls for spontaneous, autonomous, collective activity, "fusions of desire" which could help participants to escape the prison of "the normal." Implicit in this is a critique of the prevailing orthodoxies of revolutionary thought, namely Marxism and specifically its glorification of proletarian revolution, 'the masses,' 'the worker's struggle,' the vanguard party; Marxism and the banality of its categories. Rather than a class war, Hocquenghem imagines a "war of civilization" that includes sexual, cultural, psychic and ecological dimensions. In this war, he advocates an alliance of autonomous desire-based movements (the gay movement, the women's movement, the ecological movement, wildcatters, etc.). Citing D&G, he dreams of a new communalism based on "the abject desire to be loved," which must eventually dissolve the foundational structures of Humanism and

[29] The introduction is translated into English and published as "Anal Terror" in issue 3 of the journal *Baedan.*
[30] Preciado, "Anal Terror," in *Baedan: Journal of Queer Time Travel,* p. 144.
[31] Translated into English by Daniella Dangoor as *Homosexual Desire*, Durham: Duke University Press, 1993.

supersede the limits of the Human all together. He calls homosexual desire "the killer of the civilized ego."[32]

Unlike D&G and the preceding links in the Nietzsche chain, Hocquenghem does not write about Dionysos by name. And yet, a careful reader cannot help but call to mind the Dionysian implications of his proposals: "sexual communism," "anal-groupings," multiplicity of desire, the implosion of binary thought, wildness, the abandonment of traditional politics, the "grouping of desire."[33] More so than Hocquenghem's writings, the influence of Dionysos can be seen in the actual tactics of the FHAR group: satire, cross-dressing, obscene chants, phallic songs. At one point they stormed a radio broadcast on homosexuality, like thyrsos-bearing maenads, armed with phallic sausages, and disrupted the proceedings. In another, they staged a performative attack on an anti-abortion meeting. They even slapped a Catholic Priest with a sausage during a broadcast. Especially noteworthy were their meetings, held in the Amphitheater (that sacred space) of the School of Fine Arts in Paris. There hundreds of FHAR militants would meet regularly to debate, scheme, and ultimately to cruise, smoke, and let the meetings dissolve into orgies.

* * * * * * *

Though separated by language, an ocean, and the AIDS crisis, the queer theory of the 90s was already playing out in the streets of Paris in the 70s. What we are seeing is a recurrence over and over of a series of revelations and provocations; series of interweaving threads from different times, languages and nations which comprise a tradition characterized by labyrinthine twists. Put another way, queer theory has been born (and torn apart, and born again) multiple times before. Each time we see polytheistic, multiplicitous and Dionysian signs. Each is a descent into the underworld of desire, each an initiation, each a gaze into a mirror.

And now I must, in turn, face the audience and reveal the song of my own method. I want to take the queer theoretical mode championed by Sedgwick and turn it inside out. I'm not aiming to prove the queerness of Dionysos (others have sufficiently proven this point).[34] Rather than excavate the queer content in Dionysian myths, I want to locate Dionysos within queer theory. Where queer theory speaks of desire, the death drive, the self-shattering power of *jouissance*, the overcoming of the distinction between pain and pleasure in ecstasy, I will choose to speak directly to the god who is of and in all of the above. In this I've employed a heterogenous set of tools and techniques sacred

---

[32] Hocquenghem, *Homosexual Desire*, p. 150.

[33] Ibid, p. 111.

[34] See "The Queerness of Dionysos" in *Ecstatic* by H. Jeremiah Lewis, *Myths and Mysteries of Same Sex Love* by Christine Downing, or *The God of Ecstasy* by Arthur Evans.

to the Wild One: impersonation, the subversion of borders and binaries, the exploration of mysteries, the keeping of secrets, bricolage, liminality, altered states of consciousness, spirit-working, animism, conversations with vast forces which transcend the human but are irreducible to the One.

As in Nietzschean becoming, queer theory must help us to transform life itself into a work of art, or we will have to destroy it in the process. For Nietzsche, this meant transcending all the binary couples which had previously structured his life—Nietzsche *contra* Wagner, Dionysos and Apollo, Dionysos versus the Crucified—and arriving finally at the singularity with which he signed his final letters: simply *Dionysos*. Or as the bone tablets from Olbia put it: "Peace. War. Truth. Lie. Dionysos." and "Life. Death. Life. Truth. Zagreus. Dionysos."

* * * * * * *

If the reader will play along just a moment more, I'd like to propose that answers to many of the questions posed by contemporary queer theorists can be answered by the ancient myths and mysteries of Dionysos. Though our time together is presently coming to a close, allow me to sketch out the trajectory what just such an endeavor could look like. Imagine how Prosymnos might reply to Leo Bersani's question "Is the Rectum a Grave?" In what ways does the story of Ampelos—who risked his life by riding the wild bull and died for it, being transformed into the blood of the grape—explain the dilemma posed by Tim Dean's *Unlimited Intimacy*? Imagine Lee Edelman's *No Future* as told by Ariadne or the maenads. How does the cautionary tale of Pentheus' demise augment Judith Butler's argumentation about performativity and control in *Gender Trouble*? What does the centrality of performance in Dionysian worsphip indicate about the queer theoretical framework of performativity? In what ways would ritual entheogen use alter Preciado's experimental inquiry into gender and pharmaceuticals in *Testo Junkie*? And when we read *Cruising Utopia* by José Esteban Muñoz, might we in fact imagine the elusive mountain Nysa as precisely what we are looking for?

As of yet these questions remain speculation. But what becomes increasingly clear is that queer theory can be understood as a mirror held up to Dionysian myth and mystery; a diffraction, a multiplication, a return.

Neve Antheus is devoted to Dionysos and his retinue. He also maintains cultus for a whole host of queer ancestors. Sometimes that work takes the form of writing and underground publishing. Most often it takes the form of late nights spent frantically reading by candlelight. He also arranges flowers, writes poetry and talks to spirits.

[19]

Polytheism and the *Euthyphro*

EDWARD P. BUTLER

In this reading of the *Euthyphro*, Socrates and Euthyphro are seen less in a primordial conflict between reason and devotion, than as sincere Hellenic polytheists engaged in an inquiry based upon a common intuition that, in addition to the irreducible agency of the Gods, there is also some irreducible intelligible content to holiness. This reading is supported by the fact that Euthyphro does not claim the authority of revelation for his decision to prosecute his father, but rather submits it to elenchus, and that Euthyphro does not embrace the 'solution' of theological voluntarism when Socrates explicitly offers it. Since the goal of this inquiry is neither to eliminate the noetic content of the holy, nor to eliminate the Gods' agency, the purpose of the elenchus becomes the effort to articulate the results of this productive tension between the Gods and the intelligible on the several planes of Being implied by each conception of the holy which is successively taken up and dialectically overturned to yield the conception appropriate to the next higher plane, a style of interpretation characteristic of the ancient Neoplatonists.

The *Euthyphro* comes at the very beginning of the traditional arrangement of Plato's dialogues—traditional at least as far back as Thrasyllus—and, at least for us, tends to set the stage for the unfolding of Plato's thought, though the relative dearth of attention paid to it in antiquity stands in contrast to the importance assigned to it today. This fact should, indeed, alert us to the possibility that typical modern approaches to the dialogue are motivated by typically modern concerns. It is most well-known for the so-called 'Euthyphro dilemma' it has imparted to the philosophy of religion. This problem is concisely stated in the dialogue at 10a: "Is the holy [*hosios*, also frequently translated 'pious'], holy because it is loved by the Gods, or loved [by them] because it is holy?" Without wishing to discount the significance of the abundant reflections upon this problem in philosophy after antiquity, or to deny that we can see ancient Platonists on many occasions wrestling with the 'Euthyphro problem,' albeit not explicitly linked to this dialogue, it would not be unfair, I think, to say that thinkers after antiquity have approached the problem within the framing of monotheism. Some scholars, to be sure, particularly recently, have displayed greater openness than others to situating the piety of Socrates and of Plato *within* Hellenic polytheism, rather than on a trajectory away from it and toward some variety of philosophical monotheism; Mark McPherran and Jon Mikalson, in particular, stand out in this regard. To be open to this requires acknowledging, among other things, that the absence, in a given dialogue or even generally, of explicit affirmations, much less elenctic justifications, of elements utterly basic to the worldview of a Hellenic polytheist cannot be taken as manifesting a lack of support for them. It seems too often as though Socrates is on trial again in the pages of modern scholars who demand from him and from Plato an arbitrarily high threshold of proof that they identify with the tradition of Hellenic polytheism, or define that tradition so narrowly as to ensure that they do not.[1] While in many respects it is quite difficult to say something novel about Plato, in *this* respect, that is, insofar as one would speak about Plato the polytheist, it still is not.[2] This essay is not about polytheism as a mere socio-historical fact in the *Euthyphro*; rather, it concerns the meaning and value of the *Euthyphro* for the polytheistic philosophy of religion. Therefore, I do not intend to concern myself a great deal with the abundant secondary literature on the dialogue, but rather with reading the text, thinking along with it and around it, but informed particularly by hermeneutic strategies characteristic of the Neoplatonists.

---

[1] Examples of this tendency in the literature abound. For example, Kofi Ackah declares the "dialectical result" of the dialogue up to 11a to be that "piety understood as a relationship between humans and externally existing, fully anthropomorphic gods has no probative basis and is logically incoherent," ("Plato's *Euthyphro* and Socratic Piety," *Scholia* 15 (2006), p. 30), when demanding proof for the existence of the Gods is far from being the goal of this Platonic dialogue; nor is it clear how such positive ontological results are supposed to be produced from the dialectical procedure. Similarly, Roslyn Weiss argues "that it does not follow from Socrates' engaging in sacrificial rites either that he believes in the gods to whom he sacrifices or that he regards such activity as pious," and even dismisses his final words at *Phaedo* 118a as a "genuine expression of piety," ("Virtue Without Knowledge: Socrates' Conception of Holiness in Plato's *Euthyphro*," *Ancient Philosophy* 14 (1994), p. 272 n. 23.). Weiss takes no account of the testimonies elsewhere in Plato, or in Xenophon, to Socrates' belief in the Hellenic Gods, despite the fact that her thesis concerning the non-epistemic character of Socratic piety would be entirely consistent with sincere participation in the Hellenic theophany. McPherran, at least, does not deem to accuse Socrates of having forsworn his several civic oaths, "all of which called the gods of the state as witnesses" ("Does Piety Pay? Socrates and Plato on Prayer and Sacrifice," p. 95).

[2] 'Still' in the sense that there are definite indications of positive movement toward at least the openness I described; Gerd Van Riel's *Plato's Gods* (Farnham: Ashgate, 2013) being a prominent example. My reference to Plato here, rather than to Socrates and Plato, represents an initial acknowledgement that I see Plato's depiction of Socrates in the so-called 'early' dialogues as part of a theoretical continuum with Plato's 'late' metaphysics, and not as a categorically different undertaking.

At stake in the *Euthyphro*, clearly, is the relationship between theology and philosophy. Euthyphro is a diviner, Socrates a philosopher: one of the things we must measure for ourselves is just how great this difference is, and what is its true nature. This difference can be exaggerated. As McPherran points out,[3] Socrates' interactions with his *daimonion* do share certain traits with divination, and Socrates does upon occasion speak of himself as a sort of lay *mantis* (e.g., *Phaedo* 85b; *Phaedrus* 242c). Euthyphro, for his part, is akin to Socrates in more than just the ways he cites himself at the beginning of the dialogue, and of which modern readers are too derisive. It should not be, after all, an affront for Euthyphro to express such a kinship.[4] Moreover, since the later antique Platonic tradition regarded the etymologies *à la* Euthyphro in the *Cratylus* (396d & sqq.) not as mocking, but as sincere, the notion that Socrates and Euthyphro have each something to learn from the other is not outlandish. In this sense, we may see Euthyphro and Socrates as engaged in the same work, broadly conceived: namely, out of a personally experienced sense of divine vocation, trying to grasp for themselves, and not merely through passive participation in the social dimension of cult, something about the nature of the Gods and about the nature of the cosmos as the Gods would know it. Hence Proclus[5] sees Socrates in the *Cratylus* as mediating between Euthyphro's 'imaginative' (*phantastikos*) and passively given (*boskêmatôdeis*, literally as of what is fed to domesticated animals) conceptions about the Gods, and his own characteristically 'scientific' (*epistêmonikos*) understanding, by assuming a 'doxastic' mode in the *Cratylus* etymologies, one, that is, in which there is at once that which is the object of belief or *doxa*, such as the proper names of Gods who are the objects of experience and religious regard, *and also* intellectual insight, as we see in the interpretation Socrates develops from examining the names of the Gods as modified words or strings of words. In this doxastic labor Socrates recovers from the names given to the Gods in the theophanic experience of the ancients that moment of cognitive and intelligible *response* to theophany that embodies, inseparably, the presence of the Gods and of the human agent *together* in the

---

[3] "Socratic Reason and Socratic Revelation," *Journal of the History of Philosophy* 29.3, July 1991, pp. 345-373.

[4] One interesting commonality between them not cited by Euthyphro himself is a strong concern with purification. While commentators have often remarked upon Euthyphro's concern with *miasma* as exceptional, typically in support of arguments that Euthyphro's religious orientation lies outside the mainstream of Athenian religious life, somewhere on the 'Orphic' spectrum (e.g. Kahn, "Was Euthyphro the Author of the Derveni Papyrus," pp. 56-7), they have not tended to relate this to Socrates' own conception of elenchus as "a kind of ritual purification of the soul," (McPherran, *Religion of Socrates*, p. 152), and to the (much debated) 'Orphic' aspects of Plato's own thought.

[5] *In Platonis Cratylum Commentaria*, ed. Pasquali, pp. 67.24-68.9.

encounter.

The contrast between Socrates and Euthyphro against a shared background of common effort is echoed in something Socrates says at 3d, namely that Euthyphro is not in danger of prosecution from the people because he does not impart his wisdom (*sophia*) to others, or rather, we might say, that as a diviner Euthyphro shares only the *results* of his inquiry. Socrates is ironic, or perhaps merely polite, in attributing to Euthyphro a wisdom withheld, when the wisdom in question can only be attributed, first, to the Gods themselves, and second, to the one who can arrive at an adequate *interpretation* of what is conveyed to the diviner, and through them to a wider public. Even if Euthyphro possessed the wisdom to interpret the results of his divination, this would bear an ambiguous relationship his job description, so to speak, as a diviner.[6]

It must be said, in this connection, that Euthyphro never claims in the dialogue to have been specifically directed by the Gods to do anything. Can we, then, simply *assume* that Euthyphro is acting as a result of some kind of divination? I do not see how we can. It is, rather, Euthyphro's father who is explicitly said to have sought out a religious adviser (*exêgêtês*, 4c). Even if we accept that Euthyphro would regard himself as an exegete adequate for his own purposes, Euthyphro simply does not ever frame his decision in a manner that presents it as the result of any kind of divination. All that we can see from what is on the page is that Euthyphro has *inferred* his responsibilities through analogy with myths. Plato therefore does not stage in this text a direct confrontation between reason and revelation. It would have been awkward, no doubt, for Euthyphro to say that he had been directed to this course of action by a God, and for Socrates to proceed to interrogate that revelation, especially since, as McPherran points out,[7] Socrates speaks in his own case of receiving divine direction from divination and from dreams, as well as from his divine sign or *daimonion*. However, as McPherran goes on to argue, Socrates does nevertheless have a way open to him to criticize any given interpretation Euthyphro offers of the revelation he has received without resorting to impiety, and we ought not assume that Plato felt incapable of presenting such an inquiry in a suitable fashion. Indeed, the manner in which the discussion proceeds would seem to suggest that Euthyphro is not to be understood as acting on a specific divine direction, but rather on a general conception of what counts as pious behavior,

---

[6] See Aaron Landry, "Inspiration and Τέχνη: divination in Plato's *Ion*," *Plato Journal* 14 (2014), pp. 85-97 for a nuanced treatment of the issue of the diviner's knowledge. Even Theoclymenus, Socrates' example of possession divination, from *Odyssey* 20.351-7, is able to interpret his divination (20.367-70) (pp. 90-1); and Diotima, from the *Symposium*, is at once diviner and philosopher (pp. 92-3). See also chap. 3, "Divination and its Range of Influence," in Jon D. Mikalson, *Greek Popular Religion in Greek Philosophy* (Oxford: Oxford University Press, 2010), pp. 110-139.

[7] "Socratic Reason and Socratic Revelation," p. 351.

a conception which is in broad terms within the boundaries of what generally counts as piety among his peers, though his application of these norms has led to a result that will surprise those peers.[8] This makes the move to an inquiry into the *nature of piety* a natural one—in fact, a move that Euthyphro has already implicitly made himself. In this respect, we may class Euthyphro among those clergy of whom we read in the *Meno* that Socrates has had conversation, inasmuch as they wish to give a reasoning account of their ministry (*Meno* 81a). Or at least, that Euthyphro has a tendency in this direction, inasmuch as he seems to have a certain inchoate sense that reasoning should play some role in his religious life, even beyond the necessity for interpreting his direct communications from the Gods, so that his piety can inform even those decisions he makes *without* recourse to divination. In this respect, it may be significant that it is within the time it takes for his father's messenger to seek out the advice of the exegete that his hired man dies, though the death is directly caused by his father's negligence (4d). Nor are we told the result of the consultation with the exegete. It seems that Plato feels no need to even provide the materials for a confrontation between reason and revelation as such.

Most notably in this respect, when given the opportunity by Socrates to render his stated beliefs mutually consistent by straightforwardly affirming that holiness just *is* an effect of divine will, Euthyphro does not do so, clearly wishing to preserve the noetic integrity of the notion of holiness (10a-c). What troubles Euthyphro, or at least perhaps does so once Socrates has pointed it out, is that he has no *rational* means for adjudicating between two conflicting pious duties: reverence for the law, and reverence for his father, whom he would prosecute under the law. Euthyphro's intention is to prosecute his father as the law would demand, and he sees this as following from a universal, implicitly rational maxim that the law should apply to everyone equally (4b). We know from *Gorgias* 480c that Socrates does in fact agree that one should try to see ones friends and family prosecuted if they have done wrong. But how has Euthyphro gotten to this recognition? He doesn't seek to justify this maxim, or his intended actions, through reason, or at any rate, only through a particular kind of reasoning, namely arguing that for him to prosecute his father in this fashion honors a principle established by the Gods when, for example, Zeus overthrows Kronos. We should not be too quick to dismiss this line of thought. Analogy is a form of reasoning, and the transition from the reign of Kronos to

---

[8] Jon D. Mikalson, *Honor Thy Gods: Popular Religion in Greek Tragedy* (Chapel Hill, NC: University of North Carolina Press, 1991), pp. 198-201 argues persuasively that "Euthyphro's concept of piety" as displayed in the dialogue, "echoes similar thoughts found throughout Greek tragedy," and that "scattered and fragmentary parallels for Euthyphro's ideas appear in other sources for popular religion," hence "his conception of piety was not idiosyncratic," (201).

that of Zeus as recounted in Hesiod does lead to the establishment of a more just order among the Gods, one chiefly operating through persuasion and the balancing of honors (*timai*) rather than force of will (Ouranos) or calculation (Kronos).

Euthyphro's application of analogy implies that a principle can be univocally applied to Gods and to humans, despite their different ontological status: "they are inconsistent in what they say about the Gods and about me" (6a). This again suggests that Euthyphro is really seeking, whether he recognizes it or not, an exercise of reason that would transcend the division between humans and the Gods. Nor does Euthyphro see a *symbolic* interpretation of the myth, even though he emphasizes to Socrates the supra-rational nature of the events treated in myths. For when Socrates expresses doubt that there could really be war between Gods, Euthyphro characterizes such truths as 'marvelous' and 'astonishing' (6b, c), but does not draw the further conclusion that just insofar as these mythic events are *mysterious* that they might *not* therefore provide simple, unproblematic analogies to human behavior. Daniel Werner's recent study, "Myth and the Structure of Plato's *Euthyphro*,"[9] though highlighting the importance for the dialogue of Euthyphro's "adherence to traditional myth," fails to even recognize the possibility of a pious *and* symbolic hermeneutic of myth beyond the simplistic opposition of *mythos* and *logos*. The issue cannot be reduced, as Werner would wish, to a matter of an "acceptance" or "rejection" of traditional myths, or of whether "acceptance" of the myths is "loose" or "wholesale" (p. 46). Mythic reception is hardly so simple. We should not assume that Plato would be averse to a symbolic hermeneutic of myth. In the critique of mythic poetry in the *Republic*, myths requiring esoteric (or 'hyponoetic,' *Rep.* 378d) interpretation are not suitable for unmediated, simplistic application, which is why it is questionable to impart such myths to children, who are not capable of advanced theology, or to inhabitants of a 'fevered' city whose state of total mobilization, a permanent state of emergency, may render them similarly impaired. Such symbolic interpretation has as its guiding principle, not the reduction of 'irrational' myth to some purified *logos*, but the pious regard for the Gods as being "each the most beautiful and best thing possible" (*Rep.* 381c).

Insofar as problematic myths like these shed light in particular upon the *ontological difference* between humans and Gods, however, it may well be these myths that interest us most of all. To guide us in their interpretation, however, we shall need philosophical, ontological tools. Once these were developed within Platonic schools, the interpretation of such myths flourished, not in a defensive posture, but rather for the genuine ontological value such myths have to offer.[10] But in the *Euthyphro*, the difference between humans and Gods is

---

[9] *International Philosophical Quarterly* Vol. 52, No. 1, Issue 205 (March 2012), pp. 41-62.
[10] See, e.g., Lamberton, *Homer the Theologian*; Struck, *Birth of the Symbol*.

approached obliquely, through a series of hypotheses about the nature of holiness all of which have a domain of valid application, but all of which also contain some seed of their dialectical reversal, which will urge us further along in a manner that, in fact, sketches for us the outlines of the structure of being. This, at any rate, is the style of positive interpretation of dialogical refutation favored in the later Platonic schools, and which serves us better than other interpretive hypotheses with respect to this dialogue, if we do not assume that Plato intends to portray Socrates as overturning, rather than merely refining, popular conceptions of piety.[11]

* * * * * * *

The essential question in the *Euthyphro*, and in the Platonic approach to theology generally, I would argue, is the relationship between the singular (the unique or 'peculiar') and the common. When Euthyphro chooses to treat the events of myth just like worldly events, and looks to define holiness according to what the Gods choose, he chooses in favor of the singularity of the Gods as individuals, rather than orienting himself to divine *attributes*. He affirms the integrity of the Gods by affirming the unique, unrepeatable nature of the mythic event, which can offer a paradigm for practice precisely insofar as it does *not* depend upon some further principle which it merely instantiates, and which would therefore demand a prior elucidation. At the same time, he searches for a universality which would not compromise singularity.

From the perspective of later Platonic philosophy of religion, Euthyphro indeed shows the proper instincts at least, in that he wishes *both* to secure the ontological priority of henadic individuals (the unique Gods) to the eidetic or formal in its entirety *and* to pursue an *eidos* of the holy—for Euthyphro does not accept the proffered voluntarism in which the holy would be holy purely by virtue of the Gods' having chosen it. We do not have to assume that, as R. E. Allen would have it, Euthyphro is simply a theological voluntarist who misunderstands his own position.[12] Rather, we can see Euthyphro as experiencing a legitimate pull in both directions, and that preserving and articulating this tension, rather than collapsing it into one pole or the other, is the Platonist's legitimate aim as well. This tension can be seen as driving the *Euthyphro*'s dialectic.

Euthyphro realizes in an inchoate fashion that affirming divine individuality—and, inherently, plurality—ought not lead to a skeptical or nominalistic rejection of the eidetic altogether. 'Holiness' ought to have *something*

---

[11] See Mikalson (2010) for an extended defense of the mainstream nature of at least some version of all of the models of piety proposed in the *Euthyphro*.

[12] *Plato's* Euthyphro *and the Earlier Theory of Forms: A Reinterpretation of the* Republic (Abingdon, Oxon: Routledge, 1970 [repr. 2013]), p. 44.

common to it, though he is correct to reject that such a common substance—or a common substance for any of the virtues—will subordinate the Gods *existentially*, and Plato does not press such a conclusion, either. The Good, rather, as we will see from the *Republic*, is beyond substance (*ousia*), which in the later development of Platonism was elucidated, in conjunction with the henology of Plato's *Parmenides*, as expressing the primacy of the unitary or singular (*heniaios*), of individual existence (*hyparxis*), over the ideal or formal.[13] Hence the 'Euthyphro problem' is really that of how the common emerges from the singular. The singulars 'down here,' so to speak, everyday units, may indeed be ontologically posterior in many ways to the forms they participate, but the *ultimate* singulars, the Gods, eternally *generate* their community. Moreover, even if we had no Gods, we would have to be able to at least conceive such autonomously good agents in order to secure the metaphysical possibility of freedom. It solves nothing to either reduce these agents to arbitrary, and hence unfree choices, *or* to a good which arbitrarily chooses them.

We see a reflection of this problem of peculiarity in the discussion of conflicts among the Gods (7b-d). Insofar as the conflicts between the Gods are understood to be *peculiar* to each, they lack, by definition, objective resolutions. In this way they are like disputes over the Good among us, which in our case produce enmity (7d). This is not to say that enmity results in the divine case, and Socrates would certainly reject that it does. But when the conflicts among the Gods are understood as strife among absolutely unique individuals, all of whose attributes are also taken as wholly unique to each of them, there can necessarily be no formalization of the conflict as embodying a conflict of objective principles that might therefore be mediated. Dispute on this plane, the plane of pure singulars, is always a dispute over each separate act (8e), and any resolution will also be unique. Hence for us as well, when we take ourselves existentially, that is, as singulars, each problem of the application of principles is occurring as it were for the first time, every time. If Euthyphro is going to stay on the plane of singulars—which is in one respect a *low* plane of being, when it pertains to singulars such as us, but in another respect *the highest*, when it pertains to *a priori* singulars such as Gods—then only a *singular* judgment, such as an act of divination, can justify his act.

Euthyphro does not resort to this, however, inasmuch as he continues to accept Socrates' challenge to him to produce *universality*, something that can be affirmed as true of *all the Gods*, without restriction, and hence something true of them *qua* Gods. This is the breakthrough in which we are invited to participate: an inquiry into the Gods as a *kind* of thing, with an essential nature, a nature of Godhood. At the beginning of the Platonic enterprise, therefore, we are advised

---

[13] Cf. "Polytheism and Individuality in the Henadic Manifold," *Dionysius* Vol. 23, 2005, pp. 83-104.

that the inquiry will extend even this far. But where we mistake the enterprise is in seeing its end as placing a reified essence prior to the existence of the Gods, or, for that matter, affirming a wholesale subordination of other individuals to the Idea. Moreover, what prevents the latter is precisely that very Platonic piety which will not subordinate the Gods in this fashion. Hence other singulars are saved, too, in varying degrees, and with a status doubtless 'problematic,' by that philosophical piety which saves the Gods. Saving the singulars *is the problem*, and this is what recognizing Platonic piety, not toward the Idea, but toward the *immortals*, and toward the possibility of fellowship with them in and through our mortal being, allows us in turn to understand about the entire Platonic project.[14]

The dialectical ascent, then, begins in earnest from 10a-c, where Socrates poses to Euthyphro the question of whether he wishes to regard holiness as simply a passive quality of things resulting from their having been chosen by the Gods. That it should be merely an implicitly arbitrary choice and a resulting *pathos* of something, rather than a relationship more fundamental and even in some way constitutive for both, is the bottom, baseline position, but one which also, if we read it proleptically, reflects, just by virtue of being the lowest, something of the pure causal activity of the highest principle, for the Gods as the ultimate agents will indeed, in the ultimate development of antique Platonism, possess this sheer sovereignty over Being in the last analysis. Conceiving of the holy in this fashion would also be consistent with the Platonic doctrine regarding *powers*, and therefore would conceive that which is holy as the receptacle of divine power. Thus in the *Republic* (477c-d), we read that powers (*dynameis*) can be discriminated in no other way than by that to which they are relative and by that which comes about through them.[15] A power, thus, has no intrinsic character but what it is in that which it effects, and thus this putative definition of holiness may be regarded as the 'power' definition. Powers are therefore, in themselves, pure relations, and holiness the pure power of relation to the Gods, without any further intelligible determination, as *transcending* the intelligible. The proper understanding of the ontological status of the powers of the Gods lies on the far side of the investigation Socrates and Euthyphro are now undertaking, however, not to mention on the far side of the historical development of Platonism in antiquity. Therefore, Euthyphro correctly refuses to stay at this position as it is prereflectively articulated, and not ripe to be grasped, even though it would be

---

[14] I have developed this at further length through a reading of the *Phaedrus* and *Symposium* in "Plato's Gods and the Way of Ideas," *Diotima: Review of Philosophical Research* 39, 2011 (Hellenic Society for Philosophical Studies, Athens), pp. 73-87.

[15] Cf. Hans-Georg Gadamer's discussion of this doctrine in "The Dialectic of the Good in the *Philebus*," pp. 117-118 in *The Idea of the Good in Platonic-Aristotelian Philosophy*, trans. P. Christopher Smith (New Haven: Yale University Press, 1986).

consistent with the intuition of the sovereign power of divine choice. He wishes, instead, to pursue the *choiceworthiness* of that which the Gods choose.

In addition to the desire for a substantial notion of the holy, however, Socrates points out a problem forcing the ascent, by posing the question of fear and reverence at 12a-b. We have reverence for something in regard to a virtue it possesses, while we fear something simply because of its action or possible action upon us; and yet insofar as reverence is a part (*meros*) of fear (12c), we see again the emergence of something with eidetic content from out of something conceived as a pure relation. Socrates thus presents Euthyphro with another implicit figuration of divine production.

The structural consideration with respect to fear and reverence leads Socrates in turn to the notion of holiness as a part of justice, as reverence is a kind of fear. Now it is a question, not of something structurally homologous to the relation between the Gods and the (eidetically) holy, but of something that might begin to speak to the nature of holiness itself. The question of piety as a part of justice concerns the place that piety, the activities specifically directed toward the Gods in devotion (*therapeia*), has in the system of the cosmos, of the total well-ordering of things. It takes up again the purely interactional or relational conception of the holy as that which is chosen by or beloved of the Gods. This conception is enriched, however, through recognizing that holiness thus conceived is an attribute, not of the holy thing in isolation, but of an economy of devotion. It represents an advance in this respect. But given its wide-reaching significance, how can this economy be just one part of the whole of justice, just one activity among the many activities of necessity and of choice that fill up a life?

This question concerns the status of the Gods as a particular class among beings, a portion of the cosmos. Eventually Platonists will come to recognize that the Gods cannot just be certain things among all other things. Hence, at the beginning of this journey, Socrates asks the *aim* of attending to the Gods. It cannot have as its aim supplying some need, and hence making the Gods *better* in some way (13c-d). This would be the case if the Gods were solely part of the cosmic system, immanent in it without remainder. There is something limited and misleading, therefore, about the economic model, at least if we understand it as a crude exchange. To every stage of the dialectic corresponds some belief or practice which the dialectical progression does not demand be abandoned, but for which rather it poses a problem, and solving this problem will save what is true in it. The priestesses and priests mentioned in the *Meno*, like Diotima in the *Symposium*, were not looking for something to supersede their devotional works, but for a way of articulating the relationship of these acts to the world.

If Socrates is holding the Gods' transcendence—at least partially or in some respect—of the cosmic economy in his pocket, so to speak, this is not at any rate an insight available to Euthyphro. The next step in the dialectic, accordingly, comes with Euthyphro's substitution of a sublimated economy for the crude one based on need: service (*hypêretikê*) to the Gods in pursuit of their work (*ergon*) (13d-e). The importance of the relationship of service to the Gods is emphasized by its reemergence at a crucial moment in the *Parmenides* (134d-e), where the mastery-and-service relationship between the Gods and ourselves, insofar as it parallels the relationship between the forms and our knowledge of them, poses what is termed the 'greatest difficulty' with respect to the theory of forms, if it be poorly understood, for it implies that "we do not rule the Gods with our authority, nor do we know anything of the divine with our knowledge, and by the same reasoning, the Gods likewise, being Gods, are not our masters and have no knowledge of human affairs," (134e, trans. Fowler, mod.).

In the Platonic consideration of the economy of mastery and service, we glimpse the economy of recognition that Hegel would articulate so many centuries later. The difficulty of this relationship, embodied in Euthyphro's inability to say what is the work of the Gods in which we serve them, lies in the fact that there are relationships the very *idea* of which makes necessary reference to that which lies outside the realm of the *ideal*. It is not simply that we lack the knowledge we would need to assist the Gods properly in their work, but rather of conceiving, in the first place, a work as common to them and to us. Knowledge in itself is the grasp of the formal by something not solely formal, namely the soul; so too, the *mastery* exercised by the Gods over us involves essentially entities which in a certain respect would not *exist* for them. Hence, we do not see ourselves in the myths. We may *analogize* ourselves to figures in the myths, as Euthyphro does when he analogizes himself to Zeus and his father to Kronos, or, more humbly, as when we see ourselves in the mortals portrayed in myth, but we are not straightforwardly there, in that world. Those mortals, too, can only be the object of analogy. In this way, there is something in the devotional economy that transcends the economy of myth, which like the economy of the ideas or forms is fundamentally intellective. Here we see how a simplistic opposition of *mythos* and *logos* cannot do justice to the labors of Plato and Platonists. Myths have two faces, one of which looks back to the singularity of the Gods and of revelation, the other of which looks forward to hermeneutic exegesis and the ideas which emerge from it. The limitation of analogy lies in its potential obstruction of the recognition of the procession of being, with its necessary moment of *disanalogy*. Devotion must incorporate the alterity that makes it possible for Gods and mortals to recognize one another in the full alterity of their divergent existential conditions.

From the holy as simple object of divine intention, Socrates and Euthyphro passed on to the notion of a devotional economy of holiness, which has now been refined implicitly from the gross economy of exchange to the sublimated economy of recognition. This economy of recognition transcends even the plane by which the Gods give form to the cosmos, namely the plane of mythic relationships and reciprocal action *within* the divine sphere. The economy of devotion, properly understood, therefore, transcends the economy of demiurgy. This would have to be the case for polytheism not to collapse into intellect-ualized cosmotheism, and for piety as a distinct activity to disappear. This is the recognition entailed in the reformulation McPherran offers of the conception of divine service in response to Socrates' forceful hint at 14c that Euthyphro has come very near the solution to the nature of holiness before turning aside.[16] For McPherran, the positive Socratic conception of piety is accordingly "that part of justice that is a service of humans to gods, assisting the gods in their primary task to produce their most beautiful product." But we can see that something has dropped out of consideration in order to formulate this definitive statement, which is both *action-based* and focused purely on *human* action. This is a serviceable definition of piety as a human virtue or activity, but not, it would seem, of *holiness* as embodying, or at least *including*, the choice-worthiness of the objects of *divine* choice. This latter, rather, has been pushed back out of view, implicit in the notion of the Gods' 'task.' For what makes something a task of the Gods? Is it simply that They have taken it up, or is it the task's intrinsic value?

Accordingly, when the difference between humans and Gods is elided, at least aspirationally, in Plato's *Republic*, the discrete virtue of piety vanishes altogether into that of justice, which is simply the proper *adjustment* of powers in the soul, in society, and in the cosmos to one another.[17] There is a sense in which everything, simply by fulfilling its nature and playing out its role in the

---

[16] "Piety, Justice, and the Unity of Virtue," *Journal of the History of Philosophy* 38.3 (July 2000), pp. 302-3.

[17] Cf. McPherran, "Piety, Justice, and the Unity of Virtue," pp. 324-5, 326-7.

cosmic system, is holy or is expressing piety, but does the attempt to define piety truly dissolve it? Or perhaps the worship of the Gods is something really distinct in itself, but is nevertheless undertaken purely for the sake of the cosmos? This is the position suggested by the notion that piety is "the science [*epistếmê*] of sacrifice and prayer" (14c), the object of which is to "bring salvation to individual families and to states" (14b). The way in which this position is described, both in its recourse to a notion of science, and in its salvific application not to the individual as such, but to greater social units, suggest that it is the highest point achieved by the intellectualized conception of piety, insofar as the latter will only with difficulty recognize the particular, by a process of determining 'down' to it by increasingly finer sortal 'nets.' Salvation, at any rate, as the product of devotion, is indicated by Socrates to be very close (14c) to the solution of the problem of what holiness or piety is with respect to its intelligible content, unless the nearness he indicates, but does not specify, is instead the notion of service in a noble work. Or can it be both, in the sense that the state of our souls in our disposition toward the Gods, that is, the *pure relation* among Gods and mortals, is itself the work, to which of necessity we are peculiarly qualified?

A relationship of *justice* toward the Gods is paradoxical to the degree that they do not need anything from us, and cannot be bettered by our attentions to them (15a-b), even if a beautiful work could be achieved by them and ourselves in concert. They must therefore *in themselves* remain in some respect outside the economy of reciprocal benefit that they underwrite. Even justice most widely and sensitively conceived will thus fall short in capturing what piety is, though it can go a very long way. The very best account we can give of religious life in terms of reciprocal exchange (*do ut des*), even refined to the ultimate degree, still lets something escape. The Gods, to exist in the way the Hellenic tradition intuitively grasps them—because we must recognize that Socrates at no time in this dialogue, or elsewhere, really, introduces novel, controversial premises concerning the Gods, but at most sets the consequences of one intuition against another—must not exist solely in the economy of piety, and therefore the inquiry into the nature of piety has run its course, with the Gods Themselves as its remainder and its precondition. But piety's epistemological virtue is just that this immanent inquiry should reveal the objects of its peculiar concern in this light: the Gods would be of all things what concretely instantiates such self-sufficiency.

The course of this dialectic has therefore proceeded along two tracks, one explicit, in which an intelligible content has been sought for holiness or piety, the progress of which has at every stage also revealed a corresponding, *implicit* conception of piety, in which the holy is so inseparable from divine activity itself as to escape any intelligible framing we might design for it. The circle to which Socrates refers, then, at 15b-c, is not a vicious one, unless we are convinced that it is a failure to have elucidated the series of meanings attributable to piety, their sufficiencies and insufficiencies, and also to recognize in the end that there is something more than intelligible embedded in the concept. In this respect, Socrates' reference to his ancestor Daidalos suggests not merely that the argument has gotten away from Euthyphro, but the magic of ensoulment showing itself and arising through the effort at understanding. It is true that in a certain respect, when Socrates urges Euthyphro to "begin again at the beginning" with him (15c), the putative positive conception of piety discerned by McPherran at 14b has been undermined. The notion of service to the Gods in support of a work of theirs has only a relative stability; to return again to the beginning is to return to the motor that has driven the dialectic all along, namely the creative tension between the impulse to compromise none of the Gods' agency, and the understanding that the Gods, being Gods, must have a will that is good, too, and hence this goodness is there to be found in the choices they make.

Euthyphro is often treated with rather more scorn by modern commentators than Socrates' other interlocutors, despite the fact that none of them hold up particularly well to Socrates' scrutiny. Some of this, I believe, is attributable to a bias against Euthyphro's religiosity, which is bound to please neither the atheist nor the monotheist. Euthyphro, in any case, as I have remarked, deserves credit for one thing, at least: he never seeks to jettison the notion of some intelligible content for the concept of the holy. He tries, instead, to hold together the search for this intelligibility and his intuition that there is something irreducible in the relationship to the living Gods. In this, Euthyphro shows himself a true Hellene, we may say, in refusing to divorce the Gods from the world and from reason, nor divorce *these* from the Gods. Whatever transcendence is accorded the Gods, it will not be of the sort that Kierkegaard demands for his God, namely the suspension of all rational and moral claims in the face of the divine command.

For failing to adopt this Kierkegaardian solution, or the alternative of an intellectualized piety refined virtually to the point of atheism, Euthyphro is branded a shallow thinker who cannot see clearly enough to embrace either 'genuine' theology or rationality. But in refusing this dichotomy, Euthyphro remains true to the fundamental theological intuitions of his culture, and I would argue that Socrates and Plato would not wish him to do otherwise. Euthyphro may not be a gifted dialectician, but his project is theirs as well, a project in which the transcendence of the Gods in Hellenic theology will ground the cosmos and our free exercise of reason, not suspend it. It's not insignificant, in this light, that Euthyphro seeks divine sanction for recourse to the Athenian justice system, and his transgressiveness lies solely in that he would allow the law to be applied within his family, rather than shielding them.

Socrates, however, has by the end of the dialogue shown it to be thoroughly problematic to attempt to justify social action by recourse to theology. But this is because Euthyphro has tried to do so, as it were, without the Gods themselves. Euthyphro tries to match mythic incidents to worldly problems as simple precedents, a portion of myth to a part of the world, but this part-to-part correspondence will undermine the whole-to-whole relationship of the Gods to the social and the cosmic order, the same whole-to-whole relationship that any living thing has to the cosmos, for the Gods are for Euthyphro and Socrates alike living immortals, and not abstract principles or mere formulae that can be applied indifferently, in their personal absence. But this does not leave only divination, on the one hand, and a godless reason on the other, a dichotomy alien, I believe, to the mainstream of Hellenic thinkers.[18] Socrates' own piety, on the testimony of Plato and of Xenophon alike, argues rather for an integration of reason and revelation in a unified soteriology.

Edward Butler received his doctorate from the New School for Social Research in 2004 for his dissertation "The Metaphysics of Polytheism in Proclus." Since then, he has published numerous articles in academic journals and edited volumes, primarily on Platonism and Neoplatonism and on polytheistic philosophy of religion. He also writes *Noēseis*, a regular column for Polytheist.com, and is on the editorial board of *Walking the Worlds*. More information about his work can be found on his site, Henadology: Philosophy and Theology (henadology. wordpress.com).

---

[18] Even Werner, in an account otherwise hostile to Hellenic theology, recognizes that Euthyphro's rejection of the voluntarism Socrates offers him is at least in part due to the fact that "Nowhere in the traditional myths are the gods represented as the sort of beings who definitively establish the nature of right and wrong (or pious and impious) simply through a decree or fiat," (p. 50).

Romans, Gods, Politics, and Bathrooms

VIRGINIA CARPER

Today's Pagans feel obligated to be politically involved with various Progressive causes. In response to the hyper-political environment found in Paganism, several Polytheists have suggested to place more focus on devotions to the Gods. For Roman Polytheists, there is a blueprint on how devotions to the Gods can include political actions. The Capitoline and Aventine Triads offer guidance on proper governance. The public and private virtues for Romans give a structure on how they should conduct themselves in the political arena. An example of how this is done is the manner in which pay toilets in the United States became outlawed.

T oday's Pagans feel obligated to take political action such as protesting restrictive bathroom laws or disrupting Donald Trump's rallies (if they think he is a fascist). In response to this hyper-political environment, many Polytheists have suggested that venerating the Gods not include demonstrations and protest marches. The Roman approach to Gods and politics offer an alternative to both.

For guidance on political action and devotion to the Gods, Roman Polytheists look to the Capitoline Triad of Juno, Jupiter, and Minerva as well as to the Aventine Triad of Ceres, Liber, and Libera. The Capitoline Triad represents what Romans aspire to in their government officials. Meanwhile, the Aventine Triad directs Romans to protect the rights of the poor and to prevent overreach by government officials.

I. INTRODUCING THE GOVERNING TRIADS

The Capitoline Triad

In ancient times, the Capitoline Triad watched over the Roman people and their nation. Jupiter Optimus Maximus (Brightest and Best) protected the state. In addition, Juno Regina was the guardian of Rome. Together, They guided the affairs of the Roman people. Meanwhile, Minerva was the Patron of Doctors and the Arts, promoting excellence in society and culture.

From the days of the Roman Republic, this Triad represented the ideals of statesmanship, liberty, and the arts for the Romans. Although there is no "official" Capitoline Triad today, I believe that these three Gods would oversee the affairs of nations when asked. They are willing to work in partnership with our leaders, as They did with the ancient Romans.

Although there is no Rome today, we can still appeal to the Capitoline Triad for their wisdom for our leaders and countries. They can offer their guidance and protection to us, for our governments, and in our public life. We can look to Them to show us good statesmanship as well as promoting excellence in our culture.

Archaic Triad (Original Triad)

At the founding of Rome, the original Roman Triad was Jupiter, Mars, and Quirinus (three males). As Etruscan influences grew on Romans, so the composition of the Triad changed. The Capitoline Triad that is known today is Jupiter (Best and Brightest), Juno (Queen of Heaven), and Minerva. (What is unusual about the Capitoline Triad is that it consists of two females and one male.)

During the times of the Roman Kings, the original Triad (now referred to as "Archaic") was Jupiter, Mars, and Quirinus. As the Roman God of Thunder, Jupiter was the Supreme Ruler of the Heavens. He offered governance to the Roman people. As the Guardian of the Fields, Mars was the Protector of the People. Meanwhile, Quirinus was the God of the Roman People. These Gods emphasized the ideals of a ruler in war and peace. Quirinus represented the beginning of citizen involvement in government.

Jupiter is discussed more in depth in the section on the Capitoline Triad

Mars was originally a God associated with the promotion of agriculture. As *Mars Silvanus*, He watched over the fields. When Rome expanded its boundaries, Mars became a God of War. One of the original guardians of Rome, Mars guided the Kingdom of Rome with Jupiter and Quirinus.

As One of the Archaic Triad, **Quirinus** watched over Rome. Romans regarded this God in two ways. One is that He is the deified Romulus (who was taken into the heavens by Mars, his rumored father). The other is that of Quirinus being a God of the Sabines, who was worshipped on the Quirinal Hill in Rome. However they thought of Quirinus, Romans were often addressed as "*Quirites*" in their civic role.

Etruscan Influence on the Triad

One characteristic of the multi-cultural Roman religion is the adoption of other Gods as needed. At other times, certain aspects of various Gods would be combined into one God or foreign Gods were correlated with Roman ones. Influenced by the Etruscans, the original Triad of Gods overseeing the Roman State and its citizens changed.

The Etruscans had their own Triad of Gods: Tinia, Uni, and Menrva. Their Supreme God was **Tinia** (Tin). To them, He was Father Time since He governed time as well as the skies. Meanwhile, His Wife and Sister, **Uni** was the supreme Goddess of the Etruscans. She protected them and their rulers. In addition, Uni governed all aspects of Etruscan womanhood from the wedding to nursing children. Tinia and Uni's daughter was **Menrva**, the Goddess of War, Wisdom, and the Arts. She was usually depicted with a helmet and spear. (The Roman Minerva was originally this Etruscan Goddess.)

Capitoline Triad (Jupiter, Juno, Minerva)

After the wars with the Sabines, King Tarquin Priscus asked the Deities of a shrine on Capitoline Hill to move so that he could build a temple to Jupiter Optimus Maximus. In exchange for their leaving, he promised Them a new temple elsewhere (*exauguration*). All the Gods did except for Terminus, the God of Boundaries. The Romans regarded this as a good omen. The new temple was dedicated to Jupiter, Juno, and Minerva. (However, a part of it remained a shrine to Terminus.) On the Ides of September, the *praetor maximus* (head magistrate) would drive a nail into the wall of the temple (*cella Iovis*), to ward off the plague for another year.

The main temple for the Capitoline Triad had three rooms with each God having their own space. Jupiter Optimus Maximus occupied the center *cella* (room), with Juno Regina on the left and Minerva on the right. Although the temple was built during the time of Roman Kings, it was dedicated by the first Consul of the Roman Republic.

Known as The Shining Father ("*Dies Pater*"), **Jupiter**, according to the Romans, is the Ruler of the Cosmos. The ancient Romans looked to Jupiter as the Protector of Rome and its laws. They saw Him in many aspects of governance. As a member of both the Archaic and Capitoline Triads, *Jupiter Optimus Maximus* oversaw Roman affairs. As *Jupiter Lapis*, He presided over solemn oaths. Meanwhile, *Jupiter Feretrius* presided over treaties and just wars. *Jupiter Stator* encouraged the Romans to stand their ground against the Sabines and later the Samnites.

The oldest temple for Jupiter was Jupiter Feretrius, founded by Romulus. This temple was a repository of ritual implements for dedicating treaties. To declare war, the *fetialis* (priest-diplomat of Jupiter) would hurl a spear from the temple into enemy territory. To solemnize a treaty with foreign governments, the *fetialis*, using the *lapis silex* (flint) of Jupiter Feretrius, sacrificed a pig.

The Goddess **Juno** was heavily involved in the life of Rome and her people. Today, Juno is often invoked as the Protector of the State. Her many titles give the wide range of her attributes. *Juno Regina*, as the "Queen of the Heavens," like Uni, governs all aspects of womanhood. In this aspect, She is depicted wearing a goatskin cloak, and armed with a spear.

Worshipped in each of the curiae of Rome, *Juno Curitis* protected the citizen-soldiers of Rome. In this aspect, She was the only deity universal to all of the curiae. A traditional prayer to Her was *"Juno Curitis* protect my fellow natives of the Curia with your Chariot and Shield."

The sacred geese of *Juno Moneta* warned the Romans of an impending attack by the Gauls (in 390 BCE). After Marcus Furius Camillus won the war against the Gauls, he vowed a temple to Her in 345 BCE. Besides Vesta's temple, this temple to Juno Moneta was the only other round one in Rome.

In portraying **Minerva**, people often claim that She is the Greek Goddess of Wisdom, Athena with a Roman name. Wearing her military tunic and aegis, and carrying her shield and spear, Minerva does portray the martial aspects of Athena Promachos (Athena the Champion). However, the Romans also see Her as one of the Capitoline Triad overseeing state affairs.

Adapted from the Etruscan Goddess Menrva, Minerva is also the Goddess of Wisdom, Education, and Commerce. In addition, She is the Patroness of Textile Workers, Doctors, and Artisans. Furthermore, Minerva is the inventor of numbers and several musical instruments as well.

Ovid writes:

> Pray now to Pallas, boys and tender girls;
> Whoever wins Her favor will be skilled,
> For She's the Goddess of a Thousand Works.

The Aventine Triad

In 493 B.C.E., to quell plebeian unrest, Dictator Aulus Postumius vowed a temple to Ceres, Liber, and Libera. These patron Gods of the plebeians (the common citizens) ensured the fertility of the land and protected the supply of grain. Built on Aventine Hill, the temple guarded the granary. Joining Liber and Libera, ancient Italic deities of vegetable fertility, was Ceres, who also protected the urban grain supplies.

These three Deities, called the Aventine Trio, are the plebeian counter-balance to the patrician Capitoline Triad. The two Triads kept in check any excesses of both the plebeians and patricians. For example, the office of the Tribune was under their divine protection. The tribunes protected the plebeians from patrician magistrates (*ius auxilii*), and impeded any unlawful action of a magistrate (*ius intercessionis*). In this way, the Triads oversaw law, order, and social tranquility.

As a Goddess of Agriculture, **Ceres** is another Greek God adopted by the Romans. To end a famine in 496 BCE, the Sibylline Oracles counseled the Romans to accept Her. Since then, her role in Roman life has expanded beyond agriculture to include protecting the plebeian class.

As a Goddess of the Earth, Ceres made the crops germinate and grow. In April, the Cerealia celebrates Ceres' fertility aspects as the Goddess of Grain Crops. For the public enjoyment, the plebeian aediles held games for the festival. At the end of the Cerealia, torches were attached to the tails of foxes, and then lit. The foxes were set loose to run through the streets as magic to protect the crops.

Ceres has Twelve *Indigimenta*, to help Her in her agricultural tasks. These *numina* functioned as specific aspects of Ceres. They are as follows: Vervactor who turns the fallow land, Reparator who prepares the fallow land, Imporcitor who plows with wide furrows, Insitor who sows the seeds, Obarator who plows the surface ground, Occator who harrows the fields, Sarritor who weeds the crops, Subruncinator who thins out the crops, Messo who harvests the crops, Conuector who carts the crops, Conditor who stores the crops, and Promitor who distributes the crops

A native Italic deity, **Liber** is sometimes identified with the Greek God Dionysus, because of his fertility rites. However, Liber has no association with wine, and instead is a vegetative God. He protects the maturation of boys to adulthood. On the Liberalia in March, young men would don the *toga libera*, and sacrifice to Liber as full citizens. His partner, **Libera**, protects the female seed, as He does the male seed.

II. THE ROMAN WAY

Principles of Roman Religion

Romans are guided by three principles in their Polytheism. First, *Do ut des* (I give that you may give) focuses on the reciprocity between people and the Gods. Second, *Ius divinum* (sacred law) governs the right relations between humans and Gods. Finally, *Pax deorum* (peace of the Gods) stressed maintaining harmony between people and the Gods. These principles were rooted in *pietas* (piety). For Romans, this included devotion to others, the Gods, and their communities.

Added to that are the many public and private virtues that every Roman aspires to. Of the list of private virtues relevant to political action would be *dignitas* (a sense of self-worth), *firmitas* (tenacity), *gravitas* (a sense of the importance of the matter), *prudentia* (personal discretion), *severitas* (self-control), and finally *veritas* (honesty). These particular virtues both guide the conduct of the Roman Polytheist in politics, as well as define how to be an effective advocate. Following these virtues ensures that one does not degrade those for whom you advocate nor the Gods Themselves. Furthermore, devotion to the Capitoline and Aventine Triads also stress these virtues.

Meanwhile public Roman virtues provide a structure on what to advocate for. *Abundantia* is enough food for all. *Aequitas* is fair dealing between the government and the people. When conducting affairs let *concordia* (harmony between nations and between people) and *fides* (good faith in contracts) be the guide. *Iustitia* points to having sensible laws, and *salus*, the concern for public welfare. In the throes of advocacy, *bonus eventus* (remembering important positive events) and *fortuna* (acknowledging positive events) should not be forgotten.

Therefore confronting an unfair law such as barring transgender people from receiving government services would not only require listening to the Capitoline and the Aventine Triads, but also following the virtues. The Capitoline Triad counsels how the State should govern for the welfare of all its citizens. A question that this Triad would ask is: was this law rammed through the legislature late at night, when the opposition was absent? The Aventine Triad would add, does this law banning access of transgender people to aid reflect *iustitia* and *aequitas*? Both Triads would say that this law is an example of overreach by a few and tyranny against helpless citizens. Therefore, it would be a devotion to these Gods to take action overturning this law.

Bathroom Wars

The reason why there are few pay toilets in the United States was because of a concerted effort by several groups. Since women were forced to pay to go to the bathroom, while men could use the urinals for free, many women's groups filed lawsuits. In New York, the homeless people filed a class action suit against pay toilets. The public virtues of *aequitas*, *concordia*, and *salus* were being violated.

The Committee to End Pay Toilets In America (CEPTIA) organized and galvanized action in the Midwest. In an op-ed page in the Chicago Tribune in 1972, CEPTIA wrote, pay toilets in general "are a disgrace and possibly a violation of our civil rights. In essence, they make the satisfaction of our basic biological need contingent on the availability of small change, thus exploiting human discomfort for commercial toilets." Founded by two high school students, CEPTIA alerted people of the unfairness of pay toilets through word of mouth and pamphlets left at the pay toilet facilities. They also held press conferences, offering suggestions on how to avoid paying for a toilet, and pressing for laws to end the practice. Their non-confrontational methods encouraged people to demand that their state legislatures take up the matter.

The opposition to ending pay toilets focused on public safety and constitutional rights. Store owners said that the toilets were their private property, and not a public good. Hence private property rights should prevail. Municipalities stressed protection from "drug addicts, homosexuals, and muggers." They explained that pay toilets were a public good protecting the citizenry from undesirables. However, CEPTIA and its allies countered that pay toilets were an affront to human dignity. By 1980, pay toilets were outlawed throughout the United States.

Why was CEPTIA successful? They kept to a single issue and focus. They utilized non-combative means to allow legislators to change their views.

Furthermore, CEPTIA provided help for politicians to pass laws outlawing pay toilets. They employed the personal virtues of *comitas* (courtesy) as well as *firmitas* and *gravitas*.

This example of how to overturn an unjust practice follows basic Roman virtues and principles. Since the focus was one of providing people with basic needs, piety and devotion for the Aventine Triad was demonstrated. Working through the legal system, CEPTIA and its allies prompted local and state governments to change their laws. This demonstrates devotion towards the Capitoline Triad. Using reasoned speech, CEPTIA kept the focus on the problem, and allowing the politicians and store owners to change their minds. They could agree on the basic human right to use a toilet.

When taking political action, Roman polytheists are aware of how their actions affect the *Pax deorum*. Provided they listen to the Gods, and do not substitute their will for the Gods, Romans can be successful advocates for political causes. The key is to follow the guidance of the Triads, the public and private virtues, and the principles of Roman religion.

Works Used

Adkins, Lesley and Roy A. Adkins, *Dictionary of Roman Religion*. New York: Oxford University Press. 1996. Print.

Asborn, Kevin and Dana Burgess, *The Complete Idiot's Guide to Classical Mythology*. New York: Penguin Publishing. 2004. Print.

Gordon, Aaron, "Why Don't We Have Pay Toilets in America." Pacific Standard. 17 September 2014. Web. https://psmag.com/why-don-t-we-have-pay-toilets-in-america-26efede62d6b#.g12p8e1en, <accessed 19 April 2016>.

Koebler, Jason, "When American Had to Pay to Poop." Motherboard. 13 November 2013. Web. http://motherboard.vice.com/blog/when-americans-had-to-pay-to-poop, <accessed 19 April 2016>.

Ovid, *Fasti*. Trans. Betty Rose Nagle. Bloomington: Indiana University Press. 1995. Print.

Scheid, John, *An Introduction to Roman Religion*. Trans. Janet Lloyd. Bloomington: Indiana University Press. 2003. Print.

Turcan, Robert, *The Gods of Ancient Rome: Religion in Everyday Life from Archaic to Imperial Times*. Trans. Antonia Nevill. New York: Edinburgh University Press. 2001. Print.

Warrior, Valerie, *Roman Religion: A Source Book*. New York: Focus Publishing. 2002. Print.

Virginia Carper, a Roman Polytheist, lives in the Washington D.C. area with her family. She is a Dedicant (Roman Hearth) of ADF. Majoring in Divination and Minoring in Lore, She is a Level 5 Student at the Grey School of Wizardry. She has published articles in ADF's *Oak Leaves* and *Walking the Worlds*. Her writings can be found at her blog: *Nature: Observations and Meanings* (naturemeanings. blogspot.com), and at *Witches and Pagans* (witchesandpagans.com/pagan-culture-blogs/animal-wisdom.html).

An Ontological Argument for Polytheism

STEVEN DILLON

This paper constructs several ontological arguments for Polytheism. The first ontological argument is for what is called "God," the notion of which is found to be broadly amenable to classical theism. The second ontological argument is polycentric and maintains that "God" is really just a generic way of talking about many Gods. The third and final ontological argument is monocentric and maintains that even if God is a single individual, there are still many gods. Several ontological arguments are compared and contrasted with these, and it is found that they are novel. In the first place, none of the ontological arguments of this paper argue for the existence of the divine, but instead demonstrate that the existence of the divine can neither be argued for without being presupposed, nor denied without contradiction. Moreover, the arguments for Polytheism enlisted in this paper do not much resemble an ontological argument for Polytheism given by Zeno of Citium and developed by Diogenes of Babylon. Each argument is evaluated and found to be dialectically successful.

Bertrand Russell once quipped that "…the point of philosophy is to start with something so simple as not to seem worth stating, and to end with something so paradoxical that no one will believe it," (Logical Atomism, 20). Audacity has always figured into the composition of the ontological argument. Alvin Plantinga said that "[the ontological argument] has about it an air of egregious unsoundness or perhaps even trumpery and deceit; yet it is profoundly difficult to say exactly where it goes wrong. The fact, I think, is that no philosopher has ever given a really convincing, conclusive, and general refutation—one relevant to all or most of the myriad forms the argument takes," (Plantinga, 196). And even Russell conceded something along these lines: "[t]he argument does not, to a modern mind, seem very convincing, but it is easier to feel convinced that it must be fallacious than it is to find out precisely where the fallacy lies," (History, 586).

By a strict reliance on aprioricity, this paper aspires to the level of audacity that can only be found in the ontological arguments. But, the route by which this is pursued here is quite unlike that by which it is sought in the best known ontological arguments. First, ontological arguments are universally thought to be arguments for the *existence* of something, not for the conclusion that the existence of something is a first principle. Kant was the first to name a class of arguments "ontological," and he characterized them as those which "abstract from all experience, and infer entirely *a priori*, from mere concepts, the existence of a highest cause," (Kant, 499). Graham Oppy suggests that this class of arguments is better called "*a priori* arguments for the existence of God," though he continues the established practice of following Kant's terminology (Ontological Arguments, 1). Robert Maydole says "[o]ntological arguments are deductive arguments for the existence of God from general metaphysical principles and other assumptions about the nature or essence of God," (Maydole, 553). And, of course, crucial to the best known ontological argument is that something than which nothing greater can be thought cannot exist in the mind alone, but must also exist in reality. By contrast, the arguments of this paper do not so much concern whether or not something exists as they do whether or not something's existence is a first principle—a term that will be unpacked in Section I.

Ontological arguments betray their rejection of God as a first principle in more ways than merely arguing for his existence. In Gödel's ontological arguments, God is the sort of thing that can have properties, as he is in Plantinga's so-called 'victorious modal ontological argument.' But, to have properties or features is for the way that one is to be grounded in properties or features distinct from her, thereby failing to be a *first*, or irreducible, principle. Even Anselm nowhere suggests that the greatest conceivable being cannot be argued for without being presupposed. In fact, defenders of Anselm have taken it upon themselves to exonerate his argument from charges of circularity (cf. Maydole, 561-62). But, in treating God as a first principle, the arguments of this paper have a number of advantages over such ontological arguments. For example, the arguments do not rely on controversial logic, as Plantinga's does upon the modal axiom S5 and Maydole's on the Barcan Formula. Nor do they rely on metaphysical issues about which there can be reasonable disagreement, as Gödel's does with "positive" properties. Instead, they employ elementary logic, and concern themselves only with what is arguably noncontroversial. Moreover, the arguments of this paper are impervious to several objections to ontological arguments that have been widely considered to be formidable. For example, it makes no difference to the arguments enlisted here whether or not "existence" is a predicate.[1]

---

[1] Another famous objection to ontological arguments was given by Thomas Aquinas in S.T. I.2.1. It may be over-simplified as follows: since some do not understand the term "God" to denote something that actually exists, it must be *argued* that God actually exists, not simply *insisted* upon. Thus, it does not immediately follow from the concept of God that God actually exists. But, this objection is to arguments that try to deduce the existence of God and from the concept of God no less, while none of the arguments in this paper try any such thing.

Finally, as the above makes clear, ontological arguments are overwhelmingly for "God." While one of the arguments in this paper is indeed made on behalf of what shall be called "God," though the term is understood in a way that is foreign to most ontological arguments, the second and third arguments of this paper are not: they are ontological arguments for Polytheism. While such arguments are clearly unlike more recent ontological arguments, they may not be so unlike more remote ones. For example, an ontological argument for Polytheism may have been given by Zeno of Citium. Oppy says:

> following Ferguson, Barnes suggests that there is an ontological argument in the writings of Zeno of Cition, as reported by Sextus Empiricus: "A man can properly honour the gods; a man cannot properly honour what does not exist; therefore the gods exist." But, while the argument bears some relation to, e.g., the Cartesian ontological argument, it seems doubtful that this argument qualifies as an ontological argument. In particular, it is doubtful that it should be allowed that one could reasonably hold that the first premise is known *a priori*. (Ontological Arguments, 4)

By identifying the preconditions that make it possible for man to properly honor the gods, perhaps the argument is better classified as transcendental than as ontological. However, in his discussion on Diogenes of Babylon's reformulation of Zeno's argument, Michael Papazian suggests that the property 'reasonably honored'—rendered 'properly honoured' in Oppy's citation—could be regarded as part of the concept of the gods, such that "...being worthy of honour pertains to the gods independent of whether honouring them has good consequences for humans," (Papazian, 203). Broadly speaking, there are at least two kinds of reasons: those called "epistemic," which justify belief, and those called "practical," which justify action. Insofar as the relevant premise is about there being good epistemic reasons to honor the gods, Papazian's suggestion is worth considering. Be that as it may, Papazian goes on to assert that the argument is not one for Polytheism because "the Stoics were monotheists who veiled themselves as polytheists," (Papazian, 205). Of course, whether or not this broad-brush takes, the argument could be given a polytheistic interpretation. Whatever the case, though Diogenes' reformulation does speak of the gods as being of such a nature as to exist, it does not treat "the gods" as first principles, and by that fact, sharply differs from the polytheistic argument of this paper.

My primary intention is to construct a dialectically successful ontological argument for Polytheism. An argument will be called dialectically successful if (i) its conclusion follows from its premises, (ii) its premises do not beg the question and (iii) it is not subject to parody. In this context, a parody is an attempt to undermine the logic of an argument by showing that while it may lead to the conclusion one is proposing, it also leads to conclusions that are absurd. These three conditions restrict one, in the context of a dialogue, from trying to change another's mind about a conclusion by appealing to reasons which either do not imply the conclusion, would require one to already believe the conclusion or which would require one to believe something that she finds absurd. The conditions ensure that the reasons given on behalf of a conclusion can be or are commonly accepted by the participants of the dialogue.

Some final words before moving on: first, in some parts of this paper I shall capitalize "God" but not "gods." This grammatical choice is not a kind of preferential treatment; in fact, it has nothing to do with honorific differences: it has simply served well as a device for disambiguation. Second, this is not an intellectual exercise for me: I am a devoted polytheist who would immediately and without hesitation renounce every word of this paper if it caused injustice to the gods.

I. GOD

We shall begin Section I by posing a question: is there something that cannot lack being because it just is being? What would it mean to be being itself or to be being abstracted from all qualification? Could there be such a thing? We must be careful in our answers not to place being itself into a category of being, for then it would not be being itself, but only being of a certain type. It may be asked whether being itself is itself a type of being, but this inquiry would fail to understand what it means for being to be unqualified, for if there were being that is not qualified by anything, then, *a fortiori*, it would not be qualified as being a type of anything.

One may wonder whether being itself would be that which all particular beings have in common. But, if being itself were communicable, participable or exemplifiable, then it would be or belong to the category of communicable, participable, or exemplifiable being, and thereby fail to be being *simpliciter*. What we are referring to here as "being itself" would not be that which all beings *qua* beings have in common, and in virtue of which things count as beings. Rather, it may be deduced that if there is being itself, it is irreducibly unique. This is not to say that being itself would instantiate irreducible uniqueness, it precludes all such qualifications. Being itself would be non-arbitrarily primitive. Indeed, that about which no qualification can be made is about as non-arbitrarily primitive as anything can fairly get. While it cannot be analyzed, it can be described: where being is that which *is*, being itself would be sheer *is-ness*.

As to whether or not being itself exists, consider first that predications and negations of existence come in two forms: first-order and higher-order. In first-order existential statements, we talk about objects directly, saying either that they exist or that they do not. By contrast, in higher-order existential statements, what we speak of directly are of a higher order than objects, such as concepts or concepts of concepts. We say of these higher-order subjects either that they are instantiated or that they are not. But, being itself could not be treated in a higher-order way, for then it would belong to the category of beings which instantiate higher-order subjects. Now, one might insist that this is not a category of being, for insofar as anything exists, it instantiates something or other. However, this suggestion does nothing to show that there is no category of beings which instantiate higher-order subjects: at most, it shows only that it is the most general category of being. And in any case, there could be nothing more general than being itself for being itself to instantiate. It follows that being itself has to be treated in a first-order way. The problem is that, by many lights, first-order existential negation is contradictory, for insofar as there is an object to deny the existence of, it exists. So, on this account, it is a contradiction to say that being itself does not exist.

Of course, not all thinkers endorse this characterization of existential statements, and thus resist the above objection to first-order existential negation. For example, Thomists will maintain that what is having existence denied of it in first-order existential negations is not a complete existing object, but only an essence, which is either an idea in the mind, or, in a more entitative mode of being, also that part of an object which makes it to be whatever it is. Since essences can be conceived without having to commit to their existence, first-order existential negations can amount to something like, "It turns out that this essence which I understood with existential neutrality does not in fact exist." And one may divide a thing in other ways so that the object of first-order existential negation is existentially neutral; but, the important point to realize here is that no such position can render consistent a first-order existential negation of being itself. Since being itself transcends qualification, it could not be qualified as a composite being, and therefore would have no parts for us to treat with existential neutrality. As such, it is a contradiction to say that being itself does not exist.

However, while it must be affirmed that there is being itself, it cannot be affirmed on the basis of argumentation. In order for the premises of such an argument to avoid presupposing the conclusion, being itself would have to be treated with existential neutrality, at least initially. But, then the argument would treat being itself with different senses and commit the fallacy of equivocation: initially, as something one may sensibly regard with existential neutrality, and subsequently, as something that one may not. Thus, to avoid equivocation, an argument for being itself will have to reason in a circle. As something which can neither be argued for without being presupposed nor denied without contradiction, being itself *qua* being itself is what shall be called a first principle.

Some may still protest that just because existence would be part of what it is to be being itself does not mean that it actually is. However, this suggestion fails to appreciate that it is impossible, even in principle, for that which just is being to lack being. It is not a matter of our being ignorant of whether or not there is something which just is being, but that if something does not exist, it simply is not being itself.

Note that it has not been suggested that because being itself is conceivable, it is therefore possible or necessary. Such an argument would be contrary to the position of this section; namely, that being itself is a first principle. What are on offer here are illustrations that being itself exists, not demonstrations. As such, the position of this section is invulnerable to Graham Oppy's objection that "There are naturalists—myself among them—who hold that naturalism is necessary: there are no possible worlds in which there are supernatural entities. Such naturalists do not deny that it is conceivable that there are supernatural entities: but we deny that conceivability entails alethic or ontic possibility," (Maydole,"On Ontological Arguments," 454). Interestingly, if something were qualified as existing in a possible world, or as natural or supernatural, it would thereby fail to be being itself.

One such as Oppy may concede that if being itself were a first principle, then it could neither be argued for without being presupposed nor denied without contradiction, but question whether being itself is in fact a first principle: first principles cannot be demonstrated, but it can be demonstrated that something is a first principle. Thus, the argument of this section may be stated like this:

1. A first principle can neither be argued for without being presupposed nor denied without contradiction.

2. Being itself *qua* being itself can neither be argued for without being presupposed nor denied without contradiction.

3. Therefore, being itself *qua* being itself is a first principle.

To summarize our defense of (2): since "being itself" can neither be treated in a higher-order way nor negated in a first-order way, an argument for being itself will either assume what it intends to prove or surrender its validity to equivocation.

Some may suspect that the attempt to demonstrate that being itself is a first principle begs the question against atheism or naturalism. But, atheism is at most opposed to being itself *qua* God. Moreover, while naturalism is opposed to there being any supernatural categories of being, being itself could not belong to such categories, not because naturalism is true; but, because of what being itself is. However, if it must be said that the position of this section begs the question, then it should be said to beg the question against an incoherent alternative. Finally, one may question whether the above characterization of first principles has parodic counter-examples. But, whether there is some better analysis of first principles is tangential to the point, which is that existence can neither be argumentatively attributed to being itself without vicious circularity nor denied of it without contradiction.

One need not feel compelled to affirm that there is being itself simply because it is a contradiction to say otherwise: the problem with denying that there is being itself has more to do with the underlying misunderstanding of what it is to be being itself: it just is not the sort of thing of which it makes sense to say "this does or could lack being." As such, the position espoused here is acceptable to dialetheists. Moreover, it is one thing to deny that there is being itself and another to deny that there are any beings in particular. Thus, the standard argument for metaphysical nihilism, which proceeds by way of conceptually eliminating particular beings until there is nothing left, would not in any way indicate that being itself lacks being, though so much the worse if it did.

As we have deduced, being itself is irreducibly unique—a point we shall return to in section II. We may proceed apophatically to deduce any number of things about being itself, denying of it any qualifications or categorizations. For example, if being itself were limited in any sense, say, by time, place, or composition, it would thereby fail to be being itself. As such, being itself must be "outside" of time and space, and it must be perfectly simple. In fact, being itself could not even be qualified or categorized as the totality of all things, for this would itself be a boundary or limitation. One may protest that if we must proceed apophatically, then to say anything positive about being itself, even that it "exists," is to introduce illicit qualification; but, this would only be true if the positive attribution, such as "existence," were something appended to being itself and not just a different way of understanding the same thing.

Being itself seems to be what classical theists have generally sought to identify as "God." In fact, the Scholastics referred to God as "Ipsum Esse Subsistens," or the sheer act of being itself subsisting. Such theists have of course disagreed with one another over what can truly be said of God. Some, for example, have maintained that God could not be intellective (e.g., Plotinus, VI.9.6), while others have insisted on just the opposite (e.g., Aquinas, S.T. I.14).[2] For the most part, such disagreements seem to come down to whether the controversial attributions would limit God, or whether they would instead

---

[2] Another dispute between classical theists is over what the first principle should be characterized as, unity or being? At first pass, it might seem that unity and being just refer to the same thing from different perspectives, and that such a dispute is merely semantic, for how could something precede being unless there *were* something to precede being, and how could there be any*thing* if it was prior to and thus had no unity? But, the sheer differences between the systems of thought that have followed from taking each as the first principle suggest otherwise.

qualify our understanding of God. Whatever the case, I shall continue the established practice of calling being itself "God."

II. POLYCENTRIC POLYTHEISM

As indicated above, this section will expand on the idea that God is irreducibly unique. Some have found in God's uniqueness the raw material out of which to construct arguments for Monotheism. Indeed, the term 'God' is grammatically singular and is often used to denote something particular and individual. (Cf. S.T. I.11.1-2) It is even used like a proper name.[3] But, given our understanding of God, what could it mean to say that the term 'God' denotes something like an individual? Whatever else we may say in answer to this question, because being itself transcends all categories of being, we must say that God's individuality does not *consist* in being differentiated from any kind of being. Otherwise, the individuality of God—and thus God himself—would exist only insofar as there is a kind of being to be differentiated from, thereby making God a dependent being and not transcendent. God's individuality is thus externally exclusive, or exclusive of whatever he transcends. But, is God's individuality also internally exclusive, or exclusive of whatever God does not transcend?

Strictly speaking, the only thing that God does not transcend is God, so if God's individuality excluded whatever he did not transcend, then God himself would be excluded from God's individuality. In light of section I, we must say that God's identity is inclusive of at least one. But, must we also say that it is exclusive to only one? Since being itself transcends all categories of being, it does not belong to the category of beings that could pass out of or come into existence. As such, if there were many Gods, it could never happen that all but one passes out of or fails to come into existence. If there is only one God, it could not just happen to be so, but must necessarily be so: there would have to be something inherently contradictory or incoherent about there being many Gods. But, is there?

Proclus said "all that have ever touched upon theology have called things first according to nature, Gods; and have said that the theological science concerns these," (qtd. in Dionysius: 85). Classical thinkers inclined toward

---

[3] Indeed, renowned philosopher Richard Swinburne explicitly says "I take the proposition 'God exists' (and the equivalent proposition 'There is a God') to be logically equivalent to 'there exists necessarily a person without a body (i.e. a spirit) who necessarily is eternal, perfectly free, omnipotent, omniscient, perfectly good, and the creator of all things.' I use 'God' as the name of the person picked out by this description." (The Existence of God: 7) Interestingly, Swinburne is also a Trinitarian, and has been criticized for holding to "a refined paganism" for thinking that each person in God is a discrete substance. (Leftow: 232)

Monotheism have been concerned about there being many Gods because each would have to be being itself and thus first and prior to anything else. But, how could *each* God precede everything else without also preceding each other, and thus forming a circle in which no particular deity is first, but rather is preceded by every other God? However, if each God *were* prior to everything else, then each God would precede even being related to one another, so that no God *qua* God could relate to another as something to be preceded or succeeded. Edward Butler has given an illustration in a similar context that may be helpful in visualizing this: "imagine a set of points, each of which is for itself the center of a circle of which, for the others, it lies on the circumference," (polytheist.com).

The objection being addressed here is symptomatic of a tendency to treat a plurality of Gods as if each were not really divine. For example, in S.T. I.11.3, Aquinas maintains that if there were more than one God, each would have to differ from one another, thereby requiring each to be imperfect by lacking in what another possesses. But, by assuming that the Gods would have to be differentiated from one another rather than that each is individual prior to any differentiation, this line of reasoning fails to treat the Gods as if each were really divine and thus first, thereby focusing its attention on a straw-man instead of what it is purportedly about: a plurality of *Gods*.

If we take the primacy of God seriously, we shall have to admit that the individuality of God precedes all relations, even the relations of being exclusive to only one or inclusive of many. It is for this very reason that there is nothing inherently contradictory or incoherent about there being many Gods: a plurality of Gods cannot be in contradiction or tension with one another unless they are in relations with one another; but, they would precede and thus exist prior to being in relations with one another. Objections to a plurality of Gods are really therefore objections to the Gods' being in relations with one another, not to their existence. While addressing such concerns is generally important, it is irrelevant to the project of this section, which is simply to secure the existence of many Gods.

Recall that if there is only one God it is because there could only be one God and that there could only be one God if there were something inherently contradictory or incoherent about there being a multitude of Gods. But, as we have seen, there is nothing inherently contradictory or incoherent about there being a multitude of Gods. As such, we must deduce that there could be more than one God, and therefore, that there is not in fact only one God, but many.

Each of these premises is *a priori*, and none of them take Polytheism for granted, or unfairly stack the deck against Monotheism: they simply take God's transcendence and priority seriously, and work out the logical consequences. And yet, our argument may seem obscure and puzzling, for how could a singular term like 'God' denote many individuals? The problem is not that a grammatically singular term denotes many individuals, for we regularly use such terms as "horse," "tree" and "human being" to speak generically about all that is horse, tree or human. Rather, the problem is that monotheistic connotations have been incorporated into the term "God" for us, so that our default under-standing of the term is not that it is generic, and a convenient way of talking about any God *qua* God.

Could this argument be parodied? One might attempt to use the logic of our argument to defend what is widely considered impossible or incoherent. The idea would be that objections to a presumably impossible or incoherent object—such as a square-circle—fail to take it seriously, for if there really *were* such an object, then it would precede those relations which are widely thought to entail its impossibility or incoherence. However, if it is *true* that we only think the object is impossible or incoherent because we have failed to take it seriously, then the conclusion of the attempted parody will not be absurd. On the other hand, if we think the object is impossible or incoherent because we *have* taken it seriously and found it wanting, then it is not the logic of our argument that is being parodied, but that of someone else's. In either case, the parody will not succeed.

On this understanding of Polytheism, the Gods do not arise from, nor are they brought about by some higher principle: it is "polycentric." But, suppose that this argument is unsuccessful. That is, suppose that the term "God" is not generic, and that it is denotative only of one. Even on this assumption, which would appear to make Monotheism at least *possible*, an ontological argument for Polytheism can still be given. According to this argument, the gods are created by God, and the next section will discuss what this involves.

III. MONOCENTRIC POLYTHEISM

Since God is being itself, every form of being—whether possible, actual, necessary, biological, sub-atomic, etc.—will bear some likeness or other to God, for insofar as something is, it stands in a relation of similarity to the is-ness that is God. But, if forms of being would be like God, are there standards for being like God that forms of being would have to conform to? This question is not so much concerned with whether or not there are conditions or requirements for being like God as it is with whether or not the conditions or requirements for being like God are in place because there is something that defines what it is to bear a likeness to God in the first place. In this context, a standard for being like God shall be understood as a normative representation or model of God. What would such a representation or model be like?

As particular *standards*, each would be differentiated from another by the irreducibly normative individuality that comes with being a standard. But, that by which one is different from another cannot be identical to that by which one is the same as another. As such, what these standards would have in common with each other could not be a particular way of representing or modeling God. Otherwise, the standard for being like God in that particular respect would be differentiated from the other standards by the very same individuality through which it would be similar to them. To avoid this contradiction, it must be said that what each standard for being like God would have in common would be a likeness to God in the most general of ways, or, in other words, a likeness to God *simpliciter*. The likeness to God *simpliciter* shall be called the divine image, for in resembling God, it is an image, and in resembling God as such, it is "God-like" or divine by likeness. This sort of similarity contrasts with bearing a likeness to God in some specific way, say in simplicity or immateriality, which would not qualify one as divine by likeness, but as simple, immaterial or whatever else by likeness. Since the divine image is what each standard for being like God would have in common, each standard, precisely insofar as it is a standard, would non-arbitrarily qualify as divine by likeness or as a "god."[4]

If there were standards for being like God in particular ways, then, for the same reason, there would be a standard for being like God in any way whatsoever. As the most general way of being like God, the divine image would constitute this standard, for nothing could be outside of its scope to perform this function. But, if the likeness to God *simpliciter* is what sets the standard for being like God in any way whatsoever, and each god, precisely insofar as it is a god, bears this likeness to God, then each god is by nature the standard for being like God in any way whatsoever. Every form of being that is or could be would amount to little more than an imitation of the gods, since it would only be in relation to them—or that standard for being in any way whatsoever—that anything could have an identity as one sort of thing instead of another. Consider then that, strictly speaking, the gods could not be called loving, merciful, vengeful, powerful, wise and so forth, for the gods would instead be that which love, mercy, vengeance, power and wisdom are but imitations of. From the raw, crackling ferocity of thunder to the somnolence of hoarfrost at dawn, all would be but shadows cast by the gods.

This may be all well and good, but do the gods *exist?* Consider first that, like God, the existence of the gods is not something that can be affirmed or denied in a higher-order way. As what sets the standard for being like God in any way whatsoever, there could be nothing higher than the gods for them to instantiate, nor, even if there could be, any conditions or requirements that they—as the standards for being like God in any way whatsoever—would not set and thus precede. As such, their existence must be affirmed or denied in a first-order

---

[4] Those persuaded of Polycentric Polytheism may say that while these standards non-arbitrarily qualify as divine by likeness, they do not non-arbitrarily qualify as gods. But, such polytheists could still endorse the argument, merely understanding it to be for creatures that are divine but less than Gods.

way. Clearly, on the view that all first-order existential negation is a contradiction, it is a contradiction to deny that the gods exist. But, even on views that preserve first-order existential negation, it cannot consistently be denied that the gods exist, for insofar as something would have a part that could be treated with existential neutrality, its existence would be conditioned on the existence of this part, whereas, and as we have just seen, there could be no conditions or requirements that the gods would not set and thus precede. As such, it is contradiction to say that the gods do not exist; however one goes about trying to do that.

However, while it must be affirmed that the gods exist, it cannot be affirmed on the basis of argumentation. In order for the premises of such an argument to avoid presupposing the conclusion, the gods would have to be treated with existential neutrality, at least initially. But, then the argument would treat the gods with different senses and commit the fallacy of equivocation: initially, as what would have to meet certain conditions in order to exist, and subsequently, as what sets the conditions for existing rather than what has to meet them. Thus, to avoid equivocation, an argument for the gods will have to reason in a circle. But, if the existence of the gods can neither be argued for without being presupposed, or denied without contradiction, then it is a first principle that the gods exist:

1. A first principle can neither be argued for without being presupposed nor denied without contradiction.

4. It can neither be argued for without being presupposed nor denied without contradiction that the gods exist.

5. Therefore, it is a first principle that the gods exist.

To summarize our defense of (4): since the standards for being like God in any way whatsoever can neither be treated in a higher-order way nor negated in a first-order way, an argument for their existence will either assume what it intends to prove or surrender its validity to equivocation.

One need not affirm that the gods exist simply because it is a contradiction to say otherwise: the real problem would lie in the confusion that what sets the standard for being could itself lack being, as if there could be being apart from the standard of being, which would somehow need to be given to it in order for it to exist. As such, the argument of this section does not beg the question against dialetheism. Some may suspect that it begs the question against monotheists to argue that it is a first principle that there are standards for being like God. But, Monotheism is at most opposed to there being standards for being like God *qua* deities, and the reasons for identifying these standards as gods follow from the nature of these standards, not from a concealed

[53]

commitment to Polytheism. Finally, as to whether or not the argument of this section begs the question against non-theists: non-theists can grant God's existence for the sake of argument in order to evaluate this section conditionally; but, would be directed to section I for a more relevant discussion on whether or not God exists.

IV. CONCLUDING THOUGHTS

It is easier to sink a ship than it is to build one. Unfortunately, it can be difficult to anticipate objections, and so the arguments of this paper might not have taken into account the best objections that can be made against them. This is not to concede that the best objections to these arguments will be successful, but it is to caution against an uncritical endorsement of the arguments as they stand: every argument can be improved.

Ontological arguments are supposed to have chutzpah, and by arguing that the existence of the divine is a first principle, it would appear this goal has been reached: not even the boldest ontological arguments have dared to go this far. In fact, the arguments of this paper defy typical categorizations of ontological arguments, for they are neither conceptual nor Cartesian, neither Meinongian nor definitional, etc., and this is all the more true since such categorizations tend to be of ontological arguments which take it for granted that the *existence* of the divine is not a first principle, but something that can validly be argued for.

What of the three criteria for a dialectically successful argument laid out earlier? Each conclusion was deduced from premises by valid rules of inference, and the arguments can be parsed in either propositional or predicate logic. Moreover, none of their premises were found to beg the question against non-theists or monotheists. What about parodies? Some might take issue with the ontological argument for Monocentric Polytheism in section III, maintaining that if every form of being has a standard, and every standard is a god, then there are gods of forms of being that seem beneath a god. For example, one might try to parody by asking whether there are gods of garbage, cancer or foul odors. There are several ways to respond to this. Firstly, it must be asked what the objection is intended to do: is it supposed to show that the existence of the gods can be denied in either a higher-order way or a first-order way? How is that supposed to work? Secondly, such examples betray a philosophical naïveté, in that they take it for granted that such things *are* forms of being, and not just aggregates of forms of beings. Moreover, the divinity of that which sets the standard for some strange form of being would not be sullied by that strange form of being, because it is only insofar as one sets the standard for being like God in any way whatsoever, strange ways included, that one can be called a god in the first place. Finally, if one hopes to parody the argument of section III and not some other, one must confine herself to what can be established on *a priori* grounds. But, few things can be proven to actually exist within these parameters, and possibilities come cheap.

It would seem from the foregoing that we have constructed novel, powerful, and dialectically successful ontological arguments for Polytheism.

Works Cited

Aquinas, Thomas. *Summa Theologiae*. Latin Text and English Translation, Introductions, Notes, Appendices, and Glossaries. Cambridge, England: Blackfriars, 1964.

Brian Leftow, "Anti Social Trinitarianism," in *The Trinity*, ed. Stephen T. Davis, Daniel Kendall, and Gerald O'Collins. Oxford: Oxford UP. 1999.

Butler, Edward P. "Polytheism and Individuality in the Henadic Manifold." *Dionysius* 23 (2005): 85.

_____. http://polytheist.com/noeseis/2016/02/10/nature-gods-ii-first-intelligible-triad/

Kant, Immanuel. *Critique of Pure Reason*. Ed. Marcus Weigelt. Trans. F. Max Müller. New York, New York: Penguin Classics, 2007.

Maydole, Robert E. "The Ontological Argument." *The Blackwell Companion to Natural Theology*. Ed. William Lane Craig. Ed. J.P. Moreland. Chichester, U.K.: Wiley-Blackwell, 2009.

Oppy, Graham. "Maydole on Ontological Arguments." *Ontological Proofs Today*. Ed. Mirosław Szatkowski. Piscataway, NJ: Transaction , Rutgers U, 2012.

_____. *Ontological Arguments and Belief in God*. Cambridge: Cambridge UP, 1995

Papazian, Michael. "The Ontological Argument of Diogenes of Babylon." *Phronesis* 52.2 (2007): 188-209.

Plantinga, Alvin. *The Nature of Necessity*. Oxford: Clarendon, 1974.

Plotinus. *The Enneads*. Trans. Stephen Mackenna. Ed. John Dillon. Burdett, New York: Larson Publications, 1991.

Russell, Bertrand. *The History of Western Philosophy*. London, UK: Simon & Schuster, 1972.

_____. *The Philosophy of Logical Atomism*. 1st ed. Abingdon, Oxon: Routledge, 2010.

Swinburne, Richard. *The Existence of God*. Oxford: Oxford UP. 2004.

Steven Dillon is a Pagan thinker and long time devotee of Diana, whom he first met through Stregheria. Author of *The Case for Polytheism* (Iff Books, 2015), Dillon's non-fiction work is focused on developing philosophical foundations for Pagan beliefs and practices. Prior to becoming Pagan, Dillon studied to be a priest in Catholic seminary, where he majored in philosophy.

The Polytheism of the Epicureans

PAUL TERENCE MATTHIAS JACKSON

Epicureans have been branded atheists since antiquity, but although they might have held unorthodox beliefs about divinity, they did nevertheless believe in gods, however unorthodox their beliefs about them were.

They did not believe in the Olympians that Hesiod and Homer had depicted, but anthropomorphic yet bizarre gods: although these were compounds of atoms, they were immortal, unlike any other compound in the Epicurean universe, and there was quite possibly an infinite host of such deities, all alike and all nameless.

These gods were not considered figments of the imagination by the Epicureans, but as real, living entities that actually existed, remotely, somewhere out there in the cosmos, doing very little aside from maintaining their supremely peaceful, painless, and tranquil dispositions. And these gods needed to be considered real in order to be genuine, ethical models for mankind to follow, which was their main function within the Epicurean world-view. The atoms of these gods, like everything in existence, were held to be perpetually in motion, constantly being emitted from their bodies as images that then travelled directly to the minds of mankind and thereby presented a true depiction of divinity, of peacefulness, and above all, of happiness, which would then be examples for individual Epicureans to follow on their individual journeys towards ἀταραξία, tranquility.

EPICUREAN RESISTANCE TO ORTHODOXY

Greek religion almost certainly predates the eighth century B.C. epic poems of Homer and Hesiod, but nevertheless these seem to have been a common source for future orthodoxy, with Farrington (1967, 66) writing that "hitherto the Greeks had relied on Homeric and Hesiodic myth." Despite the decentralisation of Ancient Greece, with *poleis*, or city-states, often at odds with one another, and despite local variations, Kearns (in Hornblower & Spawforth(2003), 1300) concludes that this orthodoxy "presented a recognisable picture throughout the Greek world" and had "enough in common to be seen as essentially one system, and [was] generally understood as such by the Greeks."

But in the sixth century B.C. there was a marked shift away from reliance upon Homeric and Hesiodic mythologies and their supernatural explanations for natural phenomena. In Asia Minor, Thales was perhaps the first to think in this more scientific way, reasoning and rationalising, trying to make sense of the universe for himself rather than merely accepting what others told him. Thales paved the way for other philosophers who would share his resistance to orthodoxy and his rationalistic approach, and DeWitt (1954, 107) argues that it was against the likes of Homer and Hesiod that Epicurus came to position himself: "as for the poetical components of the traditional curriculum, Homer, Hesiod, and Theognis, there can be no doubt that his [Epicurus'] attitude was hostile. With the genealogies of the gods he could have had no patience." Indeed, Diogenes of Oenoanda captures the Epicurean criticism of Homer:

> [Let us then contradict Homer, who] talks all sorts of nonsense about them [the gods], [representing them sometimes as adulterers, sometimes as] lame, [sometimes as thievish, or even as being struck by mortals with a spear,] as well as introducing the craftsmen to produce inappropriate portrayals. Some statues of the gods shoot [arrows and are produced holding] a bow, [represented] like Heracles in Homer; a bodyguard of wild-beasts attends others; others are angry at the prosperous, like Nemesis according to popular opinion.[1]

EPICUREAN ATHEISM

Bearing in mind such criticism, it might not seem so surprising that Epicureanism came to be seen as atheistic, and indeed Gordon (1996, 100) writes that by the second century A.D. it had become conventional among non-Epicureans to regard Epicureans as atheists. An example of this type of attitude is evident in Lucian's parody *Zeus Rants*. The parody shows the conflicting Stoic and Epicurean ideas about the nature of the gods, with the Stoic Timocles and the Epicurean Damis debating their very existence. Timocles attests that Damis does not think that gods exist, asking, "Damis, you sacrilegious wretch, why do you say that the gods do not exist and do not show providence on behalf of men?"[2]

---

[1] "[εἴπωμεν δ' οὖ]ν πρὸς τὸν [Ὅμηρον, ὃς π]ερὶ αὐτῶν [παντοδαπὰ] λαλεῖ λα[λήματα, τοὺς] μὲν αὐ[τῶν ἀποφαίν]ων μοι[χούς, τοὺς δ]ὲ χωλούς, [τοὺς δὲ κλεπ]τικούς, [ἢ καὶ ὑπὸ θνητ]ῶν παιο[μένους δόρατι], πρὸς τῷ [προάγειν τοὺ]ς δημιουρ[γοὺς ποιεῖν ἃ μὴ π]ρέπει. τὰ [μὲν θεῶν ξόανα β]άλλει [βέλη καὶ γέγο]νε τόξον [ἔχοντα, ποιο]ύμενα ὡς ὁ Ἡρακλῆς παρὰ τῷ Ὁμήρῳ, τὰ δ' ὑπὸ θηρίων δορυφορεῖται, τὰ δ' ὀργίζεται τοῖς εὐτυχοῦσιν, ὥσπερ ἡ Νέμεσις τοῖς πολλοῖς δοκεῖ." (fr. 19 = NF 115). Translations from Diogenes of Oenoanda with my own amendments and the original are from Smith (1993; 2003).

[2] "τί φῄς, ὦ ἱερόσυλε Δᾶμι, θεοὺς μὴ εἶναι μηδὲ προνοεῖν τῶν ἀνθρώπων;" (fr. 35).

But there are at least two good reasons for this charge of atheism against Epicureans, with neither being a genuine belief that Epicureans did not believe in the existence of gods. Firstly, Gordon (1996, 101) argues that it had its "roots in philosophical discourse," which amounted to rival schools of philosophical thought purposefully misrepresenting Epicureanism as atheistic, and Obbink (1989, 220-22) specifies that the alleged atheism of Epicureanism was actually a Sceptical Academic invention, with the polemical representation of Epicurus as an atheist really a distortion of historical fact. And secondly, Obbink (1989, 188-90) also admits "atheism in the ancient world was never a well-defined or ideologically fixed position." In the ancient world, the meaning of ἄθεος could be broader than 'the theory or belief that God [or gods] does not exist,' as the Oxford English Dictionary (*OED*) (2001, 105) defines the term 'atheism,' for Philodemus in his *On Piety* classifies atheists, as Obbink summarises, into:

1. Those who say that it is unknown whether there are any gods or what they are like.

2. Those who say openly that the gods do not exist.

3. Those who clearly imply it.

And so Obbink concludes "this scheme implies that the charge of atheism could be incurred for something less than an outright denial of the existence of the gods."

EPICUREAN THEISM

And Obbink (1996, 4-6) does stress the importance of gods to the Epicureans:

One of Philodemus' main contentions in *On Piety* is that Epicurus had no doubts about the necessity of giving an account of the gods. Epicurus does seem to have placed theology first in his system: the gods are the subject of the first of the *Principal Doctrines* and stand first in the *Letter to Menoeceus*, where Epicurus asserts that the gods exist [...] the first book of Philodemus' *On Gods* deals with the irrational fear of the gods as a basic philosophical problem. The gods also have pride of place in the first colon of the Epicurean fourfold remedy.

Indeed, Epicurus himself confirms that "gods there are, since knowledge of them is by clear vision." In Cicero's *On the Nature of the Gods*, his Epicurean spokesman Gaius Velleius states that "such notions Epicurus designates by the word *prolepsis*, which is a sort of preconceived mental picture of a thing," and explains that *prolepsis*:

Is perceived not by the senses but by mind [...] by our perceiving images owing to their similarity and succession, because an endless train of precisely similar images arises from the innumerable atoms and streams to us from the gods, our mind with the keenest feelings of pleasure fixes its gaze on these images, and so attains an understanding of a being both blessed and eternal.[3]

Furthermore, Diogenes Laertius writes that *prolepsis* was a standard of truth in Epicureanism: "in *The Canon* Epicurus affirms that our sensations and preconception and our feelings are the standards of truth; the Epicureans generally make perceptions of mental presentations to also be standards."[4]

And so it seems clear that Epicureans actually did believe in gods, and that *prolepsis* revealed not only their nature but also their homes and lives.

1. The Homes of the Gods

Philodemus argues in his *On Gods* that observed phenomena "demonstrate that every nature has a different location suitable to it. To some it is water, to some air and Earth. This is also the case for animals as well as for plants and the like. And for the gods especially there has to be [a suitable location]."[5]

According to the source material, the suitable location of their homes lies distant from those of mankind. Diogenes of Oenoanda strenuously argues that immortals could not live alongside mortals, for he asks, "moreover, what [god, if] he had existed for infinite [time] and enjoyed tranquility [for thousands of years, would have got] this idea that he needed a city and fellow-citizens?"[6] And

---

[3] "non sensu sed mente cernantur [...] imaginibus similitudine et transitione perceptis, cum infinita simillumarum imaginum series ex innumerabilibus individuis existat et ad deos adfluat, cum maximis voluptatibus in eas imagines mentem intentam infixamque nostram intellegentiam capere quae sit et beata natura et aeterna" (*Nat. D.* I.49). Translations from *On the nature of the gods* with my own amendments and the original are from Rackham (1961).

[4] "ἐν [...] τῷ Κανόνι λέγων ἐστὶν ὁ Ἐπίκουρος κριτήρια τῆς ἀληθείας εἶναι τὰς αἰσθήσεις καὶ προλήψεις καὶ τὰ πάθη, οἱ δ' Ἐπικούρειοι καὶ τὰς φανταστικὰς ἐπιβολὰς τῆς διανοίας" (*DL* X.31). Translations from *DL* with my own amendments and the original are from Hicks (1931).

[5] "ἅπερ ἔδειξε[ν] ἄλλους ἄλλαις φύσεσιν οἰκείους (εἶναι) κ(αὶ) τοῖς μὲν ὑγρά τοῖς δ' ἀέρα καὶ γῆν. τ[ο]ῦτο μὲν ζῴων, τοῦτο δὲ φυτῶν κ(αὶ) 'τῶν' ὁμ[οί]ων, μάλιστα δὲ τοῖ θεοῖς δεῖ" (*On Gods* III.8.20-3). Translations from Philodemus' *On Gods* with my own amendments and the original are from Essler (in Fish & Sanders, 2011).

[6] "τίς δὲ κα[ὶ θεός, εἰ] ἦν τὸν ἄπειρ[ον χρόνον], ἡσυχάσας χι[λιάδας ἐτῶν], οὕτως εἰς ἔν[νοιαν ἂν ἦ]λθεν τοῦ πόλεως αὐτῷ χρειαν ὑπάρχειν καὶ συμπολιτευομένων;" (NF 127 and fr. 20 = NF 39).

then he answers his own question:

> Add to this the absurdity that he, being a god, should seek to have human beings as fellow-citizens. And this is the further point too: if he had created the world as a habitation and city for himself, I seek to know where he was living before the world was created; I do not find an answer, at any rate not one consistent with the doctrine of these people when they declare that this world is unique. So for that infinite time, apparently, the god of these people was cityless and homeless and, like an unfortunate man—I do not say god—having neither city nor fellow-citizens, he was destitute and roaming about at random. If therefore the divine nature shall be deemed to have created things for its own sake, all this is absurd; and if for the sake of men, there are yet more absurd consequences.[7]

Therefore according to Diogenes it is implausible to even think that the gods dwelt upon the Earth, which is what Diogenes must mean by κόσμος in the context, as the Earth had been created. The gods though, who are immortal and therefore had not been created, having existed for an infinite amount of time, must accordingly have existed before the Earth. Following this line of argument, those who claim that the gods live on the Earth would have to accept that this means the gods had previously lived elsewhere, and had at some point relocated here, which is a premise that Diogenes simply cannot accept.

More specifically, in *On the Nature of the Gods* Cicero introduces his Epicurean spokesman in the following way:

> Hereupon Velleius began, in the confident manner (I need not say) that is customary with Epicureans, afraid of nothing so much as lest he should appear to have doubts about anything. One would have supposed he had just come down from the assembly of the gods in the intermundane spaces of Epicurus![8]

---

[7] "πρὸς τῷ καὶ γελοῖον εἶναι θεὸν ὄντα ζητεῖν συμπολιτευομένας ἀνθρώπους ἔχειν. ἔτι δὲ κἀκεῖνο· εἰ γὰρ ὥσπερ οἰκητήριόν τι καὶ πόλιν ἑαυτῷ τὸν κόσμον ἐδημιούργησε, ζητῶ πρὸ τοῦ κόσμου ποῦ διέτριβεν· οὐ γὰρ εὑρίσκω κατὰ γοῦν τὸν τούτων λόγον ἕνα τοῦτον ἀποφαινομένων κόσμον εἶναι. τὸν οὖν ἄπειρον ἐκεῖνον χρόνον, ὡς ἔοικεν, ἄπολις ἦν καὶ ἄο[ι]κος ὁ τούτων θεὸς καί, ὡς ἄνθρωπος ἀτυχής - οὐ λέγω θεός - μήτε πόλιν ἔχων μήτε συμπολιτευομένας, [...] ἔρημος ἐπλανᾶτο ὁπουδήποτε. εἰ μὲν οὖν ἑαυτῆς χάριν ἡ θεία φύσις δεδημιουργηκέναι δόξει τὰ πράγματα, ταῦτα πάντα {τὰ} ἄτοπα· [...] εἰ [δὲ] τῶν ἀνθρώπων, [...] ἄλ[λα] πάλιν ἀτοπώτερα" (fr. 20 = NF 39).

[8] "Tum Velleius fidenter sane, ut solent isti, nihil tam verens quam ne dubitare aliqua de re videretur, tamquam modo ex deorum concilio et ex Epicuri intermundiis descendisset" (*Nat. D.* I.18).

'Intermundane spaces' is Rackham's translation of *intermundia*. Now Epicurus in his *Letter to Pythocles* had written:

> And that such worlds are infinite in number we can be sure, and also that such a world may come into being both inside another world and in an interworld, by which we mean a space between worlds; it will be in a place with much void, and not in a large empty space quite like void, as some say: this occurs when seeds of the right kind have rushed in from a single world or interworld, or from several.[9]

It is μετακόσμιον that Bailey translates as 'interworld.' It seems clear then that *intermundia* is Cicero's translation of Epicurus' μετακόσμια. Epicurus himself defines μετακόσμιον as μεταξὺ κόσμων διάστημα, "a space between worlds," but in order to grasp what exactly is meant by a 'space between worlds,' one has to first appreciate what is being meant by a 'world.' Bailey translates κόσμος as a 'world,' but this can be misleading because 'world' suggests a celestial body such as the Earth, whereas κόσμος can also refer to the universe. Indeed, the transliteration of κόσμος, cosmos, refers specifically to the universe rather than a celestial body. But Epicurus does again help the reader by giving his own definition of κόσμος: "a circumscribed portion of sky, containing heavenly bodies and an Earth and all the heavenly phenomena [...] it is a piece cut off from the infinite."[10] Therefore with κόσμος Epicurus seems to mean a region of the universe that contains heavenly bodies. By extension then, a μετακόσμιον, a space between those regions of the universe that contain heavenly bodies, must be a region of the universe that does not contain heavenly bodies, though Epicurus does also says that it is not entirely empty.

The nature of these interworlds is rather vague, but the important thing that the Epicureans try to convey is that the gods live remotely, away from mankind, in a potentially infinite number of such interworlds, each of which are quiet and are apart from celestial bodies, though they are not entirely empty.

In the sixth book of his *De rerum natura* (*DRN*), Lucretius further elaborates upon the homes of the gods:

---

[9] "Ὅτι δὲ καὶ τοιοῦτοι κόσμοι εἰσὶν ἄπειροι τὸ πλῆθος, ἔστι καταλαβεῖν, καὶ ὅτι καὶ ὁ τοιοῦτος δύναται κόσμος γίνεσθαι καὶ ἐν κόσμῳ καὶ <ἐν> μετακοσμίῳ, ὃ λέγομεν μεταξὺ κόσμων διάστημα, ἐν πολυκένῳ τόπῳ καὶ οὐκ ἐν μεγάλῳ εἰλικρινεῖ καὶ κενῷ, καθάπερ τινες φασιν, ἐπιτηδείων τινῶν σπερμάτων ῥυέντων ἀφ᾽ ἑνὸς κόσμου ἢ μετακοσμίου ἢ καὶ ἀπὸ πλειόνων" (*Ad Pyth.* 88-9). Epicurus also writes that that there are an infinite number of worlds in his *Letter to Herodotus* (45). Translations from Epicurus with my own amendments and the original are from Bailey (1926).
[10] "ἔστι περιοχή τις οὐρανοῦ, ἄστρα τε καὶ γῆν καὶ πάντα τὰ φαινόμενα περιέχουσα [...] ἀποτομὴν ἔχουσα ἀπὸ τοῦ ἀπείρου" (*Ad Pyth.* 88).

> Another thing it is impossible that you should believe is that any holy abode of the gods exists in any part of the world. For the nature of the gods, being thin and far removed from our senses, is hardly seen by the mind's intelligence; and since it eludes the touch and impact of the hands, it cannot possibly touch anything that which we can touch; for that cannot touch which may not be touched itself. Therefore their abodes also must be different from our abodes, being thin in accord with their bodies.[11]

This is a crucially important reference, as not only does Lucretius here state that the homes of the gods lie apart from the Earth, as *mundus* ought to be understood here, but he also gives further details about their composition: these interworlds are composed of such fine material that they cannot be touched or thereby be destroyed, like the gods who live within them. These interworlds are "hardly seen by the mind's intelligence" because of the extremely fine nature of such places.

And yet however fine this material is, it must be composed of atoms and void, for Lucretius maintains, "there is nothing which you can call wholly distinct from body and separate from void, to be discovered as a kind of third nature."[12]

2. The Nature of the Gods

Epicurus claims in his *Letter to Menoeceus* that the gods "are not such as the many believe them to be."[13] So what were they thought to be like? Firstly, in the same letter, Epicurus states emphatically that the gods were immortal:

> First of all believe that god is a being immortal and blessed, even as the common idea of a god is engraved on men's minds, and do not assign to him anything alien to his immortality or ill-suited to his blessedness: but believe about him everything that can uphold his blessedness and immortality.[14]

---

[11] "Illud item non est ut possis credere, sedes / esse deum sanctas in mundi partibus ullis. / tenuis enim natura deum longeque remota / sensibus ab nostris animi vix mente videtur; / quae quoniam manuum tactum suffugit et ictum, / tactile nil nobis quod sit contingere debet; / tangere enim non quit quod tangi non licet ipsum. / quare etiam sedes quoque nostris sedibus esse / dissimiles debent, tenues de corpore eorum. " (*DRN* V.146-54). Translations from *DRN* with my own amendments and the original are from Rouse & Smith (2006).

[12] "nil est quod possis dicere ab omni / corpore seiunctum secretumque esse ab inani, / quod quasi tertia sit numero natura reperta" (*DRN* I.430-2). Cf. also *DRN* I.511ff.

[13] "οἵους δ' αὐτοὺς <οἱ> πολλοὶ νομίζουσιν, οὐκ εἰσίν" (*Ad Men.* 123).

[14] "πρῶτον μὲν τὸν θεὸν ζῷον ἄφθαρτον καὶ μακάριον νομίζων, ὡς ἡ κοινὴ τοῦ θεοῦ νόησις

However, this is problematic: Lucretius maintains that all things are composed of atoms and void that can be broken down to these constituent atoms, meaning that compounds themselves cannot be immortal. It would follow that this *should* include gods. Sextus Empiricus captures this paradox when writing, "according to some, Epicurus in his popular exposition allows the existence of god, but in expounding the physical nature of things he does not allow it."[15] So Brown (1984, 201) concedes "the Epicurean gods, though material, were, unlike the world and its inhabitants, [the gods being] eternal and indestructible." Bailey (1947b, 1343) suggests, "Epicurus conceived them [gods] as atomic compounds, but of a texture far more subtle (*tenuis*) than anything included in our world. *Tenuis*: 'subtle,' 'fine,' 'tenuous' in the character of the atoms which compose it and in the way in which they are united." The Epicurean gods were composed of material so fine and elusive, like the interworlds that they inhabit, that they could potentially avoid fatal collisions and thereby be rendered immortal. But it is Philodemus' *On Piety* that helps most of all to make sense of the paradox. Here he explains, "for the most part they [gods] come about when they are formed from an aggregation of various similar particles."[16] Therefore, gods are composed of similar atoms, perhaps with regard to their fineness. Such a composition would be distinctive to the gods, and it is this composition of fine and elusive material that allows the gods to avoid potentially destructive collisions.

Yet Lucretius writes that all compounds are always in motion,[17] which should make them unstable and liable to lose material, even if they were to avoid potentially destructive collisions. However, it is perhaps the similarity of the atoms that the gods are composed of, thereby being mutually compatible, that curbs this instability and strengthens rather the unity of such compounds. Lucretius explains how atoms actually cohere with one another: "whatever seems to us hardened and close set must consist of elements more closely hooked and held knit deeply together by branch-like shapes."[18] Therefore these fine, elusive, and similar atoms that the gods are composed of perhaps also have

---

ὑπεγϱάφη, μηθὲν μήτε τῆς ἀφθαϱσίας ἀλλότϱιον μήτε τῆς μακαϱιότητος ἀνοίκειον αὐτῷ πϱοσάπτε· πᾶν δὲ τὸ φυλάττειν αὐτοῦ δυνάμενον τὴν μετα ἀφθαϱσίας μακαϱιότητα πεϱὶ αὐτὸν δόξαζε" (*Ad Men.* 123).

[15] "καὶ Ἐπίκουϱος δὲ κατ' ἐνίους ὡς μὲν πϱὸς τοὺς πολλοὺς ἀπολείπει θεόν, ὡς δὲ πϱὸς τὴν φύσιν τῶν πϱαγμάτων οὐδαμῶς" (*Adv.Math.* IX.58). Translations are from Inwood et al. (1994, p96). Original Greek is from U (p238).

[16] "τὰ πολλὰ [με]ν ἐπειδὰν ἐκ τῆς ὁμοίων {ἄλλων} [κἄλ]λων [ἐπι]συγκϱί[σεως ἀ]τόμ[ων γε]νηται πο[...]" (13). Translations from *On Piety* with my own amendments and the original are from Obbink (1996).

[17] *DRN* II.89-90; *Ad Her.* 43.

[18] "quae nobis durata ac spissa videntur, / haec magis hamatis inter sese esse necessest / et quasi ramosis alte compacta teneri" (*DRN* II.444-6).

a special type of bond that enhances their cohesion and unity.

And so Aëtius claims, "the same philosopher [Epicurus] says elsewhere that there are four existences immortal in their kinds, namely, the atoms, the void, the universe, the similarities."[19] Philodemus in his *On Piety* had considered what these 'similarities' are:

> [A god's] constitution out of things similar would obviously be a unified entity. For it is possible for beings constituted out of similarity for ever to have perfect happiness, since unified entities can be formed no less out of identical than out of similar elements and both kinds of entity are recognised by Epicurus as being exactly the same things, for example in his book *On Holiness*. The demonstration that this involves no contradiction may be passed over. Therefore, he was wont to say that nature brought all these things to completion alike. And that for the most part they came about when they are formed from an aggregation of various similar particles.[20]

However, these gods do lose material, as images, which must also be material, constantly stream from the gods to the minds of mankind and spark preconception. If this material was not replenished, there would surely come a point when the gods would lose all of their material and thereby no longer exist. And yet Velleius proclaims that "if the causes of destruction are beyond count, the causes of conservation also are bound to be infinite,"[21] and indeed gods might preserve their immortality in another way. According to Lucretius, the nature of the gods and the interworlds in which they reside is also similar. Therefore there would be a readily available store of similar material to replenish the gods, replacing any displaced atoms. Further, in a universe of infinite size, there are a potentially infinite number of interworlds, and so the images that the gods constantly lose might stream to the minds of mankind, but they might also happen upon other interworlds instead and thereby replenish

---

[19] "ὁ δ' αὐτὸς ἄλλας τέσσαρας φύσεις κατὰ γένος ἀφθάρτους τάσδε, τὰ ἄτομα, τὸ κενόν, τὸ ἄπειρον, τὰς ὁμοιότητας" (1.7.34 = *Dox. Graec.* P. 306 (U 355)). Translations are from Inwood et al. (1994, p96). Original Greek is from Diels (1965, 306).

[20] "στοιχ[είω]σις ὁμ[οίων οὖσα] φαίνο[ιτ'] ἂ[ν ἑν]ότης· δύναται γὰρ ἐκ τῆς ὁμοιότητος ὑπάρχουσι διαιώνιον ἔχειν τὴν τελείαν εὐδαιμονίαν, ἐπειδήπερ οὐχ ἧττον ἐκ τῶν αὐτῶν ἢ τῶν ὁμοίων στοιχείων ἑνότητες ὑποτελεῖσθαι δύνανται καὶ ὑπὸ τοῦ Ἐπικούρου καταλείπονται καθάπερ ἐν τῶι Περὶ ὁσιότητος αὐτότατα· τ[ὸ δ]ὲ μηδεμίαν ὑπε[ναν]τιολογίαν εἶναι παρα<ιτη>τέον ὑποδεικνύειν. εἴωθε τοίνυν [πα]νθ' ὁμῶς ταῦτα φύ[σι]ν ἀποτελεῖσθαι λέγειν· τὰ πολλὰ [με]ν ἐπειδὰν ἐκ τῆς ὁμοίων {ἄλλων} [κάλ]λων [ἐπι]συγκρί[σεως α]τόμ[ων γέ]νηται πο[...]" (13).

[21] "si quae interimant innumerabilia sint, etiam ea quae conservent infinita esse debere" (*Nat. D.* I.50).

these interworlds and the gods within them. Indeed, when images happen upon the minds of mankind and spark preconception, similar material might also be displaced. And so, with an endless interchange such as this, the amount of similar material would always be enough, and equilibrium would be maintained, and indeed, Lucretius does state that although there is an infinite store of material in the universe, the proportions of atoms and void always remain the same.[22] And so Bailey (1947a, 990) argues that there is a "constant supply of atoms moving in the void [which] maintains their [gods'] bodies, which are everlasting because the form [of the gods] remains the same, but the substance changes." It is Lucretius who most probably influences him: "there was always a succession of visions coming up in which the shape [of gods] remained the same."[23]

And yet, if a god constantly loses material by giving off images, and this displaced material is constantly being replaced, there must surely come a point when, although the god still exists, all of its original atoms have been lost, bringing into question whether it is still the same god anymore. This evokes the famous Ship of Theseus paradox: in his *Parallel Lives*, *Theseus*, Plutarch recalls,

> The Athenians down to the time of Demetrius Phalereus preserved the ship on which Theseus sailed with the youths and returned in safety, the thirty-oared galley. They took away the old timbers from time to time, and put new and sound ones in their places, so that the vessel became a standing illustration for the philosophers in the mooted question of growth, some declaring that it remained the same, others that it was not the same vessel.[24]

It could be argued that the god remains the same by continuity, as not all of its atoms had been exchanged at the same time.

However in his *On the Form of God* Demetrius Lacon writes, "memories are kept"[25] despite the constant interchange of atoms, and indeed that, beyond

---

[22] *DRN* I.370ff.

[23] "quia semper eorum / subpeditabatur facies et forma manebat" (*DRN* V.1175-6).

[24] "Τὸ δὲ πλοῖον ἐν ᾧ μετὰ τῶν ἠϊθέων ἔπλευσε καὶ πάλιν ἐσώθη, τὴν τριακόντορον, ἄχρι τῶν Δημητρίου τοῦ Φαληρέως χρόνων διεφύλαττον οἱ Ἀθηναῖοι, τὰ μὲν παλαιὰ τῶν ξύλων ὑφαιροῦντες, ἄλλα δὲ ἐμβάλλοντες ἰσχυρὰ καὶ συμπηγνύντες οὕτως ὥστε καὶ τοῖς φιλοσόφοις εἰς τὸν αὐξόμενον λόγον ἀμφιδοξούμενον παράδειγμα τὸ πλοῖον εἶναι, τῶν μὲν ὡς τὸ αὐτό, τῶν δὲ ὡς οὐ τὸ αὐτὸ διαμένοι λεγόντων" (*Parallel Lives* I, *Theseus*, XXIII.1). Translations from *Parallel Lives* with my own amendments and the original are from Perrin (1967).

[25] "τὰς μνήμας φυλάττεσθα[ι]" (XIII). Translations from Demetrius Lacon's *On the Form of God* are my own. Original Greek is from Santoro (2000). Of course, memories are also atomic, like everything else in Epicurean physics.

memories, "it is possible for a certain number of bodies to be kept,"[26] and so the gods could also retain original material and thereby their identity. If images were lost from their surface layer, as would be most likely, a god's core could indeed remain intact.

But regardless of the amount of material that is lost and replenished, Merlan (1960, 54) wonders how a god can remain happy, which Epicureans claims they are, if they lost any material at all:

> If the atomic complexes which are gods admittedly exchange their atoms for others which are only specifically identical, how can we still say that the happiness of the gods is an uninterrupted condition, i.e. that the gods are always happy? And the answer seems to be that an atomic complex does not lose its identity by exchanging atoms for others only specifically identical with the ones it lost.

Merlan's main point is that gods can remain happy despite losing material because the lost material is always replenished, and it is always replaced by similar material, so a god does not lose identity.

And yet Lucretius writes that "the very nature of divinity must necessarily enjoy immortal life in the deepest peace, far removed and separated from our affairs; for without any pain, without danger, itself mighty by its own resources, needing us not at all, is neither propitiated with services nor touched by wrath."[27] The loss and replenishment of atoms must be negligible as to be painless, quite possible given the fineness of their material, and this must also be how these gods can remain happy.

Moving on now to the faculties that these gods possess, Demetrius Lacon in his *On the Form of God* claims that the gods possess mind and soul: "[god] has in common with man soul. For that reason, if certain living creatures have a form made in this way, god must also be made in this way; but he will have the rational faculty and indeed together with common properties he will also have many other properties to the highest degree."[28] The gods have a body that is finer than the human mind, and therefore must possess an even finer mind and soul. Demetrius Lacon is also indicating that the gods share properties with humans, though the divine properties are enhanced.

---

[26] "δυνατόν ἐστι φυλάττεσ]θαι ποσὰ τῶν σωμάτων" (XII).

[27] "divom natura necessest / inmortali aevo summa cum pace fruatur / semota ab nostris rebus seiunctaque longe; / nam privata dolore omni, privata periclis, / ipsa suis pollens opibus, nil indiga nostri, / nec bene promeritis capitur neque tangitur ira" (*DRN* I.44-9).

[28] ἐν]ψυχίαν ἔχει κοινήν. ὅθεν οὐκ εἴ τινα ζω<ι>α μορφὴν τοιαύτην ἔχει καὶ τὸν θεὸν εἶναι δεῖ τοιοῦτον· τὸ δὲ λογιζ[ό]μενον καὶ ἄκρως γε σὺν ταυταις ταῖς κοινοτησ[ι]ν καὶ ἄ[λλ]ας πολλὰς [ἕξει]" (XVII).

Philodemus in his *On Methods of Inference* argues,

> That nothing prevents a god from being similar to man in the use of practical wisdom, since man alone of living beings in our experience is capable of practical wisdom. A god cannot be perceived of as lacking practical wisdom but can be perceived of as not having been generated and yet being composed of soul and body; with this he will be living and deathless.[29]

Philodemus like Demetrius Lacon indicates that the gods share properties with humans, like soul and body, and that this makes the gods not only rational but also alive. Indeed in Cicero's *On the Nature of the Gods* Velleius also argues that "god is a living being [...] supremely happy, and no one can be happy without virtue, and virtue cannot exist without reason."[30] Philodemus in his *On Methods of Inference* does however distinguish between gods and other living beings: "if while saying that all living things among us are destructible, we say that the gods are indestructible."[31]

Lucretius in the third book of his *DRN* reasons that the soul also makes perception possible. After explaining that the soul is a composite of breath, heat, air, and a fourth, nameless nature, he continues,

> The fourth nature must therefore be added to these [breath, heat, and air]; this is entirely without name; nothing exists more easily moved and thinner than this, or made of elements smaller and smoother; and this first distributes the sense-giving motions through the limbs. For this is first set in motion, being composed of small shapes.[32]

The suggestion is then that gods possess soul, so are alive, and so are endowed with sensation.

---

[29] "οὐδὲν [κωλύειν μὴ τῶι φρονεῖν μ]ὲν ἀνθρ[ώποις] ὡ[μοιωμένον] τὸν θεὸν ὑπ[ά]ρχ[ειν] δ[ιὰ τὸν] ἄνθρωπον φρον[ή]σε[ως μονον τῶν] παρ' ἡμῖν ζμῖν ζώιων δεκτικ[ὸν, φρ]ονησεως δὲ χωρὶς μ[ὴ νοεῖσθ,' ἀλλ]ὰ μὴ γεννᾶσθαι συνεσ[τηκένα]ι δ' ἐκ ψυχῆς καὶ σωμα[τος· καὶ ἔσ]ται ζῶιον οὖν τούτωι [καὶ ἀθ]α[νατον]" (37). Translations from *On Methods of Inference* with my own amendments and the original are from De Lacy (1978).

[30] "deus autem animans est [...] deos beatissimos esse constat, beatus autem esse sine virtute nemo potest nec virtus sine ratione constare" (*Nat. D.* I.48).

[31] εἰ' δὴ τὰ παρ' ἡμῖν ζῶια πά[ντ]α λέγοντες εἶναι φθαρτὰ τ[οὺς] θεοὺς ἀφθάρτους ὑπάρχειν λέ[γο]μεν" (34).

[32] "quarta quoque his igitur quaedam natura necessest / adtribuatur. east omnimo nominis expers; / qua neque mobilius quicquam neque tenvius exstat, / nec magis e parvis et levibus ex elementis; / sensiferos motus quae didit prima per artus. / prima cietur enim, parvis perfecta figuris" (*DRN* III.241-6).

Philodemus in his *On Piety* says, "in allowing perception and pleasure"[33] to the divine, or in other words, divinity is capable of perception and pleasure, which is in keeping with the gods' happiness. But he also writes,

> According to Epicurus, in *On Gods*, that which does not have in its nature the sensitive constitution is consistent with its divinity; and divine nature appears to be that which is not of the nature that partakes of pain [so that it [pain] necessarily creates many weaknesses] and to be a kind of divinity [i.e. sharing in pains would necessarily be a source of weakness, so that an entity that did so could be neither imperishable nor divine].[34]

Therefore although the gods can perceive pleasure, they cannot perceive pain, for this would not be in keeping with their immortality as gods are entirely insusceptible to harm. However in his *On the Form of God* Demetrius Lacon makes the comment that "the divine [...] will differ from the sensitive units and from those that do not last forever and change themselves":[35] sensitive immortals differ from sensitive mortals because the former cannot perceive pain whereas the latter can, and in fact this is what renders these mortal. The gods only perceive pleasure and not pain, as they are composed of matter that is so elusive that they evade all potentially harmful material that would inflict pain and only interact with similar, beneficial material that would thereby induce pleasure.

Accordingly Philodemus claims that the gods would survive even if any potentially harmful material chanced upon their interworld: "if they [people] inquire accurately, he [Epicurus] says, he thinks that it is possible for their [gods'] nature to exist even with many troubles surrounding it [their nature]."[36]

The anthropomorphic nature of the gods is described throughout the Epicurean corpus. Demetrius writes, "and so, after these arguments have been dealt with accurately, it is not difficult to demonstrate also, on account of these inferences, that we admit god to be anthropomorphic; it is clear that we attribute a human form to god."[37]

---

[33] "α[πολεί]π[οντες τη]ν αἴσθη[σιν] καὶ τὴν ἡδονήν" (5).

[34] "[Ἐπί]κουρωι δ' ἐν [τῶι Περὶ θ]εῶν τὸ μὴ [τῆι φύσ]ει τὴν α[ἰ]σ[θανομένη]ν σύγκρ[ισιν ἔχον] συ[μφ]ω[νον τῷ θείω·] καὶ τὸ μὴ τῆς [φυσεως ὄν] μετεχου[σης τω]ν ἀλγηδό[νων, ὥστ' ἐξ ἀν]άγκης μα[λακίας πολ]λὰς ποῆσαι, [ἡ θεια φυ]σις οὖσα [φαινεται] καὶ τις [δαιμονιος·]" (7).

[35] "τὸ θεῖον [...] παραλλάξει τῶν αἰσθητῶν ἑνοτήτων, [καὶ τ]ῶν μ[ὴ πρὸ]ς τὸν αἰῶ[να] διαμενουσῶν τε κα[ὶ α]λλαττομένω[ν]" (VIII).

[36] "εἴ γ' εὐ[σκοπουσιν] φησιν φυσιν τουτων πραγμάτων καὶ πολλῶν αὐτὴν περιεστώτων δοξ[άζειν ἐξεῖναι]" (3).

[37] "καὶ τουτων δ' οὖν περ[ι]ωδευμένων οὐ δύσκολον προσαποδοῦναι καὶ διὰ τίνας

However, this anthropomorphic nature might not be entirely consistent with the inactivity of the gods: Epicurus writes of the bliss that the gods enjoy, however in *On the Nature of the Gods* Cicero's Academic Sceptic spokesman Gaius Cotta argues that such bliss results from these gods being "entirely inactive,"[38] and that "even divine [happiness] involves being bored to death with idleness."[39] And Cotta also asks, "what need is there for feet without walking?"[40] For indeed in his *DRN* Lucretius indicates that the gods have limbs.

Demetrius Lacon tackles this argument in his *On the Form of God*:

'If indeed'- he [some Stoic or Peripatetic philosopher] says—'he [god] has human form, it is clear that he will also have eyes and so will also suffer from ophthalmia. The same [god] will also suffer in his other senses.' But this objection also contains within itself a logical inconsistency almost equal.[41]

Demetrius' argument seems to be that although the gods are anthropomorphic they do not necessarily share every single property and condition. Indeed, Epley, Waytz & Capioppo (2007, 864-66) argue, "anthropomorphism is [...] a process of inference about unobservable characteristics of a nonhuman agent, rather than descriptive reports of a nonhuman agent's observable or imagined behaviour." Therefore although gods and humans might resemble one another it does not necessarily mean that they resemble each another in every single way.

Even so, although these gods might have many properties in common with humans, the gods would possess these at the highest level, which would then mean that they are not exactly the same. And these properties might not be used in the same way either, or indeed even be used, for in his *DRN* Lucretius says mysteriously: "do not suppose that the clear light of the eyes was made in order that we might be able to see before us."[42]

In his *On Piety* Philodemus suggests that there could be a multitude of such gods: "that [it is possible even] for many eternal and immortal gods to exist."[43]

ἐπ[ὶ]σπασμοὺς ἀνθρωπόμορ[φ]ον καταλείπομεν τὸν θεόν· δῆλον δ' ὡς μ[ορφὴν τ]ὴν [ἀνθρω]π[ο]υ συ[ναπ]τ[ωμεν τῷ θεῷ" (XIV).

38 "Nihil enim agit" (*Nat. D.* I.51).

39 "ne in deo quidem esse [...] nisi plane otio langueat"(*Nat. D.* I.67).

40 "Quid enim pedibus opus est sine ingressu?" (*Nat. D.* I.92).

41 "'εἰ γὰρ ἀνθρώπου' φησίν, 'μορφὴν ἕξει, δῆλον ὡς ἕξει καὶ ὀφθαλμοὺς οὕτως <δὲ> καὶ ὀφθαλμιασει. τὸ δ' αὐτὸ καὶ ἐπὶ τῶν λοιπῶν αἰσθήσεων πείσεται.' τοῦτο δὲ καὶ αὐτὸ λῆρον [ἔ]χει παραπ[λ]ήσιον" (XVIII).

42 "lumina ne facias oculorum clara creata, / prospicere ut possimus" (*DRN* IV.825-6).

43 "πολλ[οῖς ἀϊ]δίοις [θεοῖς καθα]νάτο[ις εἶναι" (3).

And in his *On the Nature of the Gods* Cicero also indicates that Epicureans believed in an infinite number of deities:

> Moreover there is the supremely potent principle of infinity; we must understand that it has the following property, that in the sum of things everything has its exact match and counterpart. This property is termed by Epicurus *isonomia*, or the principle of uniform distribution. From this principle it follows that if the whole number of mortals be so many, there must exist no less a number of immortals.[44]

A scholion to Diogenes Laertius reads: "elsewhere he [Epicurus] says that the gods are discernible by reason alone, some being numerically distinct, while others result uniformly from the continuous influx of similar images directed to the same spot and in human form."[45] The suggestion is that although there might be a multitude of such gods, they are all similar to one another, which would correspond to their material and interworlds.

In Cicero's *On the Nature of the Gods* Cotta goes further, claiming that the Epicurean gods "are all exactly alike [...] without names."[46] Cicero here perhaps influences Merlan (1960, 56) when the latter argues that for Epicureanism "popular religion would be correct in assuming the existence of a Zeus [...] but mistaken in assuming that there is only one Zeus." However, Cicero's language is too strong, as these gods could not be exactly alike, as Rackham translates *una*, but rather similar.

3. The Life of the Gods

Lucretius beseeches:

> Put far away from you thoughts unworthy of the gods and alien to their

---

[44] "summa vero vis infinitatis et magna ac diligenti contemplatione dignissima est, in qua intelligi necesse est eam esse naturam ut omnia omnibus paribus paria respondeant. Hanc ἰσονομίαν appellat Epicurus, id est aequabilem tributionem. Ex hac igitur illud efficitur, si mortalium tanta multitudo sit, esse inmortalium non minorem" (I.50). Cf. *DRN* II.569-80.

[45] "ἐν ἄλλοις δέ φησι τοὺς θεοὺς λόγῳ θεωρητούς, οὓς μὲν κατ' ἀριθμὸν ὑφεστῶτας, οὓς δὲ καθ' ὁμοείδειαν ἐκ τῆς συνεχοῦς ἐπιρρύσεως τῶν ὁμοίων εἰδώλων ἐπὶ τὸ αὐτὸ ἀποτετελεσμένων ἀνθρωποειδῶς" (*DL* X.139). Mansfield (1993, p203) writes that "λόγῳ θεωρητός is a standard expression denoting 'entities not available to the senses but discoverable in thought'."

[46] "una est omnium facies [...] sine nominibus" (*Nat. D.* I.80-4). However, Cotta then contradicts himself, writing that "the gods are male and female," "et maris deos et feminas esse" (*Nat. D.* I.95). There is also no precedent for this in the Epicurean corpus, that the Epicureans thought that there were male and female deities.

peace, their holy divinity, impaired by you, will often do you harm; not that the supreme power of the gods is open to insult, so that it should in wrath thirst to inflict sharp vengeance, but because you yourself will imagine that they, who are quiet in their placid peace, are rolling great billows of wrath, you will not be able to approach their shrines with placid heart, you will not have the strength to receive with tranquil peace of spirit the images which are carried to men's minds from their holy bodies, declaring what the divine shapes are.[47]

And yet the Epicureans cannot have thought that the gods did absolutely nothing, for by merely existing these gods were *doing something*. Moreover, Epicurean physics holds that all atoms are constantly in motion, and furthermore these gods would be constantly undergoing replenishment of their own atoms.

Philodemus in his *On Gods* gives an insight into what the Epicureans thought the life of these gods was like. He claims that the gods "are friends to one another, even if their friendship, unlike that of human beings, does not reciprocate in mutual aid."[48] However Essler (in Fish & Sanders, 2011, 131-31) adds, "Philodemus rules out the possibility of friendship proper between humans and gods." Seneca, in his *On Benefits*, does later write that Epicurean divinity "dwells alone, without a living creature, without a human being,"[49] but here he is only trying to stress the Epicurean belief that the gods live far away from the affairs of mankind.

Philodemus elaborates upon the type of friendship these gods enjoyed, that it involved the mutual conversation of the kind engaged in by Epicurean sages, about divination and its implications for divine omniscience.[50] Indeed Rist (1972, 153) says, "Philodemus even supposes that their language is Greek or something very like it."[51] And Essler (in Fish & Sanders, 2011, 131-32) conveys that the gods not only speak and engage in conversation but also respire. And Mansfield (in Algra et al., 2010, 456) conveys the explanation from the Epicurean philosopher Hermarchus as to why the gods breathe: because gods

---

[47] "longeque remittis / dis indigna putare alienaque pacis eorum, / delibata deum per te tibi numina sancta / saepe oberunt; non quo violari summa deum vis / possit, ut ex ira poenas petere inbibat acris, / sed quia tute tibi placida cum pace quietos / constitues magnos irarum volvere fluctus, / nec delubra deum placido cum pectore adibis, / nec de corpore quae sancto simulacra feruntur / in mentes hominum divinae nuntiae formae, / suscipere haec animi tranquilla pace valebis" (*DRN* VI. 68-78).

[48] On Philodemus, *On Gods* III. 83-6.1-3.

[49] "desertus sine animali, sine homine" (IV.19.2). Translations from *On Benefits* with my own amendments and the original are from Basore (1935).

[50] *On Gods* III.4.

[51] *On Gods* III.14.4-6.

are living beings, and all living beings breathe.

Merlan (1960, 18) mentions "the well-known Epicurean assertion that the gods eat," and Masson (1907, 276-77) goes further, that "the gods require both food and drink as men do," undoubtedly also because the gods are living beings. And yet their consumption and respiration might simply amount to replenishment of atoms.

But aside from doing what is absolutely necessary for a living being, as well as philosophising, all the evidence indicates that the Epicurean gods were thought to do very little. Indeed in Cicero's *On the Nature of the Gods* Cotta says that Epicurean divinity is engaged "in ceaseless contemplation of his own happiness, for he has no other object for his thoughts."[52]

And yet these gods were not thought to sleep. Philodemus in his *On Gods* proposes, "let us consider whether one should suppose that the gods fall asleep."[53] He then remarks, "at first sight it seems inappropriate, because in these kinds of circumstances there is a violent change in living beings and one that bears close resemblance to death."[54] Therefore, as sleep was identified with death in antiquity, both would be inappropriate for an immortal.

IDEALISM OR REALISM

However, even when it is accepted that the Epicureans were theists, scholars continue to query what these gods actually amounted to. Some argue that these deities do not have to actually be biologically alive, dwelling somewhere in the universe, to be models for mankind to emulate: the Epicureans could have constructed gods in their minds to be such models.

Sedley (in Fish & Sanders, 2011, 29) puts this debate between 'idealism' and 'realism' in the following terms:

> Epicurean theology has come to be viewed as a battleground between two parties of interpreters, the realists and the idealists. Realists take Epicurus to have regarded the gods as biologically immortal beings [...] idealists take Epicurus' idea to have been, rather, that gods are our own graphic idealisation of the life to which we aspire.

---

[52]"cogitat [...] adsidue beatum esse se; habet enim nihil aliud quod agitet in mente" (Nat. D. I.114).

[53]On Gods III.11.40.

[54]"ἄτοπον μὲγ γὰρ εἶναι δοκεῖ προχείρως διὰ τὸ μετακόσμησιν νεανικὴν ἐν ταῖς τοιαύταις καταστάσεσι γινεσθαι περὶ τὰ ζῷα κ(αὶ) πολλὴν ἔχουσαν θανάτωι πρ(οσ)εμφέρειαν" (III.12.2-5), from Essler (in Fish & Sanders, 2011).

1. The Idealist Interpretation

Sedley (1998, 66), an advocate of the 'idealist' interpretation, refers to the Epicurean gods as thought-constructs, holding that the Epicurean gods were conceptual or purposeful thoughts created by mankind so as to be their own ethical models.

Sedley (in Fish & Sanders, 2011) develops and elaborates upon his earlier work, now with two main thrusts to his argument. Firstly, he argues, "once that [governing] role was eliminated and god's relevance to us was reduced to that of an ideal model, the need for him to exist objectively was likely to seem less pressing" (29). Sedley's point is essentially that if the Epicurean gods are inactive and not interested in mankind, they do not need to exist objectively so as to be an ideal model for human emulation.

Secondly, Sedley (31) analyses the Epicurean theory of preconception in close detail, making use of Cicero's *On the Nature of the Gods* in particular. Here Velleius argues that gods exist "since we [everybody] possess an instinctive or rather an innate concept of them [the gods]."[55] Sedley draws attention to Velleius' correction of himself, replacing *insitas*, 'instinctive,' with *innatas*, 'innate.' And indeed Cicero's Stoic spokesman Quintus Lucilius Balbus later uses *innatum* rather than *insitum* when he says "hence the main issue is agreed among all men of all nations, inasmuch as all have engraved in their minds an innate belief that the gods exist."[56] Sedley prefers 'implanted' as a translation of *insitas*, which is indeed the first sense of *insero*, and so argues, "knowledge of the gods then really is […] 'inborn' rather than 'implanted' in us subsequent to birth."

Sedley acknowledges, "it could then be that, on the one hand, the preconception of god is 'innate' in the sense that we are from birth programmed to acquire it […] our full realisation of that predisposition occurs […] only when images of divine beings have frequently entered our consciousness from outside" (40-1). But Sedley thinks rather that humans "fill out their innate preconception […] they had themselves visualised […] [it is] not the nature of the object that determines the preconception, but the 'innate' predisposition of the human subject" (48). Therefore according to Sedley the images of gods are not implanted in mankind subsequent to birth, and do not originate in any gods, but rather that they come from man's own mind, for mankind is born with a predisposition to mentally construct images of gods.

Sedley also wonders, "are we born already possessing some kind of awareness of the gods?" (38). However, he immediately concludes that this "idea can be quickly eliminated" as "it cannot have been hardwired into us by any divine creator" (48). Preconception is rather an "innate religious disposition

---

[55]"quoniam insitas eorum vel potius innatas cognitiones habemus" (*Nat. D.* I.44).
[56]"Itaque inter omnis omnium gentium summa constat; omnibus enim innatum est et in animo quasi insculptum esse deos" (*Nat. D.* II.12-13).

[...] to think of beings that possess precisely those capacities" that mankind aspires for. Sedley continues that preconception is "an innate desire to maximise their [mankind's] own pleasure [...] each of us has an innate propensity to imagine [...] the being [a god] we would ideally like to become" (48-9). And indeed Sedley argues that the Epicurean gods are anthropomorphic so as to facilitate such emulation, and also because the images of gods are essentially *manmade*.

2. The Realist Interpretation

Konstan (in Fish & Sanders, 2011), an advocate of the 'realist' interpretation, argues against the likes of Sedley, that the Epicureans thought that the gods are biologically alive, dwelling somewhere in the cosmos. He also analyses the Epicurean theory of preconception in close detail, making use of Philodemus' *On Gods*, countering Obbink's (2002, 215) definition of preconception as "psychological processes [...] with the human soul" (53). Rather, Konstan (in Fish & Sanders, 2011, 60) writes that according to Philodemus mind

> is said to receive συμπλοκαί, or *tangles*, of the gods,[57] from where it received also the first thoughts of them [...] 'from the first moments of birth' [...] gods are conceived [or perceived by mind] as being at the same distances as certain stars. In fact, however, they do not dwell and circulate together with the stars: rather, it is the interminglings [συμπλοκαί][58] that occur in the middle space, however far away the gods' constituent atoms [γεννητικά][59] may be.

Konstan understands that these συμπλοκαί the human mind perceives from birth are the images of the gods, whereas the γεννητικά refer to the gods themselves, from which those συμπλοκαί originate, and that the γεννητικά lie much further away as the συμπλοκαί had been travelling towards mankind from those gods. This refutes Sedley's proposal that man is born with an image of divinity that he has himself constructed. And so although one might think that they perceive gods in the vicinity of stars, they are actually only seeing the gods' images in transit.

Konstan elaborates upon his own understanding of preconception. He argues that "preconceptions are formed over time, as a result of repeated sensory (or mental) impressions—they do not come ready formed at infancy, but are acquired through experience" (67). Konstan's understanding is that preconception of the gods is not a single event, but that the conception of the

---

[57]III.8.36.
[58]III.9.21.
[59]III.9.24.

gods is enhanced after numerous preconceptions. This would explain why Epicureanism encouraged continued contemplation of the gods.

Konstan (67-68) also responds to Sedley's point about Velleius' correction of *insitas* to *innatas*. Konstan argues that "the basic meaning of *innatus*, an adjective derived from the past participle of *innascor*, is not so much 'innate' or 'inborn' as 'grown up' or 'developed,'" and indeed Lewis & Short (1917, 957) translate the root verb *innascor* as 'to grow or spring up in.' And so Konstan thinks Velleius means that the conception of the gods grows upon individuals, rather than that this conception is 'innate' or 'inborn' in them. Konstan also translates *insitas* as "'growing' […] 'implanted' on a thing," and indeed Lewis & Short (1917, 966) include 'an ingrafting' as a translation for *insitus*, and (1917, 964) to 'plant in, ingraft' as a translation for its root verb *insero*. And so Konstan does not think that Velleius is correcting himself when he replaces *insitas* with *innatas* but that he is merely clarifying himself.

Konstan and Sedley are also in disagreement over another passage from Cicero's *On the Nature of the Gods*, where Velleius says that preconception is made possible "because an endless train of precisely similar images arises from the innumerable atoms and streams **towards** the gods." [60] Rackham (1961, 50) thinks that *ad deos*, 'towards the gods,' is a scribal error and offers *ad eos*, *a deo*, *ad nos*, *a diis*, and *ad nos* as suitable and more likely corrections. He suggests that the sentence is "probably to be altered into 'streams **to us from** the gods,'" which is indeed how he translates it. Konstan (in Fish & Sanders, 2011, 70) points out that Sedley prefers not to correct the original and that he uses this reference to support his thesis that the Epicurean gods were thought-constructs: "by converging on our [human] minds they [manmade images] become our gods." Konstan contends that, whether the images come towards or from the gods, the existence of actual gods that are distinct from mankind is still indicated.

In conclusion here, Sedley (52) remarks that Epicurus would not have been "all that disconcerted" whether people adopted the 'realist' or 'idealist' interpretation. However, I argue that he would, for this is a vitally important point: the objective of Epicureanism was the acquisition of tranquility and happiness, which Epicurean doctrine, preconception, and contemplation and emulation of the divine form made possible. The Epicureans had to believe that their gods actually existed as biologically alive entities for them to be worthy of emulation, and if they were not, they could not have been worthy ethical models. The 'idealist' interpretation is complex and ambitious, but there is no explicit evidence that the Epicureans believed the gods were thought-constructs, and indeed the cumulative weight of the evidence supports the 'realist' interpretation.

---

[60]"cum infinita simillumarum imaginum series ex innumerabilibus individuis existat et ad deos adfluat" (*Nat. D.* I.49).

EPICUREAN PIETY

In his *On Piety* Philodemus argues vigorously in defence of the theism and piety of the Epicureans, and indeed for the rationale behind each.

In its first section he reveals that Epicurus himself even criticised others for not believing in gods: "those who eliminate the divine from existing things Epicurus reproached for their complete madness, as in Book 12 [of *On Nature*], he reproaches Prodicus, Diagoras, and Critias amongst others, saying that they rave like lunatics."[61]

Furthermore, Philodemus defends the sincerity of Epicurean belief in the following way:

> If he [Epicurus] had said that gods exist for the sake of social convention, they [the Epicureans] would certainly not have offered demonstrations, since there were not even any objections to tell against them, nor would they [the Epicureans] have fought against those who do away with the divine, nor would they [the Epicureans] have advanced proofs in such extensive argumentation and in the other matters connected with them [the gods] in their [the Epicureans'] books.[62]

In its second section Philodemus claims that the Epicureans observed traditional cult and worshipped and were thereby pious, and he further writes that Epicurus himself participated in the mysteries and festivals,[63] and that all acts of worship were to be conducted properly and lawfully,[64] employing objects for worship.[65] Indeed, having analysed Philodemus' *On Piety*, Festugière (1946, 92) concludes, "Epicurus, then, observed the forms of the state religion not only so as to 'obey the law,' but from genuine feeling. Nevertheless his religion was not that of the common people."[66] Of course being lawful was no bad

---

[61]"καὶ πᾶσαν μ[ανίαν Ε]πίκουρος ἐμ[έμψα]το τοῖς τὸ [θεῖον ἐ]κ τῶν ὄντων [ἀναι]ρουσιν, ὡς κα[ν τῶ] δωδεκάτω[ι Προ]δίκωι καὶ Δια[γόραι] καὶ Κριτίαι κἄ[λλοις] μέμφ[εται] φας πα[ρα]κοπτ[ει]ν καὶ μ[αινεσ]θαι" (19).

[62]"εἴ γε κα[τὰ συμ]περιφορὰν [ἔλεγε]ν εἶναι θεούς, [οὐκ] ἀποδείξεις ἔ[φερον ο]ὐδ' ὑπεξαιρέτων ἀντιπιπτόν[των, ου]δ' ἂν ἐπολέ[μουν τ]οῖς ἀναιρου[σιν, ου]δ]ὲ διὰ τοσούτων ἠργάζοντο [καὶ τοι]ούτων λόγων [πίστε]ις καὶ τῶν [ἄλλων τ]ῶν περὶ αὐ[τῶν συμ]βαινον[των ἐν βυ]βλίοις" (17).

[63]27.

[64]31.

[65]32.

[66]"Ce n'est donc pas seulement pour «suivre la loi», mais par un sentiment vrai, qu'Epicure observe les rites du culte. Néanmoins, sa religion n'est pas celle du vulgaire" (translated by Chilton, 1955, p61).

thing, but as has been demonstrated the Epicureans genuinely believed in gods anyway. And yet the Epicurean gods were not the gods of state religion, and Festugière elegantly captures this curiosity. So, the Epicureans might have attended the festivals of the gods of orthodoxy, but they did so in order to contemplate their own gods, as well to be lawful.

And in its third section Philodemus explains the Epicurean position, further defending and justifying their worship on psychological grounds, that the gods have beneficial and harmful influences upon mankind, though they do not intentionally interfere with humans, writing that "we [the Epicureans] all regard our views [about gods] as the true cause of our own tranquility."[67] He further explains the benefit of contemplating the divine nature at such occasions:

> Those who believe our oracles about the gods will first wish to imitate their blessedness in so far as mortals can, so that, since it was seen to come from doing no harm to anyone, they will endeavour most of all to make themselves harmless to everyone as far as is within their power.[68]

Festive occasions allow particular focus upon divinity, perhaps facilitating preconception, so Epicureans would then be in a better position to emulate the gods. Indeed Festugière (1946, 98) writes, "it is on festal days, when we approach the altar of sacrifice or contemplate the divine statue, that the influence of the gods makes itself more strongly felt and produces the greatest joy."[69]

Philodemus also cites the Epicurean Metrodorus as saying that it is both fitting and beneficial to emulate the gods,[70] which is made possible through worship and contemplation of them.

Throughout his *On Piety* Philodemus stresses that the benefits of worship are for the worshipper rather than those worshipped: the gods have all they need and thereby do not require worship; they are forever peaceful so cannot be moved to anger if they are not worshipped, and do not need to be appeased either; and they have no interest in the affairs of mankind, and are thus not

---

[67]"ἡμεῖς δὲ π[άν]τες ὡς ἀληθῆ τὰ δόγματα καὶ παρ[α]σκευασ[τικ]ὰ τῆς ἡμῶν αὐτῶν ἀτα[ραξ]ίας" (47).

[68]"οἱ δὲ πει<σ>θ[έν]τες οἷς ἐχρησμω[ι]δήσαμεν περὶ θεῶν πρῶτον μὲν ὡς θνητοὶ μιμε[ῖσ]θαι τὴν ἐκείνων εὐδαιμονίαν θελήσουσιν, ὥστ,' ἐπειδήπερ ἐξ ἀβλαβίας ἐθεωρεῖτο το[ῖ]ς πᾶσιν ἐρχομένη, μάλιστα φιλοτιμήσονται πᾶσιν αὐτοὺς παρεχειν ἀλύπους, ὅσ[ον ἐφ'] ἑαυτοῖς" (71).

[69]"Néanmoins c'est aux jours de fête, quand on approche l'autel du sacrifice ou contemple la statue divine, que l'influence des dieux se fait sentir avec plus de force et produit la plus grande joie" (translated by Chilton, 1955, p63).

[70]34.

benevolent towards them. And yet worship of gods is fitting for such superior beings. However, perhaps the most important reason for worship is a physical one: the gods constantly, albeit incidentally, emit images that mankind can preconceive and emulate, which in turn can result in a tranquility and happiness like that of the gods. Cicero might mock the Epicureans for emulating laziness, but this misses the point: the qualities that the Epicureans admired in their gods were their peacefulness, harmlessness, and happiness, and these were the qualities that they wanted to emulate, and it was in this way that they could be like their gods. In such a way, not only could gods be happy, but so too could individual Epicureans, and indeed society at large, though the gods could of course be harmful towards mankind, albeit incidentally, if mankind did not emulate them and thereby did not receive the incidental benefits on offer.

Epicureanism makes it clear that preconception of the divine nature is important for the happiness of mankind, but this ought not to be confused with reliance upon gods. The onus is rather on humans to facilitate preconception by attending festivals and worshipping and to act upon the images of divinity thereby received by emulating the gods. Ultimately, mankind is empowered: the gods are not benevolent, so mankind must obtain its own happiness. Epicureanism can assist, but individuals must want the assistance on offer. Indeed, Obbink (1995, 193) writes that mankind can expedite "the benefits which Epicurus thought the gods provided to humans."

Gale (2001, 12-13) speaks of Epicurus in this way:

> Despite the fact that we cannot affect the gods in any way, however, Epicurus still (somewhat paradoxically) recommends that his disciples take part in the public rituals of the state religion. Contemplation of the divine, he argues, is good for us: the perfect peace enjoyed by the gods can be a source of inspiration to us in our pursuit of the same goal. Indeed, the aim of the Epicurean is to become like the gods, to imitate their calm detachment; thus, while religious ritual cannot please the gods, it can be of great [though indirect] benefit to the worshipper.

Similarly, Santayana (1935, 30) writes that "the gods were too remote and too happy, secluded like good Epicureans, to meddle with earthly things. Nothing ruffled what Wordsworth calls their 'voluptuous unconcern.' Nevertheless, it was pleasant to frequent their temples." And Santayana , influenced most probably by Philodemus, writes, "Epicurus himself was so sincere in this belief in gods, and so much affected by it, that he used to frequent the temples" (62).

Lucretius also admits the importance of worship:

> Unless you spew all these errors out of your mind, and put far from you thoughts unworthy of the gods and alien to their peace, their holy

divinity, impaired by you, will often do you harm; not that the supreme power of the gods is open to insult, so that it should in wrath thirst to inflict sharp vengeance, but because you yourself will imagine that they, who are quiet in their placid peace, are rolling great billows of wrath, you will not be able to approach their shrines with placid heart, you will not have the strength to receive with tranquil peace of spirit the images which are carried to men's minds from their holy bodies, declaring what the divine shapes are.[71]

Here Lucretius suggests that one ought to approach the shrines of the gods, to facilitate preconception, and that this can only be done if one adopts a peaceful disposition, which will allow contemplation of divinity and in turn peace of mind for the worshipper. Therefore one should enter upon worship in the right state of mind, free of false beliefs of fearsome deities, ready to receive the real images of peaceful gods, and in this way preconception and contemplation of divinity can be facilitated. Indeed Godwin (2004, 16-17) understands Lucretius in the following way: "Lucretius depicts the wise man approaching the temples of the gods 'with a peaceful heart' and imbibing this peace of the gods into his own heart." This reference stands as the best example of Lucretius encouraging piety.

THE RELIGION OF EPICUREANISM

Such was the piety of the Epicureans, it would perhaps not be wrong to refer to Epicureanism as a religion. Indeed, Farrington (1947, 91-92) cites Gassendi:

> In the seventeenth century it was evident that Epicurus had taught a singularly pure religion, if a defective one. Drawing a distinction between the filial and servile elements in religion, the servile being those concerned with the interchange of services between men and gods, the filial with pure devotion, Gassendi emphasised the fact that it is only the servile elements of religion that are lacking in Epicurus.

Therefore, according to Gassendi at least, Epicureanism was a religion, a religion of pure devotion once all servile elements had been stripped away.

Farrington (99) also cites Sallustius' *On Gods*:

---

[71]"sed quia tute tibi placida cum pace quietos / constitues magnos irarum volvere fluctus / nec delubra deum placido cum pectore adibis / nec de corpore quae sancto simulacra feruntur / in mentes hominum divinae nuntiae formae, / suscipere haec animi tranquilla pace valebis" (*DRN* VI. 73-78).

All this care of the world, we must believe, is taken by the gods without any act or will or labour. As bodies that possess some power produce their efforts by merely existing: e.g. the Sun gives light and heat by merely existing: so, and far more so, the providence of the gods acts without effort to itself and for the good of the objects of its forethought. This solves the problem of the Epicureans, who argue that what is divine neither has trouble itself nor gives trouble to others.[72]

This further helps to explain how the Epicurean gods, thought they are not benevolent, can still bequeath benefits, incidentally.

Farrington conveys that religion "it is that constrains and holds together all humane society, this is the foundation, prop, and stay of all laws," though the "Epicurean religion could not perform what was for them an essential function of religion. Gods that took no heed whatever of bad men were useless to police the state" (110-11). Importantly, Farrington also refers to Epicureanism as a religion himself, albeit a defective one. However, this misunderstands the Epicurean belief that social harmony could actually be improved if fear was removed and individuals were empowered. Indeed Festugière comments, "it is noticeable that both [Stoic and Epicurean] doctrines touch on matters of religion. The Stoic lives in accord with the Cosmic god, the Epicurean banishes the fear of the gods and of Hades. Therefore these two systems of morality fundamentally imply a religious attitude" (1946, xiii).[73]

Festugière (94-95) describes the Epicurean religion in the following way:

> Since the gods are indescribably happy, to praise them in prayer, to draw near to them on those solemn occasions when the city offers them a sacrifice, and to rejoice with them at the arrival of festivals is to take part in their happiness. That is why the disciple of Epicurus would be faithful to the prescriptions of religion.

And so, the Epicureans worshipped the gods as it was beneficial for them, for they could partake in divine happiness merely by contemplating it, for Festugière also writes, "this religion of Epicurus is related to Plato's. Both put the goals of religious activity in the contemplation of beauty [...] the divine being, whatever its essence, is a being of perfect beauty, who lives a life of harmony and serenity [...] likewise the gods of Epicurus are filled with beauty"

---

[72]Translation by Murray (1925).

[73]"L'une et l'autre doctrine, on le voit, touche aux choses de la religion. Le stoïcien vit en accord avec le dieu cosmique; l'épicurien bannit la crainte des dieux et de l'Hadès. Dès lors ces deux morales, en leur principe même, impliquent une attitude religieuse" (translated by Chilton, 1955, pxi).

(95-6).[74] Indeed, in his *On Gods* Philodemus writes, "it [divinity] possesses beauty in plenitude."[75]

Festugière also provides a piece of evidence from the Oxyrhynchus Papyri. He introduces this as a

> Letter written by the sage [Epicurus] to an unknown friend, discovered in an Egyptian papyrus, recognised as belonging to Epicurus [...] this dogma, far from abolishing religion, should purify it; the truly pious man does not approach the gods to appease them or to obtain some favour from them, but to unite himself to them by contemplation, to rejoice in their joy, and so to taste for himself, in this mortal life, their unending happiness. (98-99) [76]

So Festugière also refers to Epicureanism here as a religion of pure devotion. He then translates the letter itself:

> <It is no proof of piety to observe the customary religious obligations—though the offerings of sacrifices> on suitable occasions may be, as I have said, in keeping with nature—nor is it, by Zeus, when someone or other goes about repeating, 'I fear all the gods, and honour them, and want to spend all my money in making sacrifices, and consecrating offerings to them.' Such a man is perhaps more praiseworthy than other individuals, but still it is not thus that a solid foundation for piety is laid. You, my friend, must know that the most blessed gift is to have a clear perception of things; that is absolutely the best thing that we can conceive of here below. Admire this clear apprehension of the spirit, revere this divine gift. After that, <you

---

[74] "Cette religion d'Epicure s'apparente à celle de Platon. Tous deux mettent le terme de l'acte religieux dans la contemplation de la beauté [...] .L'être divin, qu'elle qu'en soit l'essence, est un être parfaitement beau, qui mène une vie harmonieuse et sereine [...] De même les dieux d'Epicure sont remplis de beauté [...] 'il possède la beauté en plénitude'" (translated by Chilton, 1955, p62).

[75] I.2.7ff.

[76] "Une lettre du sage à un ami inconnu: découvert dans un papyrus d'Egypte, rapporté à Epicure [...] ce dogme, loin de supprimer la religion, doit la purifier: l'homme vraiment pieux ne s'adresse pas aux dieux pour les apaiser ou en obtenir quelque grâce, mais pour s'unir à eux par la contemplation, se réjouir de leur joie, et goûter ainsi lui-même, dans cette vie mortelle, à leur bonheur sans fin" (translated by Chilton, 1955, pp63-65 ; P.Oxyrh. II. 215 (p30) = Diels, *Ein Epikureisches fragment über Gotterverehrung*, Sitz. Ber. Berlin, 1916, pp886ff (text pp902-4)). Grenfell & Hunt (1899, p30) also examine the fragment, writing that "the principal topic discussed in the fragment is the popular idea of religion and especially of the gods, which is severely criticised by the writer [...] the author was probably an Epicurean philosopher, possibly Epicurus himself."

should not honour the gods because you think thus to gain their favour>, as people will think when they see you performing acts of piety, but only because, in comparison with your own happiness, you see how the condition of the gods is infinitely more august, according to our doctrine. And certainly, by Zeus, <when you practise> this doctrine—the doctrine most worthy of belief, <as your reason should tell you—it is of course open to you to offer sacrifices to the gods. By doing so you perform> an act which gives confidence and is a pleasure to see, if it is done at the proper time, because you honour your own doctrine by enjoying those pleasures of the senses which befit such occasions and besides you conform in some sense to religious traditions. Only be careful that you do not permit any admixture of fear of the gods or of the supposition that in acting as you do you are winning the favour of the gods. For indeed, in the name of Zeus, [as men affect to say] what have you to fear in this matter? Do you believe that the gods can do you harm? Is not that, on any showing, to belittle them? How then will you not regard the divinity as a miserable creature if it appears inferior in comparison to yourself? Or will you rather be of the opinion that by sacrificing thousands of oxen you can appease god if you have committed some evil deed? Can you think that he will take account of the sacrifice and, like a man, remit at some time or another a part of the penalty?

No doubt men tell each other that they should fear the gods and honour them with sacrifices, so that, restrained by the tribute they receive, the gods will not attack them; as a result they think that if their surmise is correct they will altogether escape injury and if it is not, all will be well because they pay homage to the power of the gods. But if these close relations <between gods and men were really to exist it would be a great misfortune, for the effect would make itself felt even beyond the grave>, after the funeral ceremonies, as soon as a man was cremated. For then men would suffer injury even beneath the earth and everyone would have to expect punishment. Moreover, I need not describe how men would have to beg for signs of favour from the gods in their fear of being neglected by them (for they would think to induce the gods in this way to communicate with them more readily and come down into their temples), any more than I can tell of the methods they would employ because of their fear of harm and so as to guard against punishment. For to speak the truth all this seems pure illusion of these people when compared with the doctrine of those who think that a life of happiness exists for us in this world and do not admit that the dead live again—a marvel not less unlikely than those which Plato imagined.

(99-101)[77]

The author of the letter is insisting that true piety involves obtaining a clear

---

[77]"<Il n'y a point piété quand on observe les obligations religieuses habituelles—bien que l'offrande de sacrifices> aux occasions convenables soit, comme je l'ai dit, chose propre à la nature—ni non plus, par Zeus, quand l'un ou l'autre va répétant: 'je crains tous les dieux, et je les honore, et je veux dépenser toute ma fortune à leur offrir des sacrifices et à leur consacrer des offrandes.' Un tel homme est peut-être plus louable que d'autres particuliers, toutefois ce n'est pas encore ainsi qu'on pose le fondement solide de la piété. Toi, mon ami, sache que le don le plus bienheureux, c'est d'avoir une claire perception des choses: voilà le bien absolument le meilleur que nous puissions concevoir ici-bas. Admire cette claire appréhension de l'esprit, révere ce don divin. Après cela, <tu ne dois pas honorer les dieux parce que tu penses, par ce moyen, gagner leur faveur>, comme on se l'imaginera quand on te verra faire des actes de piété, mais seulement parce que, en comparaison avec ta propre béatitude, tu vois combien, d'après notre doctrine, la condition des dieux est infiniment plus auguste. Et certes, par Zeus, <quand tu mets en pratique> cette doctrine, la plus digne de foi <comme ta raison doit te l'assurer, il t'est bien permis d'offrir des sacrifices aux dieux. Tu accomplis ainsi> une chose qui donne confiance et qui est vue avec plaisir, si elle vient en son temps, puisque tu mets en honneur ta propre doctrine en usant des plaisirs sensibles qui se trouvent convenir en ces occasions, et qu'en outre tu t'accommodes de quelque façon aux traditions religieuses. Veille seulement à n'y mêler ni crainte des dieux ni supposition qu'en agissant ainsi tu t'attires la faveur des dieux. Car, en vérité, au nom de Zeus (comme on se plaît à dire), qu'as-tu à craindre en cela? Crois-tu que les dieux puissent te faire du tort? N'est-ce pas là, ne regarderas-tu pas la divinité comme quelque chose de misérable si, en comparaison avec toi, elle apparaît inférieure? Ou bien serais-tu d'avis que, par le sacrifice de milliers de bœufs, tu peux, si tu as commis quelque mauvaise action, apaiser le dieu? Ou qu'il tiendra compte du sacrifice et, comme un homme, te fera remise une fois ou l'autre d'une partie du dommage?

Sans doute, les hommes se disent qu'il faut craindre les dieux et les honorer par ces sacrifices, afin que, retenus par le tribut qu'on leur porte, les dieux ne s'attaquent pas à eux: dès lors, pensent-ils, si cette conjecture est juste, de toute façon ils ne subiront aucun dommage, et, si elle n'est pas juste, comme ils rendent honneur à la puissance des dieux, tout ira bien. Mais si ces étroites relations <entre dieux et hommes existeraient vraiment, ce serait un grand malheur, car l'action s'en ferait sentir jusque par delà la tombe>, après les cérémonies des funérailles, une fois qu'on a été incinéré. Car alors, même sous la terre, on subirait un dommage et tout homme devrait s'attendre au châtiment. Outre cela, je n'ai pas à dire comment les hommes devraient mendier les signes de la faveur des dieux, dans leur crainte d'être négligés par eux (car ils penseraient amener ainsi les dieux à communiquer plus volontiers avec eux et à descendre dans leurs temples), non plus que la diversité et le grand nombre de leurs comportements eu égards à la crainte du dommage et pour se mettre en garde contre le châtiment. Car tout cela, au vrai, apparaît comme une pure illusion de ces gens-là, comparé à la doctrine de ceux qui estiment que, dès ici-bas, il existe une vie bienheureuse, et qui n'admettent pas que les morts recommencent à vivre,—prodige non moins invraisemblable que ceux que Platon a imaginés" (translated by Chilton, 1955, p65).

perception of the gods through worship and contemplation, as this is a gift from the gods that constantly, though incidentally, give off images that can then be perceived by mankind through preconception. However, simply participating in religious observance is no piety if this clear perception of the gods is not obtained, especially if participation results from fear or expectation of favour. Religious observance is acceptable, but only if a clear perception of the gods is obtained. Indeed, Summers (1995, 33) cites Bailey (1947) as writing that "it is not the act of worship that the Epicurean thinks wrong, but its motive." This all helps to further explain how the Epicureans could participate in state religion despite believing in deities who were very different from those that the state advocated.

Hadzsits (1908, 74) says that the Epicureans had "no thought of dropping religion out of life." Rather, Hadzsits argues that "Lucretius [...] espoused a system of religious and ethical philosophy" (145), and refers to Epicurus' "philosophy of religion" (160). Summers (1995, 57) concludes that "Lucretius retains a genuine religious sensibility throughout his poem," and refers to "his [Lucretius'] religion" as "mystical-transcendental contemplation."

CONCLUSION

Despite Epicurean resistance to orthodoxy, and indeed despite their own unorthodox beliefs, Epicureans were not atheists on the modern sense of the word. They believed in gods, presented evidence for their existence, described their nature, homes, and their lives. And these gods were considered to be real, living beings rather than as figments of the imagination, so important were they to Epicureans and their own individual journeys towards tranquility and happiness. Indeed, so pious were the Epicureans that, beyond a philosophy, Epicureanism might perhaps be regarded as a religion in its own right.

Works Cited

Algra, K., Barnes, J., Mansfield, J. & Schofield, M. (2010). *The Cambridge History of Hellenic Philosophy*, Cambridge: Cambridge University Press.

Bailey, C. (trans.) (1926). *Epicurus: The Extant Remains*, Oxford: Clarendon Press.

Bailey, C. (ed.) (1947a). *Lucretius: De Rerum Natura: Libri Sex, vol.II*, Oxford: Clarendon Press.

Bailey, C. (ed.) (1947b). *Lucretius: De Rerum Natura: Libri Sex, vol.III*, Oxford: Clarendon Press.

Basore, J.W. (trans.) (1935). *Seneca: Moral Essays III*, London: William Heinemann LTD; Cambridge, Massachusetts: Harvard University Press.

Brown, P.M. (1984). *Lucretius: De Rerum Natura I*, Bristol: Bristol Classical Press.

Bury, R.G. (trans.) (1935). *Sextus Empiricus: Against the Logicians, II*, London: William Heinemann LTD; Cambridge, Massachusetts: Harvard University Press.

Chilton, C.W. (1955). *Epicurus and his Gods*, Oxford: Basil Blackwell (translation of Festugière, A.J., *Épicure et ses Dieux*).

De Lacy, P.H. (trans.) & De Lacy, E.A. (trans.) (1978). *Philodemus: On Methods of Inference*, Bibliopolis.

DeWitt, N.W. (1954). *Epicurus and his Philosophy*, Minneapolis: University of Minnesota Press.

Diels, H. (1965). *Doxographi Graeci*, Berolini, apud Walter de Gruyter et Socios.

Epley, N., Waytz, A. & Capioppo, J.T. (2007). *On Seeing Human: A Three-Factor Theory of Anthropomorphism*, in the *Psychology Review 14:4*.

Essler, H. (2011). 'Cicero's Use and Abuse of Epicurean Theology' (in Fish, J. & Sanders, K.R., *Epicurus and the Epicurean Tradition*, pp129-51), Cambridge: Cambridge University Press.

Farrington, B. (1947). *Head and Hand in Ancient Greece: 4 Studies in the Social Relations of Thought* (The Thinker's Library no.121), London: Watts & Co.

Farrington, B. (1967). *The Faith of Epicurus*, Weidenfeld & Nicolson.

Festugière, A.J. (1946). 'Épicure et ses Dieux' (in Couchoud, P.E. (collection directed by), *Mythes et Religions*), Presse Universitaires de France-Paris.

Fish, J. & Sanders, K.R. (2011). *Epicurus and the Epicurean Tradition*, Cambridge: Cambridge University Press.

Gale, M.R. (2001). *Classical World Series: Lucretius and the Didactic Epic*, Bristol: Bristol Classical Press.

Godwin, J. (2004). *Ancients in Action: Lucretius*, Bristol: Bristol Classical Press.

Gordon, P. (1996). *Epicurus in Lycia: The Second-Century World of Diogenes of Oenoanda*, Michigan: University of Michigan Press.

Grenfell, B.P. & Hunt, A.S. (edited with translations and notes by) (1899). The Oxyrhynchus Papyri Part II (Egypt Exploration Fund: Graeco-Roman Branch, London), Oxford: Horace Hart, retrieved June 24, 2014.

Hadzsits, G.D. (1908). *Significance of Worship and Prayer among the Epicureans*. In *Transactions and Proceedings of the American Philological Association*, vol.39, pp73-88, The John Hopkins University Press, retrieved September 27, 2014.

Hicks, R.D. (trans.) (1931). *Diogenes Laertius: Lives of Eminent Philosophers II*, London; Cambridge, Massachusetts: Harvard University Press.

Hornblower, S. & Spawforth, A. (2003). *The Classical Oxford Dictionary: Third Edition Revised*, Oxford: Oxford University Press.

Inwood, B., Gerson, L. P. (translated and edited with notes by) & Hutchinson, D.S. (introduction by) (1994). *The Epicurus Reader: Selected Writings and Testimonia*, Indianapolis, Cambridge: Hackett Publishing Company, Inc.

Jackson, P. (forthcoming). *Parménide chez Lucrèce*.

Jackson, P. & Césarini, C. (2015). *Epicureanism & Scepticism* (a review for *The Classical Review* of Marchand, S. (ed.) & Verde, F. (ed.) (2013). *Épicurisme et Scepticisme* (Collana Convegni 22), Rome: Sapienza Università Editrice.

Konstan, D. (2011). 'Epicurus on the Gods' (in Fish, J. & Sanders, K.R., *Epicurus and the Epicurean Tradition*, pp53-71), Cambridge: Cambridge University Press.

Lewis, C.T. & Short, C. (1917). *A Latin Dictionary*, Oxford: Clarendon Press; London, Edinburgh, Glasgow, New York, Toronto, Melbourne, Bombay: Humphrey Milford.

Masson, J. (1907). *Lucretius: Epicurean & Poet*, London: John Murray.

Merlan, P. (1960). *Studies in Epicurus and Aristotle*, Wiesbaden: Otto Harrassowitz.

Murray, G. (1925). Five Stages of Greek Religion, London: Watts & Co.

Obbink, D. (1989). 'The Atheism of Epicurus' (in *Greek, Roman and Byzantine Studies*, 30:2; Periodicals Archive Online, p187), retreived January 22, 2013.

Obbink, D. (1995). *Philodemus and Poetry: Poetic Theory and Practice in Lucretius, Philodemus, and Horace*, New York, Oxford: Oxford University Press.

Obbink, D. (trans.) (1996). *Philodemus: On Piety, Part 1*, Oxford: Clarendon Press.

Pearsall, J. (ed.) & Hanks, P. (chief editor) (2001). *The New Oxford Dictionary of English*, Oxford: Oxford University Press.

Perrin, B. (trans.) (1967). *Plutarch: Lives, I*, London: William Heinemann LTD; Cambridge, Massachusetts: Harvard University Press.

Rackham, H. (trans.) (1961). *Cicero: On the Nature of the Gods, Academica*, London: William Heinemann LTD; Cambridge, Massachusetts: Harvard University Press.

Rist, J.M. (1972). *Epicurus: An Introduction*, Cambridge: University Press.

Rouse, W.H.D. (trans.) & Smith, M.F. (revised by) (2006). *Lucretius: De Rerum Natura*, Cambridge, Massachusetts; London: Harvard University Press.

Santayana, G. (1935). *Three Philosophical Poets: Lucretius, Dante and Goethe*, Cambridge: Harvard University Press.

Santoro, M. (trans.) (2000). *Demetrius Lacon: La Forma del Dio*, Naples: La Scuola di Epicuro 17.

Sedley, D. (2011). 'Epicurus' Theological Innatism' (in Fish, J. & Sanders, K.R., *Epicurus and the Epicurean Tradition*, pp29-52), Cambridge: Cambridge University Press.

Smith, M.F. (trans.) (1993). *Diogenes of Oenoanda: The Epicurean Inscription*, Bibliopolis.

Smith, M.F. (trans.) (2003). *Diogenes of Oenoanda: Supplement to Diogenes of Oenoanda: The Epicurean Inscription*, Bibliopolis.

Summers, K. (1995). 'Lucretius and the Epicurean Tradition of Piety' (in *Classical Philology*, vol.90, no.1, pp32-57), University of Chicago Press, retrieved September 25, 2014.

Usener, S. (1887). *Epicurea*, Teubner.

Dr. Paul Terence Matthias Jackson completed his thesis on the theology of the Epicureans in 2015, when it was examined by A.G. Leventis Professor of Greek Culture at the University of Cambridge Tim Whitmarsh and Dr Carolyn Price, passing with no corrections. His publications include *The Gods of Philodemus* and *Dreams, Visions, and Epicurean Gods*, and he has reviewed for *Classical Review* and *OCR/Bloomsbury Academic UK*.

The Paradoxical Ambivalence of Giving:
Seneca and the Virtue of Clemency

GALINA KRASSKOVA

This paper explores the complex nature of clemency in the ancient Roman social and political spheres through the lens of Seneca's *de Clementia*. Positioning clemency as a type of "gift-giving," it examines why it was quite often met with ambivalence by the Romans and even considered a negative trait in a ruler and what contemporary polytheists can learn from these debates.

The medieval Icelandic epic, the poetic Edda, includes a stanza that states "tis better not to give, than to give too much, for a gift demands a gift."[1] While written roughly eight hundred years after the fall of Rome, the author of this epic could easily have been referring to early imperial Rome with these words, and the mores, evidenced by their richly nuanced complexities of *creditum*, *beneficia*, and with the rise of the Caesars, *clementia* that so defined social interactions.

It is with this latter concept of clementia that this paper is concerned. At best, clementia was an ambivalent and a very complex concept. The majority of scholars today view it as something that, to the Roman mind, was indisputably tied to hierarchy and even to tyranny.[2] Braund, in her commentary on Seneca's *de Clementia*, for instance, notes that "clementia is an imperial virtue; when clementia is shown towards fellow-Romans it is testimony of absolute power."[3] Melissa Dowling goes even further, in ascribing connotations of military conquest and the subjugation of enemies of the Roman state to the term, even when it was utilized outside of the battlefield.[4] As such, clementia carried with it the imposition of ongoing obligation, a loss of face, and even degradation.

This paper will examine the nature and reception of this virtue first and

---

[1] *Havamal*, Poetic Edda lines 145-146.

[2] See Braund and Dowling. Not all scholars agree. David Konstan presents a differing view of clementia, positing that it was "a virtue and the sign of a humane temperament" noting it was precisely Caesar's clementia that favorably differentiated him from the earlier Sulla. See Konstan, 337.

[3] Braund, 32.

[4] Dowling, *Clemency and Cruelty*, 17.

foremost through the lens of Seneca's own work *de Clementia*. As this paper will show, Seneca presented clementia as a valuable virtue, a sign of excellence in character particularly in a ruler, and a consciously cultivated corrective to the destructiveness of *ira* and *crudelitas*. The situational nature inherent in the application of clementia and clementia as a specific form of gift-giving and thus an expression of the subtle social cycle of reciprocity and dynamic exchange will be examined. Finally, the role of clementia and gift-giving in imperial Rome will be viewed against the larger backdrop of Mediterranean honor culture.

Philosophy was crucial to the way ancient polytheists navigated their world. Virtue, after all, came not from one's religion but from the study of philosophy. To quote Metellus: "Dii immortales virtutem adprobare, non adhibere debent."[5] It was through philosophical study and contemplation that one learned to behave as a fully realized adult within one's community. As contemporary polytheistic communities grow and develop, it is to be hoped that they will see the resurgence of vibrant philosophical schools once again; therefore, it is important for contemporary polytheists to have a basic understanding of the major schools. Now the Romans never really embraced philosophy in the way the ancient Greeks did. Stoicism however, fit more easily with Roman values, and it was the one philosophical school to which the Romans significantly contributed. Seneca, one the leading Roman stoics, writing under the reign of Nero, often, in his philosophical writings, wrote about issues pertaining in some way to good governance. The modern practitioner of *cultus deorum* may find much to contemplate in his writings. One of the issues he touched upon with some significance was that of clemency (*clementia* in Latin).

Clementia is a problematic word. The Oxford Latin Dictionary (OLD) defines it as the "disposition to spare or pardon, leniency; complaisance." It is also defined as a special attribute both of the Caesars and of government and law.[6] It included use in a martial context, specifically on the battlefield toward conquered enemies and also in courts of law where it extended to pleas of mercy for the convicted.[7] From this latter usage, an association between clementia and despotic power evolved, specifically during the Civil War between Pompey and Caesar. Braund notes that Cicero was instrumental in effecting this shift in association through his letters and Caesarian speeches though Caesar himself actually avoided the use of the word clementia in his *de Bello Gallico*.[8]

While Caesar writes himself dispensing clementia, in actuality he uses the

---

[5] "The immortal Gods ought to support, not supply, virtue" quoted in Aulus Gellius' Noctes Atticae (Attic Nights) 1.6.8 .

[6] See OLD entry for Clementia, ae (f). This word may also be used to refer to the mildness of weather.

[7] Dowling, *Clemency and Cruelty*, 5.

[8] Braund, 33-37. See also Konstan, 340.

word only twice in his military narrative, preferring the less charged variants of *mansuetudo, moderatio,* and *misericordia.*[9] It was only after 44 C.E., when the Senate voted to erect a temple to Caesar's Clemency that the word began to gain a somewhat positive traction in Roman political speech. Certainly by the time Seneca wrote his own treatise on clementia, he clearly positioned it as, at least in large part, an imperial virtue with the necessity of imperial rule a given.

For Seneca, however, clementia was not a negative expression of power. While Stoicism in general frowned upon clementia as a violation of necessary rule of law, Seneca took a rather more pragmatic position, approaching clementia as a good and necessary component of *humanitas,* particularly in a leader.[10] He defined clementia as "temperantia animi in potestate ulciscendi vel lenitas superioris adversus inferiorem in constituendis poenis."[11] A few sentences later, he adds nuance to this definition by noting that "hoc omnes intellegunt clementiam esse, quae se flectit citra id quod merito constitui posset."[12] While the expression of clementia here is clearly rooted in hierarchical social dynamics, there is nothing in Seneca's language to indicate that he viewed this as a particularly negative trait nor that it was purely the attribute of a despotic ruler.[13] Rather, clementia, like social interactions themselves, was viewed—at the very least—as complex and at least potentially positive.

Not only does Seneca position clementia as a guard and guide against *saevitia, crudelitas,* and *insania,* but he places it clearly on the side of reason noting "misericordia non causam, sed fortunam spectat; clementia rationi accedit."[14] Thus like other virtues in Seneca's stoic world, the expression of clementia is a clearly reasoned choice, and part of the development of a virtuous character. This holds especially true for the one in possession of ultimate power.

From the first lines of book one of *De Clementia,* Seneca positions this virtue as part and parcel of a well-lived life, offering it to Nero as a guide to excellence of behavior:

---

[9] Less charged perhaps because these words lacked military and judicial emphasis. There was no connotation of a crime having been committed which necessitated forgiveness, a gift of generosity that forever altered that status of the individuals involved, creating a social imbalance, and casting the one 'forgiven' into the status of suppliant or client.

[10] Braund, 66.

[11] 2:2:1 "self-control in the mind with the power for taking vengeance or the leniency of a superior toward an inferior in determining punishments" (All translations are mine unless otherwise specified). I used Braund's Latin text of Seneca's "De Clementia throughout this paper.

[12] 2.3.2: "Everyone understands this, that clemency is that which bends itself back away from that (punishment) which might rightly be set in place."

[13] Konstan, 344.

[14] 2.4.5 "Pity sees not the cause, but the fortune (of a situation), but clemency cedes to reason."

Scribere de clementia, nero Caesar, institui, ut quodam modo specula
vice fungerer et te tibi ostenderem perventurum ad voluptatem
maximam omnium, quamvis enim recte factorum verus fructus sit
fecisse nec ullum bonam conscientiam, tum immittere oculos in hanc
immensam multitudinem discordem, seditiosam, impotentem, in
perniciem alienam suamque partiter exultaturum si hoc iugum
fregerit...[15]

Here, in the very opening passage of his treatise on clementia, Seneca
presents it to Nero as part of that "yoke" of discipline required for the
cultivation of excellence. While the question of whether or not it is part and
parcel of imperial power is taken as a given, it is the very choice in favor of
clemency that renders that power benevolent. Seneca goes so far as to write that
"Nullum tamen clementia ex omnibus magis quam regem aut principem
decet."[16] The power inherent in *imperium* was positive only if it was twinned with
benevolence and by extension clemency.[17] All other expressions of imperial
strength were "pestifera"—noxious.[18]

Three important points may be culled from the above quoted passages.
Firstly, Seneca viewed clementia as a possible expression of imperium.
Secondly, as an expression of imperium it was not only appropriate but positive.
Finally, clementia was part of the necessary social contract. Seneca writes that
"the ruler is the bond through which the Republic itself coheres."[19] This was
not necessarily hyperbole nor were the more effusive passages of *de Clementia* in

---

[15] Book 1:1:1: "I have taken on the task of writing about clemency, Nero Caesar, so I
can act as a kind of mirror and give you a picture of yourself as someone who will attain
the greatest pleasure of all. Although the true satisfaction in behaving well consists of
that behavior itself and there is no adequate reward for excellence beyond excellence
itself, it is a pleasure to inspect and examine one's good conscience and then to cast
one's eyes over this enormous mass...quarrelsome, factious, out of control and likely to
run riot to the destruction of others and itself equally, if it breaks this yoke....(Braund's
translation, p. 95).

[16] Seneca 1:3:1. "There is no one in the world that clemency suits more than a king or
an emperor." (Braund's translation, p. 95).

[17] Seneca, 1:3:1-2.

[18] Later, in chapter four, Seneca further counsels Nero toward a middle way of rulership
exhorting "severitatem abditam, et clementiam in procinctu habeo." He cautioned
vigilance over oneself and one's reactions most especially in the expression of power,
telling Nero that as Emperor he must be ready to account to the Gods for all humanity
under his care. His imperium was then a sacred trust, given to him for the good of all.
Thus imperial power itself was not only taken as a given, but—at least in Seneca's work,
given his position as imperial tutor—presented as a potentially positive good.

[19] Seneca 1.4.1 "Ille est enim vinculum per quod res publica cohaeret." See also Barton,
113-115. Translation by Barton, 113.

praise of the emperor mere flattery of the young Nero, but sincere exhortation that as an emperor he might become a just and virtuous ruler.[20]

Furthermore, Seneca uses a number of colorful and visually striking comparisons in order to emphasize the value of clementia to his intended reader. In one of the most striking examples, he goes so far as to advise Nero that:

> tibi enim parcis cum videris alteri parcere. Parcendum itaque est etiam improbandis civius non aliter quam membris languentibus, et, si quando misso sanguine opus est, sustinenda est acies ne ultra quam necesse sit incidat.[21]

While this particular metaphor refers to a surgeon's knife, it clearly also calls to mind the ruler's right to sentence a subject to execution. It is a powerful image; the allusion of the keen edge, the "acies," serves double evocative duty. It may also be significant that the example used here, far from indicating that clementia may be negative, is in fact a very positive image: the surgeon's knife that brings health and healing to a damaged body.

Later, in book one, chapter nineteen, Seneca reiterates the importance of clementia toward navigating and maintaining the social contract between an emperor and his people when he writes: "excogitare nemo quicquam poterit quod magis decorum regent sit quam clementia…"[22] While Seneca clearly accepts the political and social hierarchy inherent in Roman society of his time, at the same time, his emphasis on the emperor's clemency as an expression of his ultimate power very subtly places the entire Roman people in the position of clients, with the Emperor as ultimate patron. It is this dynamic that causes scholars like Dowling and Braund to argue for a negative reception of imperial clemency.[23]

Much of the underlying ambivalence surrounding clementia lies in its role as

---

[20] Altman speculates that the flattering tone of *De Clementia* was in part "dictated by a fervent desire that the young ruler might merit such *blanditiae.*" Altman, 202.

[21] Seneca 1.5.1: "…you are showing mercy to yourself when you seem to be showing it to someone else. So you should show mercy even to citizens who deserve condemnation just as you would to ailing limbs. And if there is ever a need to let blood, you should restrain the blade to stop it cutting more deeply than necessary." (Trans. Braund, 103).

[22] Seneca 1.14.1: "No one could imagine anything more fitting for a ruler than clemency…." Trans. Braund, 127.

[23] Dowling goes so far as to speculate that Julius Caesar's consistent bestowal of clemency was one of the leading factors behind his assassination. Dowling 32-33, 37. Seneca on the other hand specifically exhorted Nero to clemency in part because it might prove a life-saving measure (noting the hostility which Sulla evoked by his lack of this virtue). See Seneca 1.11.3. Dowling discusses this briefly in her article 'The Clemency of Sulla,' p. 333-334.

a barometer of social cohesion. The bestowal of clementia was a mark of an established hierarchy and it reinforced that hierarchy (i.e. the social cohesion mentioned by Seneca in his commentary to Nero). In this way, it may be viewed as a form of gift giving. Regardless of whether or not one views such social hierarchy as positive or negative, the power dynamics of exchange may be fraught with tension.[24] German sociologist Georg Simmel noted that "beneath all exchange lies some agonistic sense."[25] According to Simmel, the exchange of gifts or favors (more intangible gifts) carried with it the imposition of a particular social identity, precisely because it was so integral to the cultivation and maintenance of social hierarchies.[26] Exchange carried with it the paradoxical ability not only to reinforce social fabric, but conversely to upend it precisely because it "invariably involved altering equals into unequals."[27] In her forward to Marcel Mauss' *The Gift*, anthropologist Mary Douglas put it bluntly: "a gift that does nothing to enhance solidarity is a contradiction."[28]

While Seneca viewed clementia in a positive light, his opinion (as expressed in *De Beneficiis*) of gift-giving, or *beneficium*, in general was not quite so sanguine. Beneficium might all too easily turn to *creditum*—debt.[29] Creditum in turn might corrupt the beneficium: instead of giving for the sake of giving (what Italian scholar Li Causi calls *dedi ut darem*), one begins to give with the expectation of gratitude or of a gift given in return.[30] According to Seneca, the real virtue of gifting lies in the ethic and spiritual gesture of the gift, not the actual material goods or favors exchanged and, moreover, it should be done *without* the expectation of reciprocal recompense.[31] The giving of any type of gift or favor (ostensibly even clementia) requires special care, lest the giver be transformed into a creditor, and the cycle of gift giving into an unhealthy and embarrassing dependence (or addiction).[32] It is therefore incumbent on the giver to maintain

---

[24] Beidelman, 228.

[25] Simmel, 46.

[26] Beidelman, 229.

[27] Beidelman, 232. Depending on the circumstances surrounding the exchange, the receiver might well be placed (psychologically if not in actuality) in the position of suppliant or client. This is one of the arguments that both Dowling and Braund offer against a positive view of clemency.

[28] Mauss, vii.

[29] Li Causi, 233. See also *De Beneficiis* 1.11-12 for the potential poison inherent in a gift.

[30] Li Causi, 2008, 99. "I gave that I might give."

[31] Seneca, *de Beneficiis*, 1.11-12.

[32] Li Causi, 2009, 239. I have paraphrased from li Causi's original Italian: "Quello che Seneca vuole fare vedere, in altri termini, e che, se non si sta attenti alle dinamiche 'analogiche' della comunicazione attivata dai nostri gesti, un beneficio puo facilmente trasformarsi in 'creditum' (o addirittura in usura) e il donatore di conseguenza puo trasformarsi nel creditore di un capitale simbolico, creando cosi nel beneficato quella

and reinforce right attitudes and relationship with the receiver, always noting that the true benefit lies in the desire to give, not the tangible items given.[33] Unfortunately, with the case of clementia as opposed to beneficium, while the two concepts are related, the situation is a bit more complicated.

Marcel Mauss, in his seminal work *The Gift*, cautions the reader that every gift "is received with a burden attached."[34] Essentially, there "are no free gifts; gift cycles engage persons in permanent commitments that articulate the dominant institutions."[35] They reinforce the prevailing power dynamics that define social interactions within a given community and shore up prevailing power structures. The giving of a gift has the potential to affect, either by reinforcing or by challenging, prevailing status. Status, an awareness of one's place and reputation within a particular group, one's social standing, is inherently connected to honor and by extension to social obligations. Within the dynamic of exchange, both the one giving and the one receiving are bound up in a cycle of reciprocity and mutual obligation.[36] One's status depended on it and that status was a very public thing.

Carlin Barton, in his study of Roman honor culture, notes that "Romans expected of one another a high degree of behavioral finesse…lapses were noted."[37] Lapses might lead to shaming and loss of [social] status, and so these social expectations inherent in maintaining 'face' and moreover, the consequences of not do so effectively, served as a powerful self-corrective. Barton notes that "long years before Virgil or Statius created their personifications, *fama* and *rumor publicus* acted as the custodians of the *mores* of the citizens."[38] This is not insignificant either in light of the public nature of imperial clementia or in light of the force potential [public] loss of face carried within the bounds of a Mediterranean honor culture.

The emphasis placed on honor and shame in Mediterranean societies is

---

che Rosa Rita Marchese ha recentemente chiamato la 'vergogna della dipendenza."

[33] Ibid, p. 243.

[34] Mauss, p. 41.

[35] Ibid, ix.

[36] Mauss briefly discusses ancient Roman laws and gift giving tropes, but focuses overmuch on the speculative power inherent in the actual objects or favors exchanged rather than placing the power in the underlying social dynamic being established by means of the exchange (and to which the objects were tangential). There is something rather simplistic about Mauss's neat *do ut des* equation that doesn't always take into account the needs, nuances and complexities of social interactions. At the same time, within Roman society, both public beneficia and clementia carried a certain charge and the latter could be cast in a very negative light, as Lucan did with Caesar's clementia in his "Bellum Civile."

[37] Barton, 20.

[38] Ibid, 21.

remarkably consistent.[39] Honor was (and is) strongly linked to both social and economic status within a given community and while strict interpretations of what constituted 'honor' might vary somewhat between classes, there was a terrifyingly public dimension to its development, maintenance, and expression in ancient Rome.[40] Honor became a bench mark by which one's conformity to prevailing social mores might be gauged.[41] Barton discusses this when he notes that "the values of the ancient Romans…were overwhelmingly those of a warrior culture" with attendant emphasis on status, social competition, and the rewards of maintaining and bettering one's status through glory.[42] Privacy was not necessarily a consideration. In fact both Cicero and Pliny the Younger, as well as other ancient authors, caution against the license that was believed to overcome a man without the custodian of the public eye to reign in his behavior.[43] Honor was then a deeply public expression of personhood. Barton goes so far as to attribute the survival of the Republic for centuries sans a dedicated police force to the power of this type of social and cultural constraint.[44] The question then becomes, in light of this, not whether or not clementia was a positive virtue, but rather whether one's social status might be damaged by receiving it.

Obviously the most notable exemplum of clementia in action—for good or for ill—may be found in accounts of Julius Caesar. Braund ascribes to Caesar responsibility for changing the way clementia was used in political discourse and both she and Dowling reference Cicero's abundant usage of the term with respect to Caesar throughout the civil war.[45] In her article on Caesar's clemency, C. Coulter notes that Julius Caesar had a reputation for clemency from his early life pointing out that Suetonius refers to him as "natura lenissimus" (by nature very mild) and records several early instances, prior to Caesar's command in Gaul, wherein he displayed notable clemency.[46] Despite this, his clementia was not always well received.

Lucan, in his *Bellum Civile*, excoriates Caesar for showing clementia during the Civil War. In book two, Lucan begins a passage detailing an episode of

---

[39] Coombe, 221.

[40] Coombe, 228.

[41] Coombe, 231. See also Michael Herzfeld's "Within and Without: The Category of Female in the Ethnography of Modern Greece" in *Gender and Power in Rural Greece*, edited by Jill Dubisch, pp. 215-233. Princeton: Princeton University Press, 1986.

[42] Barton, 13.

[43] See Suetonius, *Tiberius*, 42.1, Pliny the Younger, *Epistulae* 3.3.4, and Cicero, *de legibus* 2.15.37.

[44] Barton, 23.

[45] Braund, 35. See also Dowling, 20-24.

[46] Coulter, 314. See also Suetonius, Julius LXXIV.

Caesar's clemency with the words "ecce, nefus belli."[47] It sets the tone for the exemplum which follows: that of Caesar pardoning Domitius at Corfinium. In pardoning him Lucan puts these words in Caesar's mouth: "'vive, licet nolis, et nostro munere' dixit, 'cerne diem.'"[48] A little later in the same passage, Lucan notes of Domitius: "...quanto melius vel caede paeracta parcere Romano potuit fortuna pudori!"[49] Here, Domitius receiving clementia *from Caesar* was viewed as a direct blow to his honor as a Roman man.[50] It is unclear, however, whether the damage to his honor arose from the dispensation of clementia, or the fact that it was Caesar dispensing it, thus highlighting Domitius' failure in battle.

Cato the Younger preferred to commit suicide rather than receive the *clementia Caesaris* at the end of the Civil War. In both cases, however, this seems to have had far more to do with dislike of Caesar himself and a belief that his actions in usurping power were unjust than a negative view of clementia as a particular trait.[51] It is worth noting that the negative shadow of Sulla still spread itself strongly over Caesarian politics. The Elder Seneca, for instance, strongly criticized Sulla's *lack* of clementia, gauging the absence of clemency to be a fault in a leader.[52] Fear that Caesar would turn into another Sulla may in fact have colored contemporary accounts of his behavior and motivations, particularly when those accounts arise from supporters of Pompey.[53]

Seneca on the other hand, far from criticizing the twinning of clementia with ultimate power, favored it as a high and necessary good, to be cultivated by a ruler. He writes that "clementia, in quamcumque domum pervenerit, eam felicem tranquillamque praestabit, sed in regia, quo rarior, eo mirabilior."[54] These are powerful words and he goes a step farther. In the same passage, he positions clementia as something that highlights a power unique to the Emperor: 'occidere contra legem nemo non potest, servare nemo praeter me."[55] He does the same thing in the following chapter noting both that "magnam

---

[47] Lucan, 2.507 "behold: a war-crime." (all Lucan translations are mine).

[48] Lucan, 2.512-513 "live against your will. Consider this day as my gift to you."

[49] Lucan, 2.17-18. "how much better if he had been slain—Fortune would have been able to spare Roman shame."

[50] This situation, however, is somewhat unique given that Domitius was an enemy soldier captured after an unsuccessful skirmish, during a civil war, as opposed to a civilian facing charges in a court, or before the Emperor in time of peace.

[51] Konstan, 343.

[52] See Dowling, *Sulla,* 331.

[53] This may also have been one of influences behind Caesar subtly and not so subtly casting himself as another Marius in his de Bello Gallico.

[54] Seneca, 1.4.4: "clemency will make any house it enters happy and calm. But in a palace its rarity will make it more amazing." (Braund translation, 103).

[55] Seneca, 1.4.4: "to kill in defiance of the law is open to anyone. To preserve life is open to no one except me." (Braund translation, 103).

fortunam magnus animus decet, qui, nisi se ad illam extulit et altior stetit, illam quoque in terram deducit," and also "servare proprium est excellentis fortunae."[56] For Seneca, inasmuch as he was presenting his ideas on clementia to Nero, its exercise had the potential to increase the emperor's good reputation, and to stand as a testament to his ultimate power.

Mauss discusses the mutual obligations inherent in the relationship between giver and receiver as a type of spiritual bond.[57] Seneca in turn alludes to the divine nature of clementia when he draws a comparison, in 1.7 between the clementia shown by the Gods to erring mortals and the clementia that might be shown by the emperor to the people in his reign. In 1.8 he compares the constraints and obligations of clement rulership with slavery, again drawing a strong parallel between the emperor and the Gods:

> est haec summae magnitudinis servitus, non posse fiery minorem; sed cum dis tibi communis ista necessitas est. nam illos quoque caelum alligatos tenet, nec magis illis descendere datum est quam tibi tutum: fastigio tuo adfixus es.[58]

Here, the question of personal honor does not arise. Rather the dispensation of clementia is a matter of duty, obligation, and even the constraints of just leadership. Clementia was the sign of a humane ruler. According to Seneca, the expression of clementia by the emperor was a mark of his godlike position and status. In this way it reinforced that prevailing power dynamics inherent in Roman governmental structure, but at the same time had the potential to greatly benefit everyone involved.

Regardless, clementia was not an easy trait to categorize in the Roman world. On the one hand, it was something to be sought in a leader (as opposed to *crudelitas*), on the other the very fact that one man had the power to bestow clementia pointed to social inequality, and potentially rendered the one receiving clementia in the socially subordinate position of client. Many scholars like Dowling, Barton, and Braund, view imperial clementia as an indication of tyranny. Clementia, particularly in warfare, was a clear sign of the victor's power and one may extrapolate from this that in government it was a clear sign of the

---

[56] Seneca, 1.5.1 "Greatness of spirit adorns greatness of standing. If the spirit does not exalt itself to match its station or stand above it, it drags that station down too, down towards the ground." (Trans. Braund, 105) and Seneca 1.5.7: "to save a life is the prerogative of exalted rank." (Trans. Braund, 105).

[57] Mauss, 13.

[58] Seneca, 1.8.1 "this is the slavery experienced by the highest importance—to be unable to become less important. But that constraint you share with the gods. The fact is that they too are held fettered by heaven. It is no more possible for them to come down than it is safe for you to do so: you are nailed to your pinnacle." (Trans. Braund, 109).

lack of power of those being ruled.[59]

At the same time, Seneca positions clementia as a virtue for both the common man and the emperor, and recommends it as a curative to the destructtiveness of *ira* and *crudelitas*. While it might imply a relationship between superior to inferior, that relationship might be situational and need not automatically imply tyranny. In 44 B.C. E, the Roman Senate erected a temple to clementia, and Seneca is not the only author to advocate for its expression. Dowling notes, for instance, that "Publilius tells us that clemency triumphs over opposition, while cruelty hurts the cruel individual worst."[60] Not only was Caesar renowned for his clementia (despite his detractors, who criticized him for the same trait, proving that it's impossible to please everyone) but after his initial severity in avenging Caesar and gaining imperium, Octavian as Augustus was noted for his clementia.[61]

Ultimately, clementia is something of a situational virtue. As an oblique form of gift giving it may, at times, have been an uncomfortable trait for Romans, particularly the Roman elite. At the same time, it was not necessarily a negative one. Gift-giving, the exchange of items and/or favors, inevitably carries with it certain tensions. It is an ambivalent exchange.[62] As a means of navigating social hierarchy, the cycle of exchange was also a means whereby "face" might be gained or lost. As such, clementia, an aspect of gift-giving intimately connected to imperium was dangerous virtue, an ambivalent trait, fraught with the potential for abuse. Despite these dangers and discomforts, however, it remained a means whereby those in a superior position might hold social "conversations' with those in an inferior position. It contributed to the smooth governing of a nation and was, in the end, both desired and sought by those being governed.

Bibliography

Altman, Marion. 1938. "Ruler Cult in Seneca." *Classical Philology*. Vol. 33, No. 2: 198-204.

---

[59] Dowling, 17.

[60] Dowling, 30.

[61] Suetonius, for instance, references it in *Augustus* 24.1, 21.2. and 57.2 and while Dowling notes (67) that this may have been in part, Augustan propaganda, it is significant that Augustus' portrayal of clementia was viewed as both positive and beneficial to the Republic. It is further significant that in 27 B.C.E. the Senate voted to bestow upon Augustus a golden shield, to be displayed in the Curia, on which were inscribed the words: *virtus, pietas, clementia, iustitia.* The inclusion of clementia in this inscription indicates that it was not an unwelcome trait in the eyes of the Senate for a ruler.

[62] So much so, that Professor Bruce Grant once referred to it as 'a martial art.' Private communication, November 2005.

Barton, Carlin. 2001. *Roman Honor.* Berkeley: University of California Press.

Beidelman, T.O. 1989. "Agonistic Exchange: Homeric Reciprocity and the Heritage of Simmel and Mauss." *Cultural Anthropology*, vol. 4, No. 3: 227-259.

Braund, Susanna. 2009. Seneca, *De Clementia.* Oxford: Oxford University Press.

Caesaris, C. Iuli. 2009 *Commentariorum: libri VII de Bello Gallico cum A. Hirti Supplemento,* Oxford, UK: Oxford Classical Texts.

Carson, R.A.G. 1957. "Caesar and the Monarchy." *Greece & Rome,* vol 4, No. 1: 46-53.

Coombe, Rosemary. 1990. "Barren Ground: Re-conceiving Honour and Shame in the Field of Mediterranean Ethnography." *Anthropologica* Vol. 32, No. 2: 221-238.

Coulter, Cornelia. 1931. "Caesar's Clemency." *The Classical Journal.* Vol. 26, No. 7: 513-524.

Dowling, Melissa. 2000. "The Clemency of Sulla." *Historia: Zeitschrift fur Alte Geschichte.* Bd. 49, H. 3: 303-340.

_____. 2009. *Clemency and Cruelty in the Roman World.* Ann Arbor: University of Michigan Press.

Fears, Rufus, J. 1975. "Nero as the Vicegerent of the Gods in Seneca's de Clementia." *Hermes* 103:486-496.

Gilmore, David (editor). 1987. *Honor and Shame and the Unity of the Mediterranean.* Washington, DC: American Anthropological Association.

Herzfeld, Michael, 1980, "Honour and Shame: Problems in the Comparative Analysis of Moral Systems." *Man* vol. 15, No. 2: 339-351.

Konstan, David. 2005. "Clemency as a Virtue." *Classical Philology* Vol. 100, No. 4: 337-346.

Li Causi, Pietro. 2009. Fra *Creditum* e Beneficium: La Pratica Difficile Del 'Dono' nel de Beneficiis di Seneca in *I Quaderni Del Ramo d'Oro on-line* n.2, 226-252.

_____. 2008 La teoria in azione. Il dono di Eschine e la riflessione senecana sui beneficia in *Annali Online di Ferrara*—Lettere vol. 1, 95-110.

Lucani, M. Annaei. 1926. edited by A.E. Housman, *Belli Civilis: Libri Decem.* Oxford, UK: Oxford Classical Texts.

Mauss, Marcel. 2000. *The Gift.* New York: W.W. Norton.

Seneca. 1962. Translated by R. Gummere, *Ad Lucilium Epistulae Morales Vol II,* Cambridge, MA: Harvard University Press Loeb Classical Library.

Galina Krasskova is a polytheist, Heathen author and academic. She holds a Masters degree in Religious Studies and has done graduate work in Classics. She blogs regularly at http://krasskova.wordpress.com.

Idunn: Goddess of the Heart

DAGULF LOPTSON

Iðunn is a goddess who has been traditionally been associated with fertility and the rejuvenation of the earth, due to her role as the deliverer of the apples of imortality to the gods. In this article, the traditional role of Iðunn as a goddess of fertility is challenged, and instead she is presented as a goddess who is primarily associated with the heart and the role that the heart plays in religious, devotional practice, drawing this association by referring to Snorri´s list of kennings in *Skaldskaparmal*. The story of Iðunn's abduction by Þjazi is then reframed into a narrative describing the necessity of sacrifice and worship in the empowerment and rejuvenation of the gods. Loki's role as a god of sacrificial fire is also brought to the forefront, along with a brief summary of Loki, Iðunn, Bragi, and Sigyn's roles as deities who embody the ritual actions of religious sacrifice within a Heathen context.

This article is an attempt to demonstrate the importance that devotional practice holds for the reawakening of modern Heathenry, and seems to have held in ancient times as well. Due to a lack of historical evidence for how ancient Heathens worshipped their gods and experienced them on a one-on-one basis, I have often heard it suggested by modern Heathens that a worship of the gods based on devotional practices is a contemporary invention. This would imply that direct experience and involvement with the gods was not a matter of concern for ancient Heathens, and is therefore unnecessary today (or at worst, hubristic). However, when viewed in the proper context, we have at least one surviving story that seems to have encoded the necessity of devotional practice within it: that of the theft of Iðunn's apples. This story also reveals Iðunn to have a very direct connection to the practice of devotion, if not being the very personification of religious devotion itself.

The story of Iðunn's abduction by the giant Þjazi is found in the skaldic poem *Haustlöng* ("autumn-long"): a poem attributed to the Norwegian skald Þjóðólfr of Hvitnir and preserved in Snorri Sturluson's *Skaldskaparmal*. Turville-Petre dates the original poem to about 900 AD,[1] implying that Iðunn

---

[1] Turville-Petre, E.O.G. *Myth and Religion of the North: The Religion of Ancient Scandinavia.* Westport, Conn.: Greenwood, 1975. 186

was a goddess well known in Þjóðólfr's day. The time period in which he was writing would also imply that the story itself and the images it contains were authentically Heathen in origin. Þjóðólfr's poem about the theft of Iðunn and her apples was inspired by a shield that was given to him as a gift from a man named Þórlief, which was decorated with the image of Óðinn, Loki, and Hænir being confronted by the giant Þjazi. The poem, which I will examine later in this article, tells the story of how Loki was captured by Þjazi and tortured until he agreed to bring him the goddess Iðunn and her magical apples that prevented the gods from aging. According to Snorri's retelling, Loki later borrows Freyja's falcon form, transforms Iðunn into a nut, and carries her out of the clutches of the giant and back to Ásgarðr.

Iðunn is largely a mysterious goddess, who doesn't appear to have any historical cult or place names. All we know of her comes from Snorri, who tells us that she is the keeper of the apples that grant the gods their youth:

> Idunn is his [Bragi's] wife. She keeps in her casket apples which the gods have to feed on when they age, and then they all become young, and so it will go on right up to Ragnarok.[2]

Rudolph Simek translates her name as "the rejuvenating one," and interprets her as a fertility goddess due to her association with apples, which could be interpreted as symbols of fertility.[3] Turville-Petre notes that the story of Iðunn's apples may have been foreign in origin, as cultivated apples were not known in Scandinavia until the Middle Ages. However, the Old Norse word commonly translated as apple (*epli*) does not only mean "apple," but is also applied to other round fruits and even acorns. Like Simek, Turville-Petre also assumes that the fruits and nuts in Iðunn's only surviving story are symbolic of fertility.[4]

Though it seems very tempting to pigeonhole Iðunn as a fertility goddess due to her association with fruits and renewal, an examination of Snorri's list of kennings in *Skaldskaparmal* tells a very different story. According to Snorri, these are the kennings that can be used for the human heart:

> Hjarta heitir negg. Þat skal svá kenna, kalla korn eða stein eða **epli** eða **hnot** eða mýl eða líkt ok kenna við brjóst eða hug, kalla má ok hús eða jörð eða berg hugarins.

---

[2] Sturlason, Snorri. *Edda*. Trans. Anthony Faulkes. London: Dent, 1995. 25

[3] Simek, Rudolf. *Dictionary of Northern Mythology*. Repr. Ed. Cambridge: brewer, 1996. 171-172

[4] Turville-Petre, E.O.G. *Myth and Religion of the North: The Religion of Ancient Scandinavia*. Westport, Conn.: Greenwood, 1975. 186-186

The heart is called bosom. It shall be referred to by calling it corn or stone or **apple** or **nut** or ball or the like, and referring to it in terms of breast or thought. It can also be called house or ground or mountain of the thought.[5]

Given that these kennings appear in the same book as both versions of Iðunn's abduction, it seems certain that Snorri would have been aware that the apples of Iðunn and the nut that Loki transforms her into are both kennings for the heart. The words *epli* (apple) and *hnut* (nut) appear in both the list of kennings and in Snorri's version of the story.

With that in mind, rather than interpreting the story of Iðunn as one of a fertility goddess being kidnapped by the forces of the underworld (as it is commonly presented) it may be more accurate to say that the "apples" of Iðunn are actually the hearts which are the keepers and expressers of religious devotion. If that analysis is correct, then this story may also reveal the understanding that the Old Norse people had of religious devotion and the effect it had on their gods. The explanation of the myth that I will be providing was written with the assumption that my analysis of Loki as the god of sacrificial/cremation fire (which I have already written extensively about in this publication and others) is correct.

The story begins with Hænir, Óðinn, and Loki travelling in the wilderness. The gods come across a herd of oxen, kill one of them, and attempt to cook it in an earth oven (subtly pointing to the understanding that the gods are fed through burnt offerings). However, no matter how much they try the gods can't cook the meat. Without the fire, the offering cannot be transmitted to the world of the gods for their benefit. Above them, in an oak tree (a tree associated with lightning and the sacred fire from heaven that lightning creates) the giant Þjazi appears in the form of an eagle. Þjazi tells the gods that if they give him a share of the food (the sacrificial offering) then the oven will cook the meat.

Though the etymology of Þjazi's name is uncertain, it is possible that his eagle form (connecting him to the sky) embodies the lightning that strikes the oak tree, through which the sacramental fire is lit and sacrifices can be made. This may explain why until the eagle descends from his oak tree, the gods are not able to cook their meat. This may also be an echo from Vedic mythology, in which Indra (the thunder god) steals soma (the sacred drink of the gods) in the form of an eagle.[6]

The gods agree to Þjazi's terms and the meat finally cooks. The eagle drops from the tree and sits on the oven, and begins to gorge himself on the whole

---

[5] Sturlason, Snorri. *Edda*. Trans. Anthony Faulkes. London: Dent, 1995. 154
[6] Turville-Petre, E.O.G. *Myth and Religion of the North: The Religion of Ancient Scandinavia*. Westport, Conn.: Greenwood, 1975. 187

ox. This angers Loki, who grabs a pole and drives it into the eagle's body. The eagle flies away, but because Loki is embodiment of the sacred fire, he can't let go of the other end of the pole (he burns at the end of the pole like a torch) and is carried up into the air.

As Loki is the vehicle that carries the devotional offerings to the gods so that they can eat, he is the obvious choice for Þjazi to kidnap in his quest to gain the "apples" of Iðunn, as he is the only one who is able to deliver the devotional offerings they represent. By Loki giving the offerings to Þjazi instead of the gods, Þjazi will become the object of worship that benefits from their power. The eagle carries Loki along a very rough ride, until Loki pleads for mercy. The eagle only agrees to free him when Loki agrees that he will get Iðunn to leave Ásgarðr with her apples.

When Loki returns to Ásgarðr, he leads Iðunn into a forest where he claims to have found some noteworthy apples, and tells her to bring her own apples with her so that she can compare them. Once she is exposed, Þjazi arrives in the eagle shape, snatches Iðunn, and carries her away to his home in Þrymheimr ("thunder-home," further emphasizing his connection to lightning). The gods are badly affected by Iðunn's disappearance and begin to grow grey and old. Without Iðunn, who is the embodiment of ritual devotion, and the offerings of the heart that she gives to the gods every day, the gods begin to wither. This part of the story in particular reveals that the ancestors seemed to hold the belief that it was their devotional acts that kept the gods young and vibrant, and that without the offerings of the heart the gods would grow weak and feeble. Devotion then is the force that empowers the gods and gives them their strength.

When the gods discover Loki's role in Iðunn's disappearance, they bind him and threaten him with death or torture. Loki agrees to go find Iðunn if Freyja will lend him her falcon shape. He then flies to Jötunheimr, finds Iðunn in Þrymheimr, and transforms her into a nut. This transformation into a nut seems strange at first glance. Why transform her at all? Why a nut? Her transformation seems important to the story because it hints to Iðunn's connection to the heart and its kennings, so that the true meaning of this story might be emphasized.

Loki takes the nut up in his claws (as the sacrificial fire, he is yet again the deliverer of the offerings and devotion that bring the gods their strength) and flies her back to Ásgarðr. Þjazi realizes what has happened, and causes a storm wind when he flies after Loki in his eagle form. When the gods see Loki flying with the nut and pursued by the eagle, they bring out loads of wood shavings, and when Loki flies over Ásgarðr's wall they set fire to the wood. The eagle is unable to stop, his feathers catch fire and he falls to the ground. The fire in this story seems to represent two functions: it emphasizes the return of Loki (the sacrificial fire) and the devotional offerings (in the form of Iðunn/the nut) that he carries. It may also represent the exorcizing power of fire to destroy or disempower hostile wights. After Þjazi falls to the ground the gods kill him.[7]

With this new context, it is revealed that Iðunn and her apples both hold a special significance to devotion and worship of the gods, and that the gods themselves rely on the hearts of human beings for their vitality and strength. The kennings for the heart reveal it to be the imagined seat of the consciousness (the *hugr*), and it is through our consciousness that human beings can perceive the gods, reflect on them, commune with them, and transmit offerings to them from our hearts translated into ritual action. This story would imply that far from being distant forces that we have no hope of influencing or affecting, the gods were imagined to be dependent to some degree on the worship given to them by humans, delivered through the vehicle of sacrifice (as embodied by Loki in this narrative).

The apples that are representative of ritual worship appear a second time in the poem Skírnismál, in which Freyr's servant Skírnir is sent to persuade the giantess Gerðr to marry him. Freyr sends Skírnir to Gerðr with golden apples and the ring Draupnir (which appear to be bribes) and Freyr's own sword (which is "plan-B" in case the bribes don't work).

> 19. Epli ellifu hér hef ek algullin,
> þau mun ek þér, Gerðr, gefa,
> frið a kaupa, at þú þér Frey kveðir
> óleiðastan lífa.

> 19. Apples against old age I have here, all gold,
> and those I'll give you, Gerd,
> to purchase peace, so you might call Frey
> not the loathsomest creature alive.[8]

Turville-Petre notes that the words *epli ellifu* in the poem are usually translated as "eleven apples," while they might be emended to *epli ellilyfs*, "apples of old-age medicine."[9] If this is correct, these apples are surely the same ones that Iðunn gives to the gods, and the implication may be that if Gerðr aggrees to marry Freyr, she will be elevated to the position of a goddess and will be able to partake of her own worship.

Iðunn's pairing with Bragi (the god of poetry) as her husband also makes a great deal of sense when she is viewed as a goddess of devotion rather than a goddess of fertility. It is through sacred words: prayers, poetry, song, etc., that

---

[7] Sturlason, Snorri. *Edda*. Trans. Anthony Faulkes. London: Dent, 1995. 59-60

[8] *The Elder Edda: A Book of Viking Lore*. Trans. Andy Orchard. New York, 2011. 62

[9] Turville-Petre, E.O.G. *Myth and Religion of the North: The Religion of Ancient Scandinavia*. Westport, Conn.: Greenwood, 1975. 175

our devotion is communicated to the gods, all of which are embodied by the gods' poet Bragi. Though there is no evidence of a cult of Iðunn, Bragi, Loki, or Sigyn, it is worth noting that these four deities in particular seem to embody the essential functions of ritual worship as required by the gods for their empowerment. I interpret Sigyn with her bowl and snake (images that often accompany European goddess of healing, power, and destiny) as the goddess who pours the ritual offerings into her husband Loki, the sacred fire, thus granting the gods victory (as her name "victorious-girlfriend" implies). Sigyn is also known as the *galdr hapt*, (meaning the "*galdr*-fetter") in the skaldic poem *Þórsdrápa*. As "fetter" is actually a kenning for "deity" according to Snorri in *Skaldskaparmal*,[10] this makes Sigyn the goddess of *galdr*, i.e magical poetry or ritual song. This is arguably the same magical poetry of worship that is embodied by the god Bragi. Loki is the sacred fire who transmits the offerings and worship embodied by the goddess Iðunn from the human world into the world of the gods. There, Iðunn feeds the gods her "apples," which strengthen and rejuvenate them.

While a great emphasis has been placed upon the pursuit of knowledge and scholarship in modern Heathenry as a reconstructive act and a way of understanding the old religion, I believe that the story of Iðunn is instructive of the vital role that ritual devotion held in the religion of the ancient Scandinavians. In my previous article: *Askr and Embla: Microcosms of the Macrocosm*, I demonstrated that trees were often used as symbols for human beings in the Eddas and Sagas, and the same case could be argued here. Iðunn's "apples" are the hearts that grow within each worshipper (symbolized by Iðunn's apple trees), which are the food that feed the holy powers. This story is, in my mind, not only instructive but also cautionary. The gods have gone a very long time without the praise and worship that *Haustlöng* tells us is the only thing that sustains them and gives them strength. The powers have weakened, and the doorway through which their offerings were received (Loki, the sacrificial fire) has been demonized and bound by the god's detractors, closing the doorway and starving the gods of their offerings. It is only through devotion that the gods can be strengthened and reawakened, which is I why I see the suppression and downplaying of the devotional impulse within modern Heathenry to be so misled and detrimental.

It is my hope that Heathens might reexamine Iðunn's mythos and her message of the importance of the heart, and that in our pursuit of knowledge and authenticity the heart of our spirituality not be ignored or overshadowed. After all, *Haustlöng* makes it clear that the gods depend on it.

---

[10] Sturlason, Snorri. *Edda*. Trans. Anthony Faulkes. London: Dent, 1995. 88

Bibliography:

E.O.G. Turville-Petre. *Myth and Religion of the North: The Religion of Ancient Scandinavia.* Westport, CT: Greenwood Press, 1975.

Snorri Sturluson. *Edda.* Tr. Anthony Faulkes. London: Everyman's Library, 1995.

The Elder Edda: A Book of Viking Lore. Tr. Andy Orchard. New York: Penguin Classics, 2011.

Dagulf Loptson has been a devotee of Loki for 20 years and counting, following a childhood love-at-first-sight encounter. Despite his insistence that he was a Heathen, many gods from different traditions have become a part of his life over the years, who he loves and honors with the precarious balance of a trapeze artist. He is the author of the devotional book *Playing With Fire: An Exploration of Loki Laufeyjarson* (available through Asphodel Press) and is a regular columnist at Polytheist.com on his blog Ørgrandr Lokean. When he's not writing about gods, he's an artist, tattoo apprentice, and horror movie junkie.

"Would the Real Philosopher-King Please Stand Up?": Hadrian and the Philosophers

P. SUFENAS VIRIUS LUPUS

While many people may argue that the Emperor Marcus Aurelius was the ideal "philosopher king," the present article instead argues that the Emperor Hadrian could equally well vie for the title. He and his adoptive mother, the Empress Plotina, were interested in Epicureanism, and their correspondence on the succession of the Epicurean school in Athens survives in inscriptions. Two other clues—the fanciful name of a savory dish, and Hadrian's sepulchral epigram—also might hint at Epicurean tendencies. Two dialogue texts which place the Emperor Hadrian in discussion with the philosophers Epictetus and Secundus (both real philosophers, though the texts are later and fictitious), as well as other details of his portrayal and understanding, demonstrate that posterity likewise thought of Hadrian as a philosophically-inclined Emperor. A translation of the *Altercatio Hadriani Augusti et Epicteti Philosophi* completes the present article.

With the American system of education being what it currently is, and the general knowledge of world history being rather lacking at present, it is a wonder if anyone in the U.S. can name a single Roman Emperor. Many will say "Julius Caesar"—even though he wasn't an Emperor at all—and some others might be able to come up with Augustus. Those who have studied early Christianity might come up with the apparent epitome of evil and excess, Nero, while those with more of a taste for the lurid and scandalous will recall Caligula (despite the third-century CE teenage Emperor Elagabulus being even more shocking in his behavior than either of these on their worst days, if sources such as the *Historia Augusta*[1] are to be given credence!).

But, were they asked to name a "good" Roman Emperor—despite the idea of the "Five Good Emperors" being anachronistic, and attributed to Machiavelli—many might suggest Marcus Aurelius, who is often thought to be

---

[1] Anthony R. Birley (trans.), *Lives of the Later Caesars: The first part of the Augustan History, with newly compiled Lives of Nerva and Trajan* (London and New York: Penguin Books, 1976), pp. 290-316.

a "good" Emperor because he was also a philosopher, and (perhaps more influentially) is spoken well of by Christians and treated relatively well by Christian history. Further, he is often praised and characterized by modern atheists as a forerunner to their own theological position based on certain statements in his misleadingly modern-titled *Meditations*[2]—and this despite the fact that he was as polytheistic as any of his predecessors or successors, even being convinced by the snake puppet oracle of Glykon to take certain actions against the Marcomanni and the Quadi which resulted in catastrophic failure.[3]

The actual facts on the ground seem to be that Marcus Aurelius was a rather reluctant Emperor, someone who might have preferred to be a common person rather than in the position that was imposed upon him by rules of succession put in place by the Emperor Hadrian, and his actual principate was not as successful, peaceful, or by any means ideal in comparison to his predecessors. His Stoic philosophy (a philosophical school whose precepts are often praised for their supposed similarity to, and even forerunning of, Christian and later forms of monotheism) was not necessarily something favored nor promulgated widely by his political policies, and his philosophical writings that have Stoic sympathies were not meant for wider consumption.[4] While his principate is not more blameworthy nor deserving of criticism as many other less effective, successful, or renowned Emperors, it is likewise not especially distinguished or praiseworthy, either. It was ultimately Marcus Aurelius' succession policy, which put his son Commodus on the imperial throne after a period in which Commodus was co-emperor with his father, that brought the Antonine Dynasty and the longest period of relative stability and success of the Roman Empire to an end. From the time of Nerva, Emperors had been appointed for merit rather than by blood relations,[5] and the breaking of this set of precedents with the accession of Commodus as sole Emperor lead to a great decline in the Empire, briefly and intermittently stabilized by some of the Severans, before the majority of the third century CE's succession of

---

[2] C. R. Haines (ed./trans.), *Marcus Aurelius* (Cambridge: Harvard University Press, 1999), pp. 2-343. One of the most (mis-) quoted pieces of the *Meditations* from Book II.11 (pp. 32-35) seems to be—devoid of context—a paraphrase of the Epicurean paradox on theodicy, but in reality it does affirm Aurelius' acknowledgement of the existence of Deities.

[3] A. M. Harmon (ed./trans.), *Lucian, Volume IV* (Cambridge: Harvard University Press, 1925), pp. 235-238.

[4] Anthony R. Birley, *Marcus Aurelius: A Biography* (London and New York: Routledge, 1993), pp. 211-223.

[5] Though Trajan, Hadrian, Lucius Verus and Marcus Aurelius did share close ties both by heredity and marriage amongst themselves. For a succinct treatment of Hadrian's succession policies, see Thorsten Opper, *Hadrian: Empire and Conflict* (Cambridge: Harvard University Press, 2008), pp. 216-221.

"barracks Emperors" who did not last long before being deposed militarily, and who generally did not establish dynasties nor have the time to appoint qualified successors.

The debates on the politics of succession for Roman Emperors could occupy a great deal of space, but the purpose of the present discussion is not to use such politics as a measure of philosophical merit, but instead to use the example of Marcus Aurelius and his renown as a "philosopher-king" (and often an over-idealized one at that) to then compare with a counter-example of someone many modern people might not associate with philosophy at all, but who was closely identified with philosophy and philosophical activities during and after his term as Emperor: Publius Aelius Hadrianus, better known as Hadrian, who was responsible for ensuring the eventual accession of Marcus Aurelius as Roman Emperor. Hadrian is said in the *Historia Augusta*[6] to have been philosophically inclined. Flavius Philostratus' *Life of Apollonius of Tyana* also records that Hadrian was interested in the life and work of its subject,[7] who was a neo-Pythagorean wonder-worker closely associated with magic, and who was even worshipped as a philosopher-hero after his death. But there is other more direct as well as indirect evidence for Hadrian's involvement with and interest in other schools of philosophy. We will examine his affiliations with Epicureanism here, as well as two later textual sources which attribute philosophical dialogues to him and the philosophers Epictetus (not to be confused with the actual Stoic philosopher who was Hadrian's contemporary and likely acquaintance) and Secundus. Finally, the earlier of these two texts, the *Altercatio Hadriani Augusti et Epicteti Philosophi*, will be given in an English translation from the Latin original.

The most definitive demonstration of Hadrian's connection to Epicureanism can be found in surviving correspondence he had with his adopted mother, the Empress Plotina (the widow of the Emperor Trajan), who in a set of letters discusses the succession of the Epicurean school in Athens in 121 CE, which was subsequently inscribed on a large marble block in Athens. Plotina wrote as follows:

> What interest I have in the sect of Epicurus you know very well, lord. His School needs help from you. Since, as of now, a successor must be taken from those who are Roman citizens, the choice is narrowly limited. I ask, therefore, in the name of Popillius Theotimus, who is currently successor at Athens, that it be permitted by you to him both to make a testament in Greek concerning this part of his decisions which applies to the organization of the Succession and to be entitled

---

[6] Birley, *Lives*, p. 75.

[7] F. C. Conybeare (ed./trans.), *Philostratus, The Life of Apollonius of Tyana*, 2 volumes (Cambridge: Harvard University Press, 1912), Vol. 2, pp. 382-383.

to appoint as successor to himself one of peregrine status, if the distinction of the person should make it advisable. And that also future successors of the sect of Epicurus thereafter may use the same right which you will have granted to Theotimus, all the more so because, as often as a mistake has been made by the testator concerning the election of a successor, it is the rule for him who is the best man to be substituted by the members of the same sect in a common meeting, a procedure which will become easier if the election is made from a larger group.

Hadrian did as requested, and thus wrote to Popillius Theotimus:

I permit you to make a testament in Greek concerning those matters which pertain to the Succession of the Epicurean sect, but since he will even more easily choose a successor if he has obtained the option of appointing a successor also from *peregrini*, this too I guarantee, and it will be permitted to all others who have obtained the succession to pass on this right either to a peregrine or to a Roman citizen.

After this response, Plotina further addressed all the "Friends of Epicurus" thus:

We have now what we were so eager to obtain. For it has been granted to any successor who will lead the School of Epicurus which is at Athens both to make authoritatively every disposition pertinent to the Succession in a Greek testament and to choose as the future president of the School either a Hellene, if he so wishes, or a Roman. We owe then a debt of gratitude to him who is in truth the benefactor and overseer of all culture and therefore a most reverence-worthy emperor, to me very dear in all respects as both an outstanding guardian and loyal son. With this fine extension of authority that has been granted it is appropriate that each of those who have been trusted with the decision concerning the presidency ever try to appoint in his place the best of the fellow-sectarians and to attribute more importance to his view of the overall interests than to his private congeniality with certain members. In my opinion, therefore, it would be better not to regard any with more affection than those who win recognition as outstanding in the power of our doctrines and, accordingly, in the superiority of their own moral condition. If this were not to occur, not by the peculiar nature of the matter but by our own weakness or through some other accidental impediment, I think it the duty of him who will plan for the society's program to aim at the man who will please all in common and not just at the one who will please him personally. But, by Zeus, I do not at all think that he who once lays hold of the advantage which has come to him from the doctrines and who has gratitude for his joint perception of such, with his habit of living by a fixed principle which would not allow him to abuse the great gift, I think that he will not only not fail to dispose by testament so that … the preservation of dignity of that position …[8]

In 125 CE, Hadrian again reiterated his earlier decision to the Athenians:

…Once again I say what I decided for Popillius Theotimus and deified Plotina, my most revered mother, that I gladly grant that it be permitted to whoever preside on each occasion over the Succession to dispose of it by a Greek testament, whether they wish to choose a Hellene or a Roman…Romans…disposed…who explained these matters to her and to all the Epicureans in common. Farewell…March at Athens in the consulship of Valerius Asiaticus for the second time and of Aquilinus.[9]

It is likely that Hadrian's philosopher friend, Heliodorus, was an Epicurean and succeeded to the head of the school in Athens.[10]

A second sympathy of Hadrian with the Epicurean philosophy may be discerned in the term *tetrapharmakos*, the "fourfold cure," which was a Greek term designating a drug made from wax, tallow, pitch, and resin. However, it is also known from the Epicurean philosopher Philodemos, who wrote during the first century BCE, and was likewise used by Diogenes Laertius in the third century when summarizing Epicurean doctrines. In Philodemos' expression, the *tetrapharmakos* consisted of the following principles: "Don't fear the gods; Don't worry about death; What is good is easy to get, and What is terrible is easy to endure."[11] In what might seem like a random and perhaps even unconnected circumstance, the Latinized term *tetrapharmacum* was used in Hadrianic circles for something mentioned in the *Historia Augusta* as having been invented by Lucius Ceionius Commodus—better known as Aelius Caesar, the first adopted heir of Hadrian—as a pastry dish made of a sow's udder, pheasant, wild boar, and ham, which was enjoyed not only by Hadrian and Aelius Caesar,[12] but also by the later Emperor Alexander Severus. While this may have made for a hearty post-

---

[8] James Henry Oliver, *Greek Constitutions of Early Roman Emperors from Inscriptions and Papyri* (Philadelphia: American Philosophical Society, 1989), pp. 174-180.
[9] Oliver, pp. 180-181.
[10] Birley, *Hadrian*, pp. 109, 182; Birley, *Lives*, p. 75.
[11] Translation slightly modified from D. S. Hutchinson, "Introduction," in Brad Inwood and L. P. Gerson (eds./trans.), *The Epicurus Reader: Selected Writings and Testimonia* (Indianapolis and Cambridge: Hackett Publishing Company Inc., 1994), p. vi.
[12] Birley, *Lives*, pp. 80, 92.

hunting dish for Roman elites, it is clearly named after the earlier precedents in a rather complex and high-browed punning fashion. What I would suggest, however, is not that it is named after the more obvious medical concoction, but instead it might refer more to the philosophical concept, given not only Hadrian's known interest in Epicureanism, but also because of his own sense of humor which would likely have enjoyed such playful usages.

A final example of Epicurean influences in Hadrian's life and work might be evidenced in his famed poetic epitaph. The Epicurean belief in the soul did not preclude the soul's ultimate mortality, even if it persisted after the death of the body, and overall philosophers of this school were highly skeptical of mysticism and all possibilities of immortality. Hadrian's life had been marked by religious activities, and participation in the Eleusinian Mysteries on several occasions,[13] and thus it seems strange that in his declining years, and even after the deification of Antinous, that he might have become more skeptical. Nonetheless, the lines of his epitaph do paint such a skeptical picture:

Animula vagula blandula
hospes comesque corporis,
quo nunc abibis in loca
pallidula rigida nudula,
nec ut soles dabis iocos

Little soul, little wanderer, little charmer,
body's guest and companion,
to what places will you set out for now?
To darkling, cold and gloomy ones—
and you won't make your usual jokes.[14]

Anthony Birley suggests that despite his varied religious and mystical activities during life, that a return to the skeptical viewpoint may have its evidence in this poem, highly influenced by the Roman Republican poet Ennius, who was known to have been a favorite poet for Hadrian,[15] and whose work

---

[13] See P. Sufenas Virius Lupus, "'I Have Seen The Maiden': Hadrian, Antinous, and the Eleusinian Mysteries," in Melitta Benu et al. (eds.), *Queen of the Sacred Way: A Devotional Anthology in Honor of Persephone* (Asheville, NC: Bibliotheca Alexandrina, 2012), pp. 164-172; "Demeter and Goetia: The Eleusinian Mysteries and the Strange Case of Hadrian and Antinous," in Melitta Benu and Rebecca Buchanan (eds)., *Potnia: A Devotional Anthology in Honor of Demeter* (Asheville, NC: Bibliotheca Alexandrina, 2014), pp. 261-272.

[14] Birley, *Hadrian*, p. 301.

[15] Birley, *Hadrian*, p. 302; Anthony R. Birley, "Hadrian's Farewell to Life," *Laverna* 5 (1994), pp. 176-205 at 202-205.

has also been found in the Herculaneum Library which contained a great deal of Epicurean philosophical texts, including those by Philodemos from which the *tetrapharmakon* has been derived.

It is mentioned in the *Historia Augusta* that a philosopher named Epictetus was acquainted with Hadrian.[16] It seems very likely that this Epictetus was the famed Stoic philosopher and former slave whose works have survived and was a contemporary of Hadrian, and who was known to have been the teacher of Arrian, who was also a friend of Hadrian.[17] What influence Epictetus and his Stoicism might have had on Hadrian is not certain, and cannot be easily discerned. However, this connection most likely lead to the composition of the question-and-answer dialogue text known as the *Altercatio Hadriani Augusti et Epicteti Philosophi*.[18] It is clearly not a record of the actual philosopher Epictetus

---

[16] Birley, *Lives*, p. 75.
[17] Birley, *Hadrian*, p. 60.
[18] Lloyd William Daly and Walther Suchier, *Altercatio Hadriani Augusti et Epicteti Philosophi* (Urbana, IL: The University of Illinois Press, 1939).

and Hadrian's interactions, though some scholars and consumers of the text have taken it as such since its composition, which likely occurred in the later second or early third centuries CE; it does not bear any particular sympathies to a Stoic viewpoint in the materials enumerated within it. This text did inspire the creation of another dialogue text, however, which features a philosopher known as Secundus the Silent Philosopher and the Emperor Hadrian having a similar interaction (though the Emperor speaks and the philosopher writes his answers on a wax tablet). The historicity of this text is likewise doubtful, but the existence of a philosopher called Secundus—who was a teacher of Herodes Attikos—is fairly certain, and it seems possible that Hadrian would have encountered him in Athens in about 125 CE.[19] This originally Greek text was translated into Arabic, Syriac, Armenian, and Ethiopian, and exists in many manuscripts.[20]

These two philosophical texts both include questions on gods, which are interesting in juxtaposition with one another. The Epictetus text first asks "What are the gods?" and the following reply is given: "A constellation of eyes, the spirits of understanding; if you fear, they are fearful; if you are temperate, they are sanctified."[21] Later, the text again asks, "What is a god?" and the response is "That which maintains all things."[22] The Secundus text asks and answers:

What is God?

A self-formed good, an image of many shapes, an eminence too lofty to be seen, a conformation with many aspects, a problem hard to understand, immortal intelligence, an all-pervading spirit, an eye that never closes in sleep, a power known by many names, light that prevails over all.[23]

While all of these statements are more philosophical in nature than cultic or theological, nonetheless they do not present any characteristics which are diagnostic for identification of a particular philosophical viewpoint. The Secundus text lends itself much more to a monotheistic interpretation, certainly, which might be why it was preserved in so many manuscripts and was translated

---

[19] Birley, *Hadrian*, p. 182.
[20] Ben Edwin Perry (ed./trans.), *Secundus the Silent Philosopher: The Greek Life of Secundus, Critically Edited and Restored So Far As Possible, Together with Translations of the Greek and Oriental Versions, the Latin and Oriental Texts, and a Study of the Tradition* (Ithaca: Cornell University Press, 1964).
[21] Daly and Suchier, p. 106 §39.
[22] Daly and Suchier, p. 106 §60.
[23] Perry, pp. 78-81.

as widely as it was in later (post-hegemonic monotheist) periods. Given that both of these texts are fictional, their specific partisan philosophical credentials are not as significant to consider as the fact that the interlocutor in them with each of their respective philosophers was Hadrian. For the literate traditions of later centuries, it would seem that Hadrian's inquiring philosophical mind was noteworthy among his many talents, interests, involvements, and distinct qualities. This persisted into more recent centuries, too, and even influenced the interpretation and (re-)construction of certain visual images of Hadrian: a statue in the British Museum had the Emperor's head on a body attired as a Greek philosopher, which was considered highly anomalous and unusual until it was revealed recently that it was a nineteenth century fusing of antique, separate parts into a whole that was thought to be a further example of Hadrian's philhellenism.[24] Even after death, Hadrian's philosophical tendencies continue to assert themselves in the minds of those who seek to preserve his legacy.

To conclude this brief examination, it would be worthwhile to consider what actual position a philosophical Emperor like Hadrian had in terms of alignment with one or another of the philosophical schools. While some of his actions and words seem to have Epicurean sympathies, as already discussed, it is clear by many of his other actions that he did not adhere strictly to their viewpoints, especially in terms of his approach to the existence and involvement of Deities—or, at least it would seem to be such, based on how heavily and ardently he was dedicated to or interested in some of them. Likewise, whatever merits Stoicism might have had in his eyes, it is clear that his approach to life was not in line with their most basic and overarching ethics. As he traveled far, it might seem that he would have been attracted to a Peripatetic/Aristotelian approach—indeed, the *Epistle of Fermes to Hadrian*,[25] a later medieval text, on which the more popular *Epistle of Alexander to Aristotle* was based, both detailing the wonders (including monstrous races) of the East, reflects both rulers' penchant for travel and for inquiring into and encountering wonders first-hand. And, as recorded by Philostratus, and also perhaps as apparent in other aspects of his religious engagement, it would also seem that Hadrian was greatly interested in neo-Pythagoreanism and Platonism as well. Not unlike his (and many of his contemporaries') syncretistic approach to religiosity, it appears that Hadrian was eclectic in his philosophical tastes, and did not favor one school's approach over any and all others, at least in its entirety. The physics of one school might have an appeal and an empirical validity, while the ethics of

---

[24] Opper, pp. 68-70.

[25] Henri Omont, "Lettre à l'Empereur Adrien sur les Merveilles de l'Asie," *Bibliothèque de l'École des Chartres* 74 (1913), pp. 507-515; Claude Lecouteux (ed.), *De Rebus in Oriente Mirabilibus (Lettre de Farasmanes), Edition synoptique accompagnée d'une introduction et de notes* (Meisenheim am Glan: Hain, 1979).

another may have been more applicable in particular circumstances, and yet a third might have provided a metaphysical perspective that seemed more or less meaningful in light of yet other events on a given occasion.

In this, the general syncretistic approach of the culture at the time would have had both a religious and a philosophical dimension, and an Emperor as cosmopolitan and multiculturally aware as Hadrian would thus have been able to have a wide range of options available to him when considering anything that would fall under a philosophical rubric in his life.[26] As with so many areas of our human existence, this variability by context and lack of fixed and partisan attachment to any single outlook in a pluralistic arena like late antique polytheism was (and is) eminently practical. A singular philosophical outlook and affiliation with a singular philosophical school was not necessary for Hadrian to be a successful philospher, Emperor, or Philosopher-Emperor, and indeed it would have been as inimical to him as an exclusivist monotheism would have been, no matter how much that later theological viewpoint has influenced and shaped our views of the above-discussed as well as other philosophical schools for the past sixteen centuries.

Altercatio Hadriani Augusti et Epicteti Philosophi

The text upon which my translation is based is found in Daly and Suchier's 1939 edition,[27] and the present translation was published earlier (with some slight variations) in *The Phillupic Hymns*[28] and *Devotio Antinoo: The Doctor's Notes, Volume One.*[29]

The Cross–Examination of the Emperor Hadrian and the Philosopher Epictetus

H: What will we have, if you were unbound from your girding, or if you were to denude me? Consider the body, which even you are able to instruct.

---

[26] While the authors and editor of the following collection are arguing mostly about the atmosphere Hadrian's approaches created as one favorable to the flourishing of Christianity, nonetheless their basic premise is predicated upon this exact syncretistic and eclectic, pluralistic attitude, and the circumstance that Christianity was characterized and consciously presented as more of a philosophy than a religion during the Hadrianic period: Marco Rizzi (ed.), *Hadrian and the Christians* (Berlin: Walter De Gruyter, 2010).

[27] Lloyd William Daly and Walther Suchier, *Altercatio Hadriani Augusti et Epicteti Philosophi* (Urbana, IL: The University of Illinois Press, 1939).

[28] P. Sufenas Virius Lupus, *The Phillupic Hymns* (Eugene: Bibliotheca Alexandrina, 2008), pp. 233-237.

[29] P. Sufenas Virius Lupus, *Devotio Antinoo: The Doctor's Notes, Volume One* (Anacortes, WA: The Red Lotus Library, 2011), pp. 433-438.

E: It is an epistle.

H: What is an epistle?

E: A quiet announcement.

H: What is a picture?

E: A true deception.

H: What is this you have taught?

E: We see indeed a painted apple, flowers, animals, gold, silver, and yet they are not true.

H: What is gold?

E: The purchase of death.

H: What is silver?

E: The place of envy.

H: What is iron?

E: The implement of all arts.

H: What is a sword?

E: The ruler of fortresses.

H: What is a gladiator?

E: A murderer without guilt.

H: Who are they who depart sanity?

E: They who are concerned with strange business.

H: By what consideration is a man not made tired?

E: By the making of profit.

H: What is a friend?

E: Harmony.

H: What is the longest thing?

E: Anticipation.

H: What is anticipation?

E: Sleep for being vigilant, expecting dangerous events.

F: What is that which man is not able to see?

E: Another heart.

H: By what thing do men err?

E: Cupidity.

H: What is liberty?

E: Innocence.

H: What leads and is wretched to the community?

E: Birth and death.

H: What is the best, and indeed, the worst?

E: A word.

H: What is that which is pleasing to some and displeasing to others?

E: Life.

H: What is the best life?

E: The shortest one.

H: What thing is most certain?

E: Death.

H: What is death?

E: Perpetual security.

H: What is death?

E: The fearing of many, if the wise man lives, inimical to life, the spirit of the living, the dread of parents, the spoils of freedom, the cause of testaments, the conversation after destruction, the end of woefulness, the forgetfulness after memory, the leading torch, the load of burial, the inscription of a monument; death is the end of all evil.

H: Why are the dead crowned?

E: As a testament for the crossing over of life itself.

H: Why are the dead's thumbs tied together?

E: So that he may not know that he is twain after death.

H: What is the corpse—bearer?

E: The one whom many avoid but none escape.

H: What is a funeral pyre?

E: Contentment of believers, the repayment of debts.

H: What is a trumpet?

E: A battle incitement, the army—camp signifier, an exhortation of the arena, the signal for the opening of the theatre, the funeral lament.

H: What is a monument?

E: Branded stones, the spectacle of leisurely passers—by.

H: What is a poor man?

E: Namely he whom all behold in a barren pit and yet they leave him in that place.

H: What is a man?

E: Similar to a bath: the first room is the *tepidarium*, the warm bath, in which infants are born thoroughly anointed; the second room, the *sudatorium*, the sweat—room, is boyhood; the third room is the *assa*, the dry—room, the preference of youth; the fourth room, the *frigidarium*, the cold bath, is appropriate to old age, in which sense comes to all.

H: What is a man?

E: Similar to a fruit: Fruits that hang on trees, thus even are our bodies: when ripe they fall, or else they become embittered.

H: What is a man?

E: As a lamp placed in the wind.

H: What is a man?

E: A stranger of a place, the image of law, a tale of calamity, a slave of death, the delay of life; that with which Fortune would frequently make its own game.

H: What is fortune?

[117]

E: Namely the matron of nobility impinging upon servants themselves.

H: What is fortune?

E: Without justice, the closest turning–point, the fall of the good of another; at which's coming, brilliance is shown, at which's recession, shadow is made.

H: Indeed, how many are they with fortune?

E: Three: one who is blind, who impinges where he pleases; and another who is insane, who concedes, I summon to be removed; the third is deaf, who does not favorably hear the entreaties of mercy.

H: What are the gods?

E: A constellation of eyes, the spirits of understanding; if you fear, they are fearful; if you are temperate, they are sanctified.

H: What is the sun?

E: The splendor of the spheres; which takes away and places the day; through which it is given to us to know the course of the hours.

H: What is the moon?

E: The handmaid of days, the eye of night, the torch of darkness.

H: What is heaven?

E: The summit of boundlessness.

H: What is heaven?

E: The atmosphere of the world.

H: What are stars?

E: The destiny of humans.

H: What are the stars?

E: The omens of navigators.

H: What is the earth?

E: The granary of Ceres.

H: What is the earth?

E: The cellar of life.

H: What is the sea?

E: The way of doubt.

H: What is a boat?

E: A wandering house.

H: What is a boat?

E: A guest–house where it pleases.

H: What is a boat?

E: The spirit of Neptune, the archive of a year's course.

H: What is a sailor?

E: A lover of the open sea, forsaker of firmness, a despiser of life and death, from which he is a client.

H: What is sleep?

E: An image of death.

H: What is night?

E: Rest for working, the profit of weariness.

H: What is a pillow?

E: The wish of sleeplessness.

H: Why is Venus depicted nude?

E: Nude Venus painted, Lovers are shown nude; for whom nudity pleases, it is proper to dismiss nudity.

H: Why is Venus married to Vulcan?

E: To show love by the heat of fire.

H: Why is Venus a squinter?

E: Because love is crooked.

H: What is love?

E: The annoyance of heart's leisure, shamefulness in boys, reddening in virgins, fury in women, ardor in youth, laughter in age, it is worthlessness in the mocking of fault.

H: What is a god?

E: That which maintains all things.

H: What is a sacrifice?

E: A lessening.

H: What is without fellowship?

E: Kingship.

H: What is a king?

E: A piece of the gods.

H: What is Caesar?

E: The head of light for the people.

H: What is a senator?

E: A splendid ornament of a city of citizens.

H: What is a soldier?

E: The wall of authority, defender of the fatherland, a glorious servant, an indicator of power.

H: What is Rome?

E: The fount of authority of the sphere of earth, mother of nations, possessor of things, the common–dwelling of the Romans, consecration of eternal peace.

H: What is Victory?

E: Discordance of war, love of peace.

H: What is peace?

E: Generosity of calm.

H: What is the forum?

E: The temple of liberty, the arena of disputes.

H: What are friends?

E: They are the site of support.

H: What is a friend?

E: As similar to a citrus fruit: blessed on the outside, for in its heart is concealed bitterness and malice.

H: What is a parasite?

E: Those who are baited with crumbs like fish.

P. Sufenas Virius Lupus is a metagender person, and was the founder of the Ekklesía Antínoou—a queer, Graeco-Roman-Egyptian syncretist reconstructionist polytheist group dedicated to Antinous, the deified lover of the Roman Emperor Hadrian, and related deities and divine figures—but, since eir retirement from that group in March of 2016, remains the *Mystagogos* of the Antinoan Mysteries. E is also a contributing member of Neos Alexandria and a practicing Celtic Reconstructionist pagan in the traditions of *gentlidecht* and *filidecht*, as well as Romano-British, Welsh, and Gaulish deity devotions, and continues to teach courses in these (and other) subjects to modern polytheists interested in taking them. Lupus is also dedicated to several land spirits around the area of North Puget Sound and its islands. Lupus' work (poetry, fiction, and essays) has appeared in a number of Bibliotheca Alexandrina devotional volumes, as well as Ruby Sara's anthologies *Datura* (2010) and *Mandragora* (2012), Inanna Gabriel and C. Bryan Brown's *Etched Offerings* (2011), Lee Harrington's *Spirit of Desire: Personal Explorations of Sacred Kink* (2010), Galina Krasskova's *When the Lion Roars* (2011), Tara Miller's *Rooted in the Body, Seeking the Soul* (2013), Sarenth Odinsson's *Calling to Our Ancestors* (2015), and Crystal Blanton, Taylor Ellwood and Brandy Williams' *Bringing Race to the Table* (2015), as well as various esoteric, Pagan and polytheist periodicals. Lupus has also written several full-length books, including *The Phillupic Hymns* (2008), *The Syncretisms of Antinous* (2010), *Devotio Antinoo: The Doctor's Notes, Volume One* (2011), *All-Soul, All-Body, All-Love, All-Power: A TransMythology* (2012), *A Garland for Polydeukion* (2012), *A Serpent Path Primer* (2012), and *Ephesia Grammata: Ancient History and Modern Practice* (2014), with more on the way. Lupus blogs at Aedicula Antinoi (http://aediculaantinoi.wordpress.com), and also has the "Speaking of Syncretism" column at polytheist.com.

Presocratic Theology and the Great Tablet of Thurii

LUDWIG MAISEL

The academic discussion of polytheism in general, and of Presocratic philosophy in particular, suffers from a number of false assumptions: (1) there is a natural and necessary development from polytheism to monotheism, (2) these and other categories are so universal that they can be meaningfully used in any historical context, (3) the Presocratic thinkers developed philosophy by replacing mythological accounts by rational, scientific ones, (4) as specific as possible a modern term should be found to categorize any non-monotheistic theology. How we can read the Presocratics without making these assumptions is shown by interpretations of the theologies of Thales, Anaximander and Anaximenes. That the Presocratics were read as polytheistic and religious thinkers is then demonstrated by tracing the influence of Heraclitus and Empedocles on the Great Tablet of Thurii, a Bacchic text containing a prayer. Like the other thinkers discussed, the author of this text believes in a structural unity that helps to explain the multiplicity of phenomena, but it is not monotheistic.

It will not surprise readers of this journal when I write that modern scholars have almost systematically misunderstood the theology of Greek philosophers. One problem is that the history of philosophy is often treated as a road map, from superstition to rationality, from myth to science. It would be wrong to claim that this view is still as widespread as it was a few decades ago, but nevertheless the idea that there was something inherently unstable about Greek polytheism, that it already contained the germ of its own destruction, is widespread. Martin West interpreted Aeschylus' portrayal of Zeus in the fifth century BCE as instantiating "the Greek poets' development from a pantheon of independently minded divine agents towards a quasi-monotheistic régime,"[1] and Hans Günter Zekl opined in his introduction to Proclus' commentary on Plato's Parmenides that his polytheism was anachronistic in the fifth century CE.[2]

---

[1] West, Martin L. "Towards Monotheism." Pp. 21-41 in *Pagan Monotheism in Late Antiquity*, ed. Polymnia Athanassiadi and Michael Frede (Oxford: Oxford University Press, 1999).

[2] Zekl, Hans Günter, ed. *Kommentar zum platonischen Parmenides*. (Würzburg: Königshausen & Neumann, 2010), 10. Both of these accomplished scholars, sadly, have

There is something very aggressive in the accusation of anachronism—it alleges that Proclus was wrong to be a polytheist and should have realized, as we now think we realize, that Hellenic polytheism was dying out. Were mass persecutions of polytheists justified, then, because they were successful? This appraisal amounts to blindly siding with the victors of history. It is the kind of historiography that takes it for granted that, because the religious policies of emperor Julian *did* fail, they always *had* to fail, never mind the span of his reign; or that because Manichaeism has not survived until *now*, its survival for about twelve centuries was merely prolonging the inevitable. When we confound what *is* with what *ought to be* in this manner, we surrender the explanatory power of historical investigation in favor of teleology, the investigation of which is not part of historiography.

So this is one fault, to judge people's beliefs at one point in time only on the basis of what comes before or after them. West too is guilty of this when he describes the theology of Aeschylus and his contemporaries as *from* one thing and *towards* something else rather than as a coherent worldview. But he adds another methodological error, identifying the goal as monotheism and the starting point as polytheism. For the latter, he uses the circumlocution "a pantheon of independently minded divine agents," presuming rather than stating that this constitutes *real* polytheism, whereas a cosmology in which "Zeus is the only real source of divine initiative and the other gods are supporters and executants of his will" is something in between this and *actual* monotheism. The source of this error is that he takes for granted, without reflection and without fully spelling it out, that polytheism and monotheism entail more than just the belief in many gods or one god. Polytheism is taken to logically imply that the power of each god is limited by the power of the others; no one god may be dependent on the other, or their plurality is in danger.[3] Monotheism, on the other hand, implies not just the existence of a single god, but also the dependence on them of everything else.

When we try to work with these categories, Aeschylus is neither fish nor flesh: he has many gods, but they are at the very least interdependent or, if West is right, all completely dependent on Zeus. The natural assumption is that we must rephrase the definition of polytheism to allow for the interdependence of gods—indeed, unless we do this, we must describe even Hesiod as a quasi-tritheist and not a proper polytheist, because all his gods are somehow genealogically dependent on Chaos, Gaia and Eros, or as a serial quasi-monotheist, because he has the rule of Zeus after the quasi-monotheistic dominance of Ouranos and Kronos. Or should we call him an atheist, because Chaos' coming-into-being is prior to Chaos,' or any god's, personal agency? The fact is

---

recently passed away, but their ideas about polytheism are not at all a thing of the past.
[3] This is itself a theological proposition.

that his gods are interdependent, yet not limited by each others' powers; the Hecate of *Theogony* 411-52 is subject to Zeus in terms of hierarchy, but she is not just "independently minded," the fulfilment of her will is equally independent. Her powers are potentially limited by the rulership of Zeus, but not actually limited by the existence of other gods of similar independence of power. Hesiod does not problematize this, and it cannot be required of us to solve his perceived inconsistencies before we are able to even *describe* the nature of his theology.

All this is just to spell out some of the presumptions we can expect from academics and must try to avoid ourselves, whether we read poets like Hesiod and Aeschylus or philosophers. We must perhaps add two more when we come to philosophy, although they are extensions of the ones we have already discussed, and they both serve to undermine the validity of polytheism. The first is the idea that the Presocratics gradually developed a form of philosophical, even scientific inquiry—and that this rational enterprise is opposed to myth and foolish devotion to the gods of myth, although of course it retains religious devotion as the proper attitude towards the single creator god whom natural theology discovers; the second is the fragmentation of polytheism into a host of distinct terms, like animism, pantheism, panentheism, henotheism or kathenotheism. To take just one example: treating pantheism as distinct from monotheism and polytheism takes it for granted that the cosmos cannot be a god in either of the other two kinds of cosmology. Adopting it as a category leads to the pervasive idea that, because the Stoics followed Plato in calling the cosmos a god, they are pantheists rather than polytheists, despite believing in a plurality of gods. Thus, while monotheism, quasi-monotheism or "monotheistic tendencies" can be ascribed to almost anyone whose theology has any sort of unified structure, polytheism is fractured into a heap of peculiar categories, none of which map very well onto historically attested belief systems.[4]

---

[4] Outside of Greek- and Jewish-influenced thought, of course, the first step is to find an equivalent to the term god, and a bias associating godhood with uniqueness and supreme power leads to monotheistic interpretations of, for example, Hindu and Zoroastrian theology. But even in reading Greek and Latin literature, the closeness of language can conceal as much as it reveals—*ho/he theos* or *deus* are often found in contexts where translating them as "God" rather than "the god" produces a meaningful sentence, but choosing such a translation reduces many other references to deities in the same work to meaninglessness or apparent irrelevance to the author's *actual* theology, mere concessions to traditional ways of speaking. Due to the threatened status of polytheism, as living traditions and as an intellectual position, and the high status of monotheism in discourse even where "effective polytheism" is the norm, I would indeed argue for the academic use of polytheism as a very wide category, but limit monotheism to a self-claimed identity. I don't see the point in limiting monotheism to, say, only groups that abjure the veneration of saints, of angels, of icons, of belief in the

For the rest of this essay, I shall firstly attempt to demonstrate what taking polytheism seriously means for the interpretation of three Presocratic philosophers, namely Thales, Anaximander and Anaximenes, traditionally considered the first three Western philosophers. My hermeneutic assumption is that these thinkers do not object to or deviate from traditional religious discourse(s) except where we can demonstrate it. Having, to the best of my abilities, shown that it is possible and sensible to read Presocratic philosophers as polytheists who worked within the religious worldview of their time, I will then attempt to show that we have evidence that they were read in this way in antiquity: I will jump forward in time to Heraclitus and Empedocles, not to give full account of their theology in this article, but to help us interpret the so-called Great Tablet of Thurii, a 'Bacchic-Orphic' gold tablet, which I believe to be inspired by them.

Thales of Miletus

There are only three pieces of information, all of them recorded by Aristotle, on which any speculation about Thales' theology rests:[5]

> 14 Gemelli: "Thales, the originator of this kind of philosophy, said that water is the *archê*, whence he also claimed that the earth is (floating) on water."

> 17A Gemelli: "And some say that it (=the soul) is mingled up with the universe, whence perhaps Thales too supposed that all things are/everything is full of gods."

> 18B Gemelli: "It seems, from what people hand down, that Thales too understood the soul to be a kinetic thing, if he really said that the (magnetic) stone has a soul because it moves iron."

In 14 Gemelli, Aristotle is claiming that Thales was the first of what we now call the material monists, and held water to be the underlying substrate of all things. Dührsen[6] (250-252) surmises that Thales' meaning is more likely to

---

trinity, etc. (that would be a theological point in itself), but in the face of practices/beliefs like these I don't believe an etic criterion for what constitutes monotheism exists, except the claiming of this identity (and sometimes using it is a matter of survival, so it would be arrogant of academia to deny it to some).

[5] I cite fragments/testimonia of the Presocratics by the numeration within the relevant philosopher's section of Gemelli Marciano, M. Laura, *Die Vorsokratiker. Griechisch und Deutsch* (2007), except where fragments are not included there, but only in Diels, Hermann, and Walther Kranz, *Die Fragmente der Vorsokratiker. Griechisch und Deutsch* (1959). Diels-Kranz are cited as "DK [number of author] A/B/C [number of testimonium/fragment/etc]."

[6] Dührsen, Niels Christian. "Naturphilosophische Anfänge." In *Frühgriechische Philosophie*

have been that all things came *out of* water. I don't think, however, that he is right in calling this a bold innovation against the traditional cosmogonies of the Greeks, which posit something like Chaos or Night as the first principle; firstly, we have only a very small remnant of cosmogonic literature, not to mention unwritten theogonies, and secondly, as Dührsen himself notes (254-254), Homer already called Okeanos the origin (*genesis*) of all gods (*Iliad* 14,201;246). As Hesiod's genealogical method shows, there is not much difference between the origin of all gods and the origin of all phenomena of the universe, as what we would call cosmological rather than theological entities, like darkness, day, ether or Tartaros, are not differentiated from 'actual' gods. I think that is is therefore rather beside the point to ask, as Robinson[7] does, whether "'water,' for example, would have been included among what [Thales] called gods." If we presuppose that Thales must have had a clear position on whether water was a god (a 'mythical' explanation) or not a god (a 'scientific' explanation), we are begging the question.

Besides, the very phrasing ("what he called gods") presupposes that gods in Thales' terminology have little to do with the traditional Greek gods. Robinson suggests (485) a meaning along the lines of "powerful life-principle." West (30) too holds that "Thales had started on the road of emancipating such terms as 'soul' and 'god' from the limitations of their conventional applications." What were these limitations? In Greek usage, justice, Zeus, fortune and the sea are all gods; that usage is surely no less wide than what West supposes was the innovative sense of Thales' usage: "forces intrinsic to the natural world."

We must treat 17A and 18B Gemelli together, because everyone else does; whether rightly remains to be seen. We have seen that commentators are uncomfortable with the idea that by "gods," Thales may have meant gods. They are much more comfortable with the idea that he meant more or less the same as what he meant by "soul." Aristotle is already making this suggestion, but we cannot really follow him in good conscience. He may already have known nothing more about Thales' meaning than we do, and his interpretation could be filtered through Old Academic psychology. But even if the gods are or have souls, it is not therefore permissible to suggest without argument that "one might wish to call divine" the soul of the magnet. This rests on the assumption that any rational thinker would wish to throw out any notion of gods out of the window as quickly as possible, and use it, if at all, only in a way that takes the traditional gods out of the picture. The conflation of "god" and "soul" amounts to equating the forces Thales posited with the natural forces of modern Physics;

(= *Grundriss der Geschichte der Philosophie. Die Philosophie der Antike*, Vol. 1). Vol 1 (2013): 237-338.

[7] Robinson, T. M. "Presocratic Theology." In *The Oxford handbook of presocratic philosophy* (2008): 486-498.

it makes sense to us, but there is no indication that it would have made sense to Thales.

Anaximander of Miletus

Anaximander's account takes the *apeiron* (the indefinite) as the source and guiding principle of the world; it is given some attributes clearly associated with divinity (it "steers everything" and is "deathless and indestrucible," 5A Gemelli), but whether he explicitly called it divine, as Aristotle does, is in doubt. Bodéüs[8] rightly cautions that the ascription of traditional divine attributes to a new entity does not constitute their transferral. What does seem to be transferred is the attribute of immortality: the gods, since they are definite and have come forth from the indefinite, ought to behave like all other things and dissolve back into the *apeiron* as "punishment" (5B Gemelli) for their transgressions, just as the *apeiron* must be punished, and lose its nature by becoming definite. It is thus in line with Anaximandrian cosmology when Cicero says that his gods come into being and are long-lived, but must pass away (9A Gemelli). More problematically, he continues: "and (Anaximander's opinion is that) these (=the gods) are the innumerable worlds." The multiplicity of worlds is otherwise attested (5C, 5D, 6A, 6B Gemelli), but it makes no sense for Anaximander to have said that the gods are an innumerable number of worlds like ours; this would not be a correction of traditional beliefs, it would be the redefinition of a word.[9] Tentatively, I would suggest that Anaximander called these worlds gods, but not the only gods.

Anaximenes of Miletus

For Anaximenes, infinite Air/Breath (*aêr*) is the primordial substance, and the substrate from which other substances form by compression and thinning out, which are caused by its constant motion (2C Gemelli). Thus compressed air constitutes the flat earth, which is carried by air, and moisture rising from it is rarefied and becomes fire; this fire then makes up the stars (4B Gemelli). The parallels with Hesiod—if we understand Chaos as air and Gaia to come forth from it, which is a conceivable reading—are clear, and show us at once that

---

[8] Bodéüs, Richard. *Aristotle and the Theology of the Living Immortals* (Albany: SUNY Press, 2000), 187.

[9] Generally, later doxography (Aëtius is a particularly egregious offender) tends to start with the word "god" or "gods" and then proceeds to various thinkers' definitions, unsystematically picking out some important entity or entities in their system, sometimes regardless of their own terminology (rather like modern scholars). This sort of presentation, of course, leads to unreliable doxographical accounts and suggests a basis for comparison between different thinkers that does not exist. I don't believe the history of how this vacuous terminology came to be, or how it was adapted and utilized by monotheists, has been written.

Anaximenes' account is more detailed than, but not in principle opposed to mythological theogony. If we could rely on the testimony of Aëtius, he would have also made air the substance of souls, but I concur with Gemelli in doubting its accuracy (15 Gemelli).

Either way, it is easy to see why he *could* have called *Aêr* a god (DK 13 A 10, not included by Gemelli), whether he actually did or not. But the parallel with Hesiod's Chaos clearly shows that *Aêr* is not a "supreme divine principle"; West again (p.32) begs the questions when he paraphrases Hippolytus' report that "gods and divine things come to be (out of air), but everything else from its descendants" (2C Gemelli): "Hippolytus also refers to 'descendants' [...] of these second-order deities." Not only are the descendants most obviously read as identical to the gods and divine things, but the gods are simply deities, not second-order ones. The bilocution "gods and divine things" even allows the interpretation that 'mythical' gods and 'rationally explained' phenomena had the same cosmological status in Anaximenes' system, just as we have claimed for Hesiod. In line with the hermeneutical assumption I have described, the most cautious interpretation of Anaximenes is that he used non-mythical language to describe a cosmogonic process, but that he did not substantially differ from the assumptions made in mythical cosmogonies.

The Great Tablet of Thurii

This gold tablet was found in a grave in Thurii in Magna Graecia in the 19th century, together with another, much more straightforward tablet that reminds the soul of the deceased of what it has to do after death (originally learnt, perhaps, in a mystery cult or from a ritual specialist) and announces its deification to it. It was inscribed in the fourth century BCE. It was first published, based on a rather poor transcript and on the basis of innumerable emendations and rearrangements, by Hermann Diels,[10] who saw in it an Orphic hymn to Demeter. The errors of its initial editor have been slowly emended over the twentieth century, and the current text, in Albert Bernabé's edition of the Orphic Fragments,[11] has not, to my knowledge, been criticized for its fundamental method, only on minor textual points.[12] I will give this current text in Greek, minus the nonsense letters that make up half of it, and a threadbare

---

[10] Diels, Hermann. "Ein orphischer Demeterhymnus." In *Festschrift Theodor Gomperz* (1902): 1-15.

[11] Pajares, Alberto Bernabé, ed. *Poetae epici Graeci: testimonia et fragmenta. Orphicorum et orphicis similium testimonia et fragmenta. Pars II. Fasciculus 2*. Vol. 2. (Leipzig: K.G. Saur, 2005), p. 66-71.

[12] In reading ΓΗΜΑΙΤΙΕΓΗ and interpreting it γῆ ματρὶ γῆ (line 1), as well as in retaining the tablet's ΠΑΜΜΗΣΤΟΙ (line 3), I am following Betegh, Gabór. "The 'Great Tablet' of Thurii (OF 492)." In *Tracing Orpheus: Studies of Orphic Fragments (Vol. 10)*. (2012): 219-225.

translation; the rest of this essay will be an attempt to make sense of it.

πρωτογόνῳ γῆ ματρὶ γῆ γᾶι ματρὶ κυβελείᾳ κόρρᾳ δήμητρος
ζεῦ ἀὲρ ἤλιε πῦρ δὴ πάντα? νικᾶι
[3] τύχα φάνης? πάμμηστοι μοῖραι σὺ? κλυτὲ? δαῖμον?
πάτερ παντοδαμάστα ἀνταμοιβή
ἀὲρ πῦρ μᾶτερ νῆστι νὺξ ἡμέρα
[6] ἑπτῆμαρ νήστιας ζεῦ ἐνορύττιε? καὶ πανόπτα αἰὲν μᾶτερ ἐμᾶς ἐπ
ἄκουσον εὐχᾶς καλὰ ἱερὰ
ἱερὰ δημῆτερ πῦρ ζεῦ κόρη χθονία
[9] ἤρως φάος ἐς φρένα μῆστωρ εἷλε κούρην
αἶα ἀὲρ ἐς φρένα

To the Firstborn, to Gaia, to Meter, to Gaia, to Gaia, to Meter, to
Kybele, to Kore of Demeter
O Zeus o air o Helios o? fire conquers? everything?
[3] o? Tyche o? Phanes? o? all-planning Moirai o you famous daimon
O father all-subduer exchange
O air o fire o Meter o Nestis o? Nyx/night o? Hemera/day
[6] o? seven days of fasting o Zeus who-digs-in? and all-seeing always
Meter my
prayers hear o beautiful holy
holy Demeter o fire o Zeus o Kore the Chthonian
[9] o? hero o? light into mind planner seizes Kore
o? Gaia o? air into mind

It is immediately obvious how much is doubtful about this text, and neither removing the question marks nor removing the words that are marked by one, neither sparse nor generous punctuation produces a text that is immediately comprehensible. Before I move on, I first want to make some points on the language, which will guide, but also limit my further interpretation. I take the entire first line to consist of datives, but from that line onwards down to the eighth, I consider it an address; I find the two final lines most difficult, and have not found a satisfactory explanation of them. I think that almost all the potential vocatives (i.e. the nouns preceded by an o? in the translation) really are vocatives, and in particular I don't see why previous editors seem to have exclusively read *kala hiera hiera* as plural neuter, "beautiful things, holy things (sacrifices), holy things," rather than as adjectives referring to Demeter: "beautiful holy holy Demeter."

Heraclitus of Ephesus

One word jumps out at any reader who has had to look up words in reading

Heraclitus: *antamoibê* (line 4) is an extremely rare word, and it is not, to my knowledge, attested before the writing of this tablet in any author except Heraclitus.[13] It means something like mutual exchange or compensation, but has a peculiar cosmological association. Like Anaximander's substances coming forth and collapsing back into the *apeiron*, it signifies the relation of Heraclitus' substrate, fire: "All things are compensation for fire, and fire of all things, like wares for gold and gold for wares" (39 Gemelli). While fire is eternal and uncreated, it is also ever-changing (40 Gemelli), and it is transformed, like Anaximenes' air, into other substances: "the changes of fire: first sea, then half of the sea earth, half *prêstêr* (storm?)." He adds, however, that the amount of material does not change from one state to the other (41 Gemelli), something that Anaximenes may not have made explicit.

It is likely that Heraclitus is referring to this process, or one analogous to it, when he says that "War is father of all, king of all, and shows some to be gods, others humans, makes some slaves, others free." (37 Gemelli.) This is just to show that Heraclitus too believes in a plurality of gods. Their substance, like that of humans, is apparently convertible into fire. All things, and this must include fire as much as everything else, are one (27 Gemelli); whether this one is the same as the one that he calls *to sophon mounon*, the sole wise thing, and which both "wants not and wants to be called by the name of Zeus," or whether that refers to, e.g., fire, is unclear. However, it does seem that the unity of all opposites is also seen as a god: "the god (is) day night winter summer war peace satiety hunger" (50 Gemelli).

I believe that this already gives us something to work with. Taking *antamoibê* in its Heraclitean sense of an exchange or compensation of substances for one another is apt: Anaximenes has already held air and fire to be so related, and Heraclitus has claimed the unity of night and day. It is not impossible that the author of the tablet's text would call this process of exchange "all-subduing father," since it would apply to all things, and bring forth all things. We might therefore paraphrase lines 4-5 as "O all-subduing father, exchange! O air and fire (by turns)! ... O night and day (by turns)!" We might also eliminate the switch from the process of exchange to the subjects of exchange by interpreting *antamoibê* as a dative: "O all-subduing father, by exchange air and fire ..., night and day (by turns)!" But we have seen that it is difficult for us to appreciate whether the substrate of fire, the totality of substances, or the process of their exchange is treated as the most fundamental principle, or even whether they are

---

[13] The connection is already noted by Bernabé, Alberto and Ana Isabel Jiménez San Cristóbal. *Instructions for the netherworld: the Orphic gold tablets.* (Leiden/Boston: Brill, 2008), p. 144. The authors here identify many of the same parallels that I find important, but they waste their energies on what seems to me a wild goose chase after an imagined syncretic Dionysos-Protogonos-Phanes-Helios.

identical. Considering that *amoibê*, from which *antamoibê* is derived, means both the process of compensation and the compensation, i.e. that by which one is compensated, perhaps we are seeing a distinction where the tablet's author would not have seen one. So much for Heraclitus.

Empedocles of Acragas

Empedocles is best known for his proposal of four fundamental elements, whose interaction is governed by two forces. The elements are fire, air, water and earth, and the forces are friendship and strife, or attraction and repulsion between different elements (19 Gemelli). The four elements are called by mythical names, Zeus for fire (also called Hephaistos, (41 Gemelli), or Titan, i.e. the sun (62 Gemelli)), Hera for air, Aidoneus (Hades) for earth and Nestis for water (17 Gemelli).

Just from this, an obvious solution appears to the rest of line 4: "O air, fire, Meter and Nestis (by turns)!" must refer to the four elements.[14] We would not need line 1's sequence of "to the Earth Meter Earth Earth Meter" to guess that Meter refers to the fourth element, since this equation is fairly well-established.[15] In addition, the list of four elements along with night and day also occurs elsewhere in Orphic literature.[16]

What looks like two equations of god and element, Zeus=Air and Helios=Fire, in line 2 might at least claim partial Empedoclean pedigree, if in 62 Gemelli Titan (=the sun) really means the same as fire. The allegoresis of Zeus as referring to air is known from Diogenes of Apollonia (in his fragment 10 Gemelli), the last Presocratic included in Gemelli's edition, but still much older than our tablet.

Things have gone smoothly so far, but they cease to do so at this point. I would like to be able to claim that line 1 is a list of names referring to Earth (Gaia, Meter, Kybele and Kore) and line 8 is another address to the four elements (Demeter=Earth, Fire, Zeus=air, Kore Chthonia=water), but while the identification of Demeter and Earth is well attested,[17] it seems eminently implausible to make Chthonian Kore, Kore of the Earth, a name for water; it is true that it has become conventional in modern scholarship to identify Empedocles' Nestis with Persephone (Gemelli does so without argument, e.g. on page 326), but the symmetry of Zeus-Hera and Hades-Persephone is surely marred by the fact that Persephone is the only one without a clear connection

---

[14] Cf. Bernabé & Jiménez San Cristóbal, p.145.

[15] See previous note. Guthrie, William Keith Chambers. *Orpheus and Greek religion: a study of the Orphic movement*. Princeton University Press, 1935, 97 seems to be the only one who holds that *prôtogonô* in line 1 refers to the Earth as well, which I consider the best interpretation.

[16] Cf. Bernabé & Jiménez San Cristóbal, p.146.

[17] Cf. Papyrus Derveni, 22.12

to the element she is supposed to represent. The ancient tradition, that Nestis is a Sicilian goddess associated with rain,[18] seems definitely preferable.

Yet unless the tablet's conception is less Empedoclean than we think (line 5 can hardly be a coincidence), we ought to understand Kore as meaning water. However, that means we cannot read line 1 as referring to Earth exclusively, and it would be awkward to find that the tablet is not addressed, like all the other tablets from Thurii that have an addressee, to Persephone-Kore alone; and it would be odd to append a single unrelated name to a list of almost certainly synonymous names. It is no very satisfying conclusion to propose that water is meant, instead, by Demeter. Is it possible to suppose that the list in line 8 is incomplete, referring to Demeter=Earth, Fire, Zeus=Air, then breaking off? Line 2 is incomplete, too. But I should stop here and admit defeat on this point.

My analysis of the Great Tablet, although not yet a full explanation, does go beyond my predecessors, for I can offer an explanation of what I think is its overall meaning. I think that, in the light of what we have seen of the theology of Heraclitus and other Presocratics, the ritual specialist behind this tablet availed themselves of what s/he saw as the penetrating insights of Empedocles and Heraclitus, although I think that s/he fitted Empedoclean ideas into a primarily Heraclitean worldview. S/he addressed their prayer, in the tradition of other bacchic tablets, to Persephone, equating her with the earth and other deities associated with the earth. This was no rationalization or demyth-ologization: it was a penetration into the deeper meaning of mythology. All these names really referred to the same powerful entity, which could be beseeched in the hopes that she would grant a blissful afterlife, even deification. But then s/he went further; I do not see anywhere in the tablet a clear reference to anything like a substrate, but the tablet's writer must have thought that the elements could change into each other. In the absence of a substrate, the only constant is change, which is apparent, even identical with the elements. For this reason, the author thought it was fitting to change their address from "father" to "mother," just as Earth would be 'compensated' for Zeus. To see this as monotheism would be a gross mistake. *Antamoibê* is not the supreme deity, on which the others depend. Instead of reifying it, we should see it as the process which we can abstract from the existence of the gods in order to describe it.[19]

To the firstborn Gaia Meter, Gaia, Gaia Meter, Kybele, the Kore of Demeter:
O Zeus-Air, o Helios-Fire [...] who are Chance [... and] all-planning

---

[18] Eustathius 1180, 14
[19] The same would go for Tyche or Chance and the Moirai or Fates, but I am unsure about quite how they fit into the overall meaning.

Fates, you famous daimon/deity, all-subduing Father, Compensation: o Air, o Fire, o Meter, o Nestis; o Night, o Day; o Zeus who-digs-in and all-seeing, ever, Meter, hear my prayers, o beautiful, holy, holy Demeter, o Fire, o Zeus, o Chthonian Kore [...] o Gaia, o Air [...]

Ludwig Maisel is a non-binary person and a student of classical philology in Germany. They are currently constructing a website about religious history at http://historyofreligiousthought.blogspot.de.

Cheaper by the Dozen:
On Swinburne's Argument Against Polytheism

JULIE MCCORD

In *Dialogues Concerning Natural Religion,* David Hume attempts to negate a version of the teleological argument by pointing out that, when presented as an analogy, it actually favors polytheism over monotheism, because we more often see complex machines or structures built by groups of people than by one person alone. At the time, given a cultural assumption that any decent religion must be built on the edifice of monotheism, this might have served well as a rebuttal of the teleological argument. Now, however, as Western culture comes back into conversation with cultures that have chosen other paths, and as we ourselves witness the rebirth of many religions once thought dead and gone, it is possible to assert in earnest what Hume argued in jest: that polytheism does, in fact, hold up to philosophical scrutiny as well as or better than monotheism. In a section of Chapter Eight of *The Existence of God* addressed to Hume's argument, Richard Swinburne recognizes this new threat and attempts to address it by making an appeal to the principle of simplicity. It is this argument that I will address here.

Behold, then, the theogony of ancient times brought back upon us.
— David Hume[1]

Introduction

In most philosophical (rather than theological) discussion, writers share a common definition of "God" that does not necessarily portray the full concept according to any one religion, but instead is a generalization composed of what is taken as a consensus of certain key traits that "God" can be said to have regardless of specific tradition. (Even this consensus can be questioned, but that is not usually the focus of philosophical discussion.) Because polytheism is a recent reintroduction into serious Western thought, no such consensus now exists about the core nature of polytheism or its gods, such

---

[1] Pojman, Louis P. and Michael Rea. *Philosophy of Religion: An Anthology. 5th edition.* (Belmont: Thomson Wadworth, 2008), 62.

as can be discussed regardless of specific tradition. The only consensus is that it indicates many in the place of One, which is substantially more vague than the philosophical definition of monotheism, which indicates not only number but also some thoughts about nature. In this paper, I have written from the standpoint of a "traditional" polytheism, that is, polytheism as I know it to be practiced and believed in those cultures which are known to me. My specific examples come from the Indo-European family of traditions—most often specifically from the Greek, as I believe that will be the most familiar to my audience. Though these examples, I will show that Swinburne's argument falls wide of the mark in its interpretation of polytheistic thought and its implications. I have endeavored, for the most part, to limit myself to concepts that are extremely common or universal not only within Indo-European tradition but in other polytheistic systems of which I am aware. These things being true, my advisor, Robert Greg Cavin, points out that Swinburne and others may disagree that the points I bring forward concerning the nature of polytheism and pluralized "gods" would necessarily be part of their generalized definition, were that to exist. Such questions, should they arise, will have to be addressed in a separate paper.

Because Swinburne's primary concern is actually the rehabilitation of the teleological argument, he begins by writing about its resiliency against other criticisms that need not concern us here. But then, on his way to a discussion about whether temporal order is more likely self-existent or the mark of a creator, he attempts to make quick work of Hume's famous polytheistic analogy in the following statement:

> But Hume's hypothesis is very complicated—we want to ask about it such questions as why there are just 333 deities (or whatever the number is), why do they have powers of just the strength which they do have, and what moves them to cooperate as closely as obviously they do; questions of a kind which obtrude far less with the far simpler and so less arbitrary theistic hypothesis. Even if Hume were right in supposing that the prior probability of his hypothesis were as great as that of theism (because the fit with background knowledge of the former cancels out the simplicity of the latter) (and I do not myself think that he is right), the hypothesis of theism nevertheless has greater explanatory power than the Humean hypothesis and is for that reason more probable.[2]

In other words, he attempts to frame a probability argument that monotheism wins. But he states that "fit with background knowledge" is

---

[2] Ibid., 68.

Hume's strength in the prior probability, weighed against the simplicity of Swinburne's theory, whereas theism then wins in final probability because of its "explanatory power." But surely, explanatory power must have some relationship with background knowledge, which has already been ceded, however reluctantly, to Hume. I will therefore treat the two points in reverse of Swinburne, addressing first the explanatory power and fit to background knowledge, and then the claim to simplicity.

Explanatory Power

Swinburne would have a difficult time proving decisively that theism is the best at explaining the universe—as surely implied by the very fact that there is still so much for him to write on the subject after more than a thousand years of debate. In fact, most of the traditional arguments for theism—the teleological argument, the cosmological argument, testimony of miracles, and indeed the religious experiences of people throughout the ages—cannot lead all the way to the conclusion that the creative agent implied by them must logically be *one* being, possessed of all the traditional perfections. They can as easily conform to the model of polytheism. Only the ontological argument explicitly demands a monotheistic concept of God, and it is an *a priori* argument, which as such makes no claims on explaining anything about the world we see. Furthermore, the main traditional stumbling block for monotheism, the problem of evil, is of no consequence to the polytheist at all. While the monotheist must guess at the reasons why an omnipotent *and* omnibenevolent single God would allow needless suffering, the polytheist has access to all sorts of explanations that need not strain his or her faith at all. As we will see shortly, the polytheistic gods are many, and not all are particularly kindly toward man: there is no impetus to assume that the very gods who formed the laws of nature were concerned about the suffering of mankind. (Indeed, this explanation specifically covers *natural* evil, which is the more difficult form for the monotheist to explain away in terms of free will.) Those gods who concern themselves with our welfare, given that they are often younger than the gods of nature, just as we are younger than nature itself, are more limited in their powers and knowledge: and then also, as John Michael Greer points out in *A World Full of Gods*, they represent what can be *conflicting goods*, which are sometimes themselves the source of suffering. (Should one take the promotion that will move one into a different city from one's friends? Friends and home are one form of good, and a job promotion is another: and yet their combination in this case produces suffering.)

Swinburne thus must attempt to weaken the analogy that also grants the teleological argument to polytheism, writing that:

> ...if there were more than one deity responsible for the order of the
> universe, we would expect to see characteristic marks of the handiwork

of different deities in different parts of the universe, just as we see different kinds of workmanship in the different houses of a city. We would expect to find an inverse square of law gravitation obeyed in one part of the universe, and in another part a law which was just short of being an inverse square law—without the difference being explicable in terms of a more general law. It is enough to draw this absurd conclusion to see how wrong the Humean objection is.[3]

Firstly, Swinburne has sidestepped the original analogy here. We might expect that if the universe were divided into physical fiefdoms, then multiple gods might govern each one differently, creating an inconstant universe. But the analogy is not to rule, but to creation: and this is not a very good representation of how human groups typically come together to create something. (For that matter, even rule within a well-governed nation tends to some comprehensible hierarchy, leading to an internally consistent system of governance.) We would be better off imagining a factory, in which many people worked in different divisions, taking on different phases in the creative process and the building of different pieces of the whole, with all phases being overseen by a manager, architect, or other leader. In this case, more typical of human production of machines and other complex objects, even though many people are working on many parts, this does not diminish the coherence of the whole. And in fact, this model also corresponds much more closely to the usual polytheistic understanding, in which there is in fact an "overseer" who is mainly responsible for the existence of general order, governing some number of "upper management" gods with such broad responsibilities as love or justice, who in turn take precedence over lesser gods whose powers are progressively more restricted in scope and then eventually, only when we reach the border between gods and nature spirits, in space. The Greek pantheon would be an obvious, well-known example, and its structure, a hierarchy of gods divided according to power and held together by familial bonds, is typical. By the time we reach the level of divinity that would confine its interests to a physical fiefdom—say, a river nymph—we have moved far below the ranks where the power to influence physical laws would reside.

But this leads to another objection to Swinburne's analysis, because, ironically enough, these polytheistic systems do not regularly assert that the gods to whom man normally has recourse are themselves also the first cause of the universe. The way that the analogy actually plays out within polytheistic systems, which perhaps is only even more true to the analogy itself, is that the gods, rather than creating the universe out of nothing, instead *impose order* on raw materials that already exist by some other cause.

---

[3] Ibid., 68.

Again, we can use the familiar Greek pantheon to illustrate this concept. The ancient Greeks experimented with several different concepts of gods connected to the first cause and the essential laws of physical nature. The best known are probably Gaea, the Earth, and Ouranos, the Sky. However, others were posited by various religious and philosophical factions, such as Phanes (Light), Nyx (Night), and Eros (Love/Attraction, alternatively named as the son of Aphrodite). None of these were considered personal gods, in the sense that they were too macroscopic to concern themselves with individual human beings, or even perhaps with humanity as a whole. They approached the threshold of omnipotence, but certainly not of omnibenevolence—as the Greeks, like many polytheists, did not assume that man was in fact the purpose and focus of all creation, at least not in the beginning.

The next generation of gods, born of these vast and inhuman forces, were the Titans. These were the first to begin to impose some sense of order onto an originally chaotic system. To do so, they had to display somewhat more of what we would define as intelligence and knowledge of what they purposed to do: they moved away from near-omnipotence in favor of near-omniscience. (According to Hesiod, the Titaness Hecate could move through all worlds and knew what was happening in each of them: this was both why Zeus awarded her honors and why she was often said to have been the one who told Demeter where her daughter Persephone had been hidden. Metis, the original goddess of wisdom and foretelling, is also a Titan.) We cannot award all the Titans near-omniscience by the broadest definition, since there is the story in which their king, Cronos, is fed a stone in the place of his youngest son, Zeus, who is then hidden away until adulthood, and Cronos apparently never knows the difference. Even so, however, Cronos retains a reputation for general wisdom and intelligence.

From the Titans, Cronos and his wife Rhea in particular, are born the Olympian gods who are today most familiar. Here the concept of moral good in the gods is introduced for the first time. Though wise, the Titans cannot be called good, as the story of Cronos eating his own children surely demonstrates. The Titans also fail to make good on a promise they made to Gaea on their ascent to power, to free their siblings, the cyclopes and the giants, from imprisonment. By contrast, the first thing Zeus does apart from freeing his own siblings from the belly of Cronos is to fulfill this broken vow. This establishes him as the origin of benevolence—the first "good" god, and the one who will from this point forward be the "overseer" who establishes that the universe runs in such a way that life, including man, will have some degree of safety. Even though the folkloric nature of some mythology ultimately calls into question the goodness of the gods in terms of their adherence to culturally-based moral standards, ultimately, this does not take away from the Olympians' *religious* standing as the ultimate source of morality and order.

But Zeus, in his evolution of morality, has had to sacrifice some degree of power and knowledge. Although it is rare, he can find himself nearly overpowered or outwitted. This, too, is typical of polytheism: the "three perfections" of omnipotence, omniscience, and omnibenevolence rarely even come close to coexisting in one being. In at least the Indo-European models, the theory of generations of gods proceeding through the qualities in this particular order is the rule. Omnipotence, or something very near it, is required for the initial creation of the raw components of the universe, but it is held by beings without any particular concern for life as we know it—and sometimes, in fact, by beings with no discernable consciousness at all. In some cases, as in the spontaneous self-creation of Gaea and with her of natural laws, the creation of the physical universe itself seems to be presented as an emergent property of the first strata of gods, a sort of natural birth, rather than as a deliberate (teleological) act. Consciousness and then morality *develop* in successive generations of gods, as they arguably might have done in corporeal beings. Swinburne's criticism bears little resemblance to this model at all.

Simplicity

The heart of Swinburne's argument, though, is that monotheism is simply to be preferred to polytheism on the grounds that it contains greater simplicity, and is thus comparatively more probable. Hume, of course, had already addressed this objection:

> To multiply causes without necessity is indeed contrary to true philosophy, but this principle applies not to the present case. Were one deity antecedently proved by your theory who were possessed of every attribute requisite to the production of the universe, it would be needless, I own (though not absurd), to suppose any other deity existent. But while it is still a question whether all these attributes are united in one subject or dispersed among several independent beings; by what phenomena in nature can we pretend to decide the controversy? Where we see a body raised in a scale, we are sure that there is in the opposite side, however concealed from sight, some counterpoising weight equal to it; but it is still allowed to doubt whether that weight be an aggregate of several distinct bodies or one uniform united mass. And if the weight requisite very much exceeds anything which we have ever seen conjoined in one single body, the former supposition becomes still more probably and natural. An intelligent being of such vast power and capacity as is necessary to produce the universe, or, to speak in the language of ancient philosophy, so prodigious an animal,

exceeds all analogy and even comprehension.[4]

To this Swinburne replies, as previously quoted:

> But Hume's hypothesis is very complicated—we want to ask about it such questions as why there are just 333 deities (or whatever the number is), why do they have powers of just the strength which they do have, and what moves them to cooperate as closely as obviously they do; questions of a kind which obtrude far less with the far simpler and so less arbitrary theistic hypothesis.[5]

This essentially leaves Swinburne with the contention that one is simpler than many, and thus more likely. But surely, if simplicity does imply probability, it cannot merely refer to numbers. To return to the analogy of building, if we see a monument like Stonehenge or one of the pyramids, we are more justified in assuming many builders than one, for two reasons. We assume many minds behind the creation of a complex object, but we also assume many bodies behind the control of such very large and heavy objects as appear, for example, at Stonehenge. We know that one person, however strong, simply could not move enormous stones by himself: so power as well as intelligence is at issue. Nor is it easy to imagine what reason one person would have to create something on such a grand scale, while we can find several potential reasons why a group of people might do so, both religious and political. On every level, the explanation of many builders conforms better to what we know and what we can reasonably guess than the explanation of only one builder. Surely, then, that makes many builders the "simpler" explanation, in that it requires fewer contortions and exceptions to make it fit the evidence. No additional variables have to be concocted or taken into account to explain that many men can build a monument: but several must be introduced to explain how it is possible or desirable for one man to do so.

The question of why there should be precisely 333 deities is a spurious one. Polytheism treats gods as a superior class of spirits, which, like any other class of spirits or other entities, might consist of any number of beings. Where there is a number attached to them at all, as a rule it is a symbolic one representing their perfection, not one to be taken literally. To return to the Greeks, the Olympian gods are numbered traditionally as twelve: but there are substantially more than twelve gods. The number is present as a numerological symbol rather than as a literal count.

Likewise, when Swinburne asks why there should be 333 deities (or some

---

[4] Ibid., 62.
[5] Ibid., 68.

other arbitrary number), it is equally fair to ask why there should be only one. He implies that order exists in the universe for man's benefit, writing that "If I am right in supposing that God has reason to create finite creatures with the opportunity to grow in knowledge and power, then he has reason to create temporal order."[6] But he has previously argued that "There is a great deal more order in the world than is necessary for the existence of humans."[7] He means the latter contention to show that mankind could exist in a less than perfectly ordered universe, and so is fit to comment on the surprising nature of that order: but we can question how he means to conform this statement to the other one. If order is imposed on the universe by a God primarily concerned with man, but is then imposed to a scale far beyond what man will actually require, is this automatically more likely than that such universal order was imposed by a generation of gods for whom the benefit of man was not yet a great concern? The reason Swinburne posits for God's interest in order beyond what benefits man is "beauty,[8]" but it would be awfully difficult to prove an objective standard for what God should consider "beautiful," except by saying that we must accept that what God created is beautiful to Him: and to posit that God's reason for order is beauty, and that we know that order is beautiful because God created it, is circular.

Why should there be only one God? If He were to exist, He would be the greatest possible anomaly in a universe where we find few others of even a modest scale. In our own observations, wherever we find that any one thing exists, we are justified in assuming that somewhere in the world there are others like it: and most often we are proven right. There is not only a single member of any species, nor only a single species of life. There is not one planet, one star, one galaxy, one comet. There is not one chemical, one element, one molecule, one atom, one atomic particle. The whole principle of existence that we can observe is that of many, not of one. (The single exception is the observation of one universe, and even that is currently being questioned.) Can we really argue that one God, Whose nature would be the ultimate violation of that principle and would require all sorts of special explanation, is a simpler explanation of godhood than many gods, whose nature would be in perfect keeping with what we see all around us? The question of why there should be 333 (or however many) of them is no more troubling than the question of why there should be eight planets in our solar system rather than ten.

Why should there be 333 gods? Because it is the nature of things that where

---

[6] Ibid., 71.

[7] Ibid., 66.

[8] As, for example: "In so far as some sort of order is a necessary condition of beauty, and it is a good thing—as it surely is—that the world be beautiful rather than ugly, God has reason for creating an orderly universe."

there is one, there are many, and because according to the myths, they are family. Why are their powers of a particular strength? Because the nature of gods accords them a range of power and intelligence, just as our nature accords a lesser range to us. What moves them to cooperate? They have common goals in the creation of the universe, and again, they are family. These answers are not so complicated that they become ridiculous—certainly not more ridiculous than the questions that must be posed to monotheism and its logical consequences. Swinburne's argument against polytheism fails, and Hume's hypothesis—his joke, made earnest by a new cultural context—stands firm.

Julie McCord is a former Archpriestess of the Fellowship of Isis. Under the name Estara T'shirai, she has contributed to several articles and books on magical and devotional practice.

Theisms

ERIK MEGANCK

From a philosophical point of view, there is no need for a fundamental contradiction between polytheism and monotheism. Actually, to me, they seem to work together as an atheist (in its 'proper' sense) critique of metaphysics. I will use two of my mentors to put up my argument, Sam IJsseling and Jean-Luc Nancy. This argument comes down to the following contentions. Polytheism cannot be not philosophical nowadays, since it cannot ignore or undo metaphysics and actually belongs to its very dissolution. Monotheism only opposes polytheism inasmuch as it is confused with henotheism. Monotheism does not—or no longer—contain an argument against polytheism, on the contrary. If they both are understood in the thoughtful, not the shallow, atheist register, they allow for a profound contemporary understanding of the world. The world no longer appears as a 'thing' that has meaning. The event of world, which is opening, is itself meaning.

Jean-Luc Nancy (Université de Strasbourg) does not need any introduction. He has (co-)written more than a hundred books on almost any subject, so it takes a really strange philosopher never to have heard of him.

Sam IJsseling (+2015) was a Dutch philosopher who came to KU Leuven (University of Louvain) in 1969 and opened many interesting philosophical paths there. He introduced Heidegger, Levinas and Derrida to his students and colleagues in a time when these authors were considered no less than subversive. He also wrote on polytheism as a critique of metaphysics. His book on polytheism, *Apollo, Dionysos, Aphrodite and the Others. Greek Gods in Contemporary Philosophy*[1] strangely enough was never translated into English. The last chapter of that book treated on polytheism and postmodern thought.

Nevertheless, he—nor Nancy, for that matter—never 'betrayed' his Christian roots—he started out as an Augustinian monk but left the congregation when he realized that the notion of 'One God' in Christianity is just as awkward as that of 'One Principle or Norm' in traditional metaphysics. However, he kept a great respect for Christianity because of its beautiful liturgy,

---

[1] S. IJsseling, *Apollo, Dionysos, Aphrodite en de anderen. Griekse goden in de hedendaagse flosofie* (Amsterdam: Boom, 1994).

art and its critical potential towards religion in general. But how can philosophical polytheism be made to rhyme with even a vague adherence to Christianity, that is after all called 'monotheistic'?

First of all, we are dealing with *philosophical* polytheism. Far from me to imply that faith and thought are opposites or subordinated one to another, as in traditional philosophy. In premodern thought, philosophy was considered the servant, *ancilla*, of theology and faith, whereas in modernity this relationship turned upside down and philosophy became the supervisor of theology and faith, telling them what and how to live their religion. More and more, the Cartesian obsession with certainty preferred scientific method over belief and faith. Later on in this article, I will show that this opposition/subordination scheme does not work, at least not any more. IJsseling realized this and he resented this scheme. But still, there is a 'difference'—a term that goes a long way with French philosophers. The difference between philosophical and theological (or religious) polytheism is not such that it would present two different modes of the same theory or paradigm or doctrine, as in 'Christian' versus' atheist' existentialism. The difference will be clarified later on. Suffice it here to say that philosophy and theology are to me not as two separate disciplines, but two tendencies of thought. When we think about the God of Christianity, philosophy can only assert that this name circulates and disrupts the worldly discourses like politics, philosophy, theology, art and literature, whereas theology can introduce different contents and become more e.g. Revelational than philosophical. I cannot even use the Bible as criterion for a difference, since the Bible has an enormous philosophical potential too.

Of course, IJsseling wrote extensively on ancient myths, but that does not necessarily mean that he wanted to reinstall or reactualize or even recontextualize or reconstruct those ancient religions. He drew on those mythical narratives to make a philosophical point, namely that the meaning of our existence is a narrative matter, not an essentialist or a rationalist one. Humans meet themselves in stories, not in definitions. Scientific definitions of human beings can all be traced back to the prototypical one by Aristotle: a rational animal. But has anyone ever felt himself or herself a rational animal? Or, for that matter, a black box (behaviorism) or a kind of clumsily embedded computer network (Artificial Intelligence) or a pitiful version of an ape (evolutionism)? But we have all at one time felt like Antigone, or like being confronted by a sphinx, or the plaything of the Moirai. As Heidegger puts it: scientific definitions are correct, but not true. Antigone is true, but not correct in a theoretical, falsifiable, conceptually clear way. She is true to life. She is, says IJsseling, more *real* than any physical woman since she has pervaded human reality for thousands of years, while we inhabit that realm no longer than less than a century. And even nowadays thousands of years later, we still experience these 'stories' as very meaningful.

[143]

All kinds of events that make up world and human existence require meaning, we are never satisfied with things-as-they-are. We want to understand—if only to control chaos and anxiety. We all have had the experience of something happening to us that we did not see coming, though, looking back, we recognize the unavoidability of the event. The Greek called this the goddess Anankè, Necessity. Science has no word for it since such events fall outside the scope of causality and prediction. In scientific discourse, the experience of the tragically inevitable is discarded as coincidence. Therefore, no wonder that polytheism reappears in the intellectual, philosophical talk after Nietzsche—who himself was a great admirer of Greek polytheism. Philosophy that strings along with Nietzsche is called post-modern. This 'post-' is rather a tricky prefix. It cannot mean 'after,' since we have not yet left modernity behind us. In 'post-,' modernity loses its original and programmatic rigidity. The key word is 'dissolution'—to some a loss, to others a gain. In polytheism, post-modern philosophy rediscovers the possibility of meaning that is not tied to a structure that depends on unity-and-unicity—of God, Reason, anything. Meaning is spread out over many stories that offer no full explanation, often contradict each other and only survive because they are told, not because they are verified.

Religious polytheism does not question the plurality of gods and demons. This plurality is the very basis of polytheist experience and faith. To question it would shift this experience to theology or philosophy or mythology or anthropology. The rites and narratives remain without reflection. Religious polytheism is not even a belief, it is simply unreflective—which is one meaning of Schelling's 'tautegorical' (*Philosophie der Mythologie*, 1856). Religious polytheism does not search for an origin of the gods, of an system that these gods might represent. There *are* many gods, and that settles it. A philosophical polytheism understands this plurality, not as a pre-given, but through the irreducibility, in principle, of this plurality. Plurality becomes interesting to philosophy when it cannot—or no longer—be subsumed under one principle—a principle that draws its strength from its unity and uniqueness—or integrated in one logically coherent system. Plurality of meaning is philosophically polytheistic in that it concerns the 'inhabitation' or circulation of several 'founding' stories that each of them 'create' the world and supply the meaning of it.

By the way, does this not hide a rigid opposition between (religious) experience and (philosophical) reflection? I do not think so. Historically speaking, experience became reflection and we cannot reverse history. We cannot abolish metaphysics to go back to what was before—which actually comes down to an argument against what is called polytheist reconstructionism. We can never experience ancient myth because we cannot subtract the effect of metaphysics, of modernity, of scientific analysis. Conceded, Heidegger, among others, points out that metaphysics is an alienating thought, but does not imply that it can be 'remedied,' that we can erase it and, by doing so, re-uncover true reality. To put this bluntly, we simply cannot get back to myth because we have had mythology. Therefore, contemporary or post-modern polytheism can only be philosophical, not as opposed to religious, but as historically 'different.' Metaphysics is not the overcoming of myth, but the effect of a shift. As Jean-Luc Nancy—whom we will meet again later on in this article—puts it:

> [...] the constitution of metaphysics itself proceeded neither by self-constitution nor by the "Greek miracle." Its provenance lies in a transformation of the entire order of "ties with the inaccessible." The West was born not from the liquidation of a dark world of beliefs, dissolved by the light of a new sun—and this no more so in Greece than during the Renaissance or the eighteenth century. It took shape in a metamorphosis of the overall relation to the world, such that the "inaccessible" took shape and functioned, as it were, *precisely as such* in thought, in knowledge, and in behavior. There was no reduction of the unknown, but rather an aggravation of the incommensurable [...] [2]

This transformation, this provenance cannot be 'undone' nor can it be 'reversed.'

The meaning of our existence is spread out over several narratives, intersecting and contaminating and contradicting each other. These narratives do not form a closed, logically coherent system and are completely free of any aspiration to form a 'total explanation' of reality, as science does. Religious polytheism would not be bothered by this, since it was never caught up in metaphysical logic. Philosophical or contemporary polytheism questions this logical imperative of *Tertium non datur*. As Jean-Pierre Vernant put it:

> Myth brings into play a form of logic that we could call, in contrast with the logic of non-contradiction as used by philosophers, a logic of ambiguity, of equivocity and polarity. [3]

IJsseling urged philosophers to allow for this ambiguity, even embrace it. He was not convinced at all by the traditional 'evidence' of unity and purity and could never go along with the analytical attempts to clean up thought according to the instructions of a metaphysics that does not think through the death of

---

[2] J.-L. Nancy, *Dis-Enclosure. The Deconstruction of Christianity* (New York: Fordham University Press, 200), 8.

[3] 'Le mythe met donc en jeu une forme de logique qu'on peut appeler, en contraste avec la logique de non-contradiction des philosophes, une logique de l'ambigu, de l'équivoque, de la polarité.' J.-P. Vernant, *Mythe et société en Grèce ancienne* (Paris: Maspero, 1974), 250.

God and has not yet heard and realized how the real world became a fable.[4]

What Nietzsche meant by this, is that there is no longer any 'external reference, no divine principle or 'outerworldly' realm where the truth value of every narrative can be established and where all narratives can be indexed and filed accordingly in the one overarching Story. This has nothing to do with relativism since this statement also presupposes an external view—outside thought? what could that mean?—from where all narratives and interpretations can be surveyed and judged—by whom or what? by thought from outside thought? by something or someone else, like science or politics?—and where this survey and judgment yields an identical truth value for all narratives and interpretations.

****

Secondly, polytheism is not exactly the opposite of monotheism. I know there's quite a lot of confusion here, but strictly speaking, it is the opposite of henotheism. The latter specifically states that there are not many gods, there is only one—or at east, there is only one true god or one 'upper god.' Polytheism and henotheism are both the result of a count, yielding respectively 'many gods' and 'one god' in the world. This 'in the world' is important, as we will see. One cannot count things that do not belong to the world. Calculus, census, counting is typical of a world that has quantity as its property. Whenever one starts to count outside this world, one ends up with nothing or infinity. Monotheism, on the other hand, claims that nothing in this world is divine, that only God is God, that divinity cannot be found amongst or be deduced from things or situations.[5] Therefore, the opposite of monotheism is pantheism, the belief or philosophical conviction that everything in de the world is divine.

It is typical of the philosophy of religion[6] since Heidegger to eagerly search for verbs other than 'be' to describe divinity. Strictly speaking, we should be satisfied with the proclamation that God and only He 'gods.' This 'godding,' again, strictly speaking, does not necessarily contain existence or unity and uniqueness. When I say that God 'gods,' cannot deduce from that that He (necessarily) exists or that He is (necessarily) one.

---

[4] I refer, of course, to those two brilliant texts by Nietzsche. The passage on the madman who proclaims the death of God is §125 of *The Gay Science* and 'How the "True World" Finally Became a Fable' is the fourth chapter of *Twilight of the Idols*.

[5] Events can be considered divine within a certain philosophical or theological frame, but an elaboration of this, following Caputo and Badiou and Žižek, would take us too far here.

[6] Actually, this is a very confusing term, dating from modernity. It suggests that philosophy is totally non-religious and that religion is totally unphilosophical, that moreover religion is a topic, an object of philosophical reflection that literally 'lies before, over against' this reflection, as if reflection has nothing to do with religion.

Of course, these –theisms are not at all clear-cut concepts. Take Hinduism, for instance—in as far as there is such a thing as thé (one) Hinduism (always and everywhere identical to itself). We know this to be a polytheism. But then, its many gods are seen as emanations of a 'higher' divinity, so henotheism. But still, this divinity, Brahman, has been proposed as inaccessible to human approach, so in a way monotheistic. It is also well known that strictly henotheistic religions like Islam and Judaism consider Christianity a polytheism in disguise because of the doctrine of Trinity. Also, Protestant Christianity considers Catholicism slightly polytheist because of its army of saints and angels and because of the magnificence of its liturgy.

The confusion between monotheism and henotheism is also typical of Western metaphysics. Where does the One Principle—be it God or Reason or Consciousness or Market or whatever—reside? At the top of the system of reality or actually also somewhat 'outside' it from where it founds the system as a whole, with itself at the top, determining all meaning within the system? I read this ambiguity—again, to be embraced—in the *Proslogion* of Anselm. He calls God that, greater and higher than which nothing can be thought. The top of the system, that is. But then he also calls God greater and higher than anything that can be thought. So, on the one hand, God is the Highest Being that holds the system together from within, but on the other hand, God can be thought as beyond all that can be possibly thought. Perhaps this is why John Caputo call God the locus of the impossible. The tension between those two divine positions, if I can call them that, where Anselm finds God, is very significant. It shows thought (and reality), the epistemological (and ontological) order, as what can never be totally enclosed, as 'excessive.' Thought is at the same time 'too much' and 'too little'—which reminds us of the Derridean supplement. Thought hides an openness where the traditional epistemological accountancy does not work well. God might be a name for this openness. As Highest Being, God is doubtless the strongest concept imaginable, as metaphysical excess God is a name beyond conceptuality that disturbs thought as a system and turns it into an open event.

Market and Reason thrive on the same ambivalence. They need to remain, in a way, independent of the system they carry, inaccessible, immune. These days, 'market' is treated almost as a natural law, whereas it is just a neo-liberal ideology. Reason, in order to protect itself from interpretation, metaphoricity, literature etc. also needs to anchor outside the system it supports.

****

Thirdly, this is also all about theism as such, apart from any modality (mono-, poly-, heno-, pan-, or even a-). Theism in philosophical, i.e. post-modern sense may refer to a system that establishes truth as follows: reality 'collects' its truth at the dwelling place of the One Highest Principle, this other world (*Hinterwelt*, as Nietzsche calls it) that can only be accessed by applying the correct epistemological strategy. To paraphrase Nietzsche: as long as we keep on using the word 'is,' we will be thinking theistically. The establishment of any truth "X *is* Y" always requires an authority at the top of the domain that is covered by '*is*,' where appeal becomes impossible without rendering the whole system absurd (in Levinassian sense), meaningless. This establishment moreover, this theistic dynamics, works independently of what exactly is installed as *theion*, as divine— God or Reason or ...

This shows atheism as an ambiguous term—again, to be embraced as such. On the one hand, there is the shallow atheism that bluntly rejects the existence of God. This is a rationalist proposition about the existence of God, only with a logical operator thrown in. This means that it is still a theism, where God at the top of the system, as Highest Being, is simply being replaced by Reason. This atheism is a theism that has removed God but has kept the rigid thought structure of the system that is typical of traditional metaphysics. Theism is the onto-theo-logical structure of thought, and this shallow atheism is just another figure of this structure.

On the other hand, there is a more thoughtful atheism, almost a mirror of the shallow one. It does not want to keep the structure of the system. It allows the 'a-' in atheism to dissolve the theist structure, leaving God and the gods alone. This is partly what Gianni Vattimo means when he says: 'Today, there are no longer strong, plausible reasons to be atheist, or at any rate to dismiss religion.'[7] The (heno)theism of metaphysics dissolves into a polytheism, into an irreducible plurality of founding narratives. Strangely enough, this dissolution does not chase God and the gods out of the system. They hang around in the a-theist world, free, not clinging to the position of Highest Being—which is why many contemporary continental (i.e. French and Italian) philosophers find the notion of *kenosis* so fascinating, thought they often misunderstand it. I would even contend that this 'a-' can be seen as the dwelling place of God or gods, as his or their proper name perhaps. Some, such as I, consider it 'divine,' the way the rigid structures of traditional metaphysics and the alleged philosophical monopoly of science dissolve.

The rehabilitation of atheism, overcoming its shallow version through philosophical reflection, has led, paradoxically enough, to the so-called 'theological turn' in French (phenomenological thought, a turn that has worried quite some philosophers (like Dominique Janicaud). They seemed to fear that philosophy sold itself out to theology. Even if this were so in some isolated cases, the theological turn proved to be an atheist turn—in the proper philosophical sense of atheism: thinking secularization, disenchantment, the

---

[7] G. Vattimo, *Belief* (Stanford: Stanford University Press, 1999), 28.

'return of/from religion' as well as the 'exit of/from religion' through.[8] This atheism relinquishes any claim on the existence, number or habitat of God or gods. It observes the circulation of a name, of names, no more—but also: no less.

So far, I have been able to share the following insights: current polytheism is unavoidably philosophical since it has 'passed through' metaphysics; philosophical polytheism does not necessarily oppose monotheism in that they both criticize metaphysics; both polytheism and monotheism are philosophical atheisms. Or to be more accurate: both polytheism and monotheism acquire their true philosophical depth through the philosophical exploration, explicitation or clarification of atheism.

****

Before I go on to explore the implications of a contemporary, post-modern philosophical polytheism that is also a 'true' atheism, there is another contemporary discussion to be touched on. It concerns the epistemological position of science today. Philosophical polytheism seems, to say the least, irreconcilable with the reductionist tendency of science. Scientific discourse considers non-scientific entities, concepts and explanations 'useless hypotheses.' The answer that Laplace gave Napoleon when the latter asked why God was absent from his five-volume celestial mechanics (1799-1825)—"I had no need for that hypothesis, Sire"—can be called programmatic. Also, what is called 'Einstein's dream'—or more officially: the Grand Unifying Theory'—is typical of the scientific mentality: to be able to deduce the whole material realm from only one equation that has the same beautiful simplicity as the famous $E=mc^2$. In order to be meaningful, reality must be reduced to its measurable—therefor predictable and, if not quite that, at least statistical—features. This reduction and with it the predominance of scientific discourse seems to be waning. Other narratives are re-entering the philosophical scene without any headstrong resistance. Which could mean that science ends up as one of many discourses— as a perspective, Nietzsche would say. Now, this contention usually meets with reactions like "Perspectives do not put people on the moon," suggesting that there must be truth in science on that ground. Of course perspectives do not do such things. But before humanity started shooting things and people at the moon, something else had to be done, something of a much huger order. The moon had to be 'disenchanted.' It had to be reduced to a lump that was open for exploitation. Once the moon was no longer a goddess or a heavenly body but had become a lump, it was just a question of calculation to land on the moon. It is not that Aristotle was too stupid to calculate the way to the moon, it

---

[8] In French: 'retour de la religion' or sometimes 'retour du religieux' and 'sortie de la religion.'

was just that this reduction, this shift in perspective had not arrived yet.

Perspectives work rather like a game. Each perspective sets out its own basic rules, and then it works. These rules cannot be justified by referring to another world. Those rules have no cause, no reason. Perspectives are manifold, there is no criterion, neither inside nor outside the world, that can legitimately reduce this manifold to a system where one of them is right and all others wrong—or in one way or another less true.

I inserted this little piece on science and perspective, not only to point at science as a henotheistic and shallow atheism, but also to tackle a much heard question concerning these perspectives., namely: what exactly are they perspectives of? Is there not somewhere an objectively true reality that reveals its perspectives according to a certain, perhaps unknown dynamics? No. There is—after Kant—no philosophical imperative whatsoever that urges us to rely on such reality. If one prefers to believe in an objective reality, then that is no more than a faith article. There is absolutely no 'proof' or any other compelling argument for objective reality, i.e. a world that has its truth, its meaning, its sense, independent of and prior to (each historical manifestation of) current thought. Paraphrasing Nietzsche: there are only perspectives, and even that is a perspective. This means that the plurality of perspectives, interpretations, discourses, styles, etc. make up what we call: world. There is an ancient Greek mythological world, a Roman world, a Christian world, a modern world, etc. And there is nothing hiding behind these worlds, neither a 'real' and objective world (of science) nor an eternal dynamics that causes the sequence of worlds (like a dialectics). World is not a representation of something else, of another and more sustaining world. World is *ex nihilo*, as we shall see later on.

****

Heidegger as well as Wittgenstein both contended that the world cannot generate its own meaning on, in or from itself. The latter first thought that the 'layer' that warranted the meaning of things in the world cannot itself belong to that world. Later, he thought that the meaning 'arrived' in the use of language. That meaning 'arrives' and is not a matter of eternity, stability and outerworldliness, has also been pointed out by Heidegger. To him, meaning can only happen within a horizon that itself cannot be part of that meaning. The truth of the world and its sources are not to be found in the world. The truth is not a thing between things or a proposition between propositions. It can therefore not be the totality of those things and/or propositions either.

Nietzsche had already denied philosophy any access to another, true world. What he considered the theological grip on thought, referring to an authority that allows you to say 'is,' has lost its strength and rigidity. God is dead. And when God has died, the realm he inhabited also loses its glamor. The other world, where the meaning of this one was supposed to be forged, remains empty from now on. There is no longer that other world to refer to when the question concerning the full meaning of this world and human existence arrises.

But if this philosophical tradition, i.e. continental critique of metaphysics, accepts that the meaning of the world does not belong to itself nor to another world, then where does the world collect or acquire its meaning? This question, of course, needs perhaps some justification in the light of a certain nihilism that is quite happy to consider a world without any meaning at all. But then again, why read this article? I would advocate a philosophical loyalty to its early inspiration, with Plato's astonishment or perplexity that there *is* meaning, that the world *is* intelligible at all. So, where does the meaning of the world come from?

A genitive can have an objective and a subjective sense. The first sense asks for a meaning that is communicated to the world, from another world. This question, however, has been declared invalid by Nietzsche. The second of subjective sense asks for the meaning that the word attributes to itself, a question that Heidegger and Wittgenstein declared invalid. So, again, what could be the meaning of the world … if any?

Meaning, says Nancy, has to be understood in the register of *ex nihilo*, *umsonst*.[9] We can, as it is, read the question concerning the meaning of the world 'beyond' its genitive sense. We can ask for the meaning(*)world, for world *as* meaning. This requires a step back—in the Heideggerian sense[10]—from the traditional system of *signification*, from the famous *adaequatio rei et intellectus*, from the vision of truth as the way this world corresponds to another world of concepts and structure. This end of the era of *signification* is Nancy's version of the 'end' of metaphysics. World takes leave of its Cartesian determination and (heno)theist structure. Its meaning becomes a matter of interpretation, of circulating narratives and perspectives. Plurality becomes irreducible. No one principle directs this circulation from without or within. In the words of, again, Vattimo: reality became

> rather the result of the intersection and "contamination" (in the Latin sense) of a multiplicity of images, interpretations and reconstructions circulated by the media in competition with one another and without any 'central' coordination.[11]

---

[9] This is a recurrent theme in the work of Jean-Luc Nancy, namely his *The Creation of the World or Globalization* (New York: SUNY Press, 2007) and his two volumes of *The Deconstruction of Christianity*, i.e. *Dis-Enclosure* (New York: Fordham University Press, 2008) and *Adoration* (2013, ibid.), passim.

[10] M. Heidegger, *Identity and Difference* (Chicago: University of Chicago Press, 2002), 49ff.

[11] G. Vattimo, *The Transparent Society* (Baltimore: John Hopkins University Press, 1992), 7.

Then, again, where does the meaning(*)world, this plurality of narratives come from, if they have no origin, no external reference, no closure? They happen, says Nancy, at the 'other *of* the world,' which is not at all the 'other *than* the world.' World itself is marked by an alterity that cannot be 'solved.' World does not so much *have* an opening, but *is* opening. This opening *is* meaning, and this constitutes world. This is, in short, my reading of what I call polytheistic mono-a-theism. The world is not a substance that contains a kind of directing office or instance that we can therefore consider divine. If there is 'divine,' it should be found in the opening that is the other of the world. Since this opening is not a structure, a presence, a power, an essence or anything like it, this monotheism is strictly atheist.

This atheism is not the proposition "God exists" with the logical operator 'negation' tagged onto it. It recognizes the circulation of the name in many of the current—literally: running through actuality—discourses. It is atheist in that it thinks world as opening, this being the event of meaning where the 'a-' resists enclosure of the world, of thought, of truth. World has lost its archaeology and teleology, has become *ex nihilo*.

****

This leaves me with one last item to solve, viz. how to understand polytheism, monotheism and atheism together. The 'a-' in atheism is key here. It dissolves all theist structures, all onto-theo-logy, all obsession with unity-unicity of traditional metaphysics. This dissolution does take place from 'within'; the dissolution happens *with* the system, not *to* the system. The 'a-' belongs to the system as its very proper dissolution. Atheism dethrones the Highest Being and with it its epistemological, ontological, ethical, political potencies. The 'one true world' becomes a manifold of discourses, interpretations, narratives that can no longer be subsumed under one principle. Because of its meaning-potential, we can call this irreducible plurality a philosophical polytheism. Because of the removal of divine representations of the world and their alleged authority, we can also call this philosophical monotheism. But again, only if we read both theisms in a philosophically (and not scientifically or logically) atheist way.

Erik Meganck studied philosophy, theology and psychology in Louvain, Antwerp, Ghent and Rome. He wrote a dissertation, *From Veritas to Caritas* , on Nietzsche, Heidegger, Derrida and Vattimo. He teaches metaphysics at the University of Louvain. His research focuses on contemporary continental critique of metaphysics and the connection between philosophy and theology/religion (in the broadest sense).

The Dawkins Delusion

WAYLAND SKALLAGRIMSSON

The aggressive arguments against spirituality made by Richard Dawkins and the New Skeptics movement cause some polytheists to adopt a detrimentally hostile attitude toward science, whereas others mistakenly attempt a (pseudo)scientific defense of their religion. However, an examination of polytheistic philosophy leads instead to a more nuanced understanding of its rationality, and the ways in which a scientific and spiritual worldview can coexist and even complement each other.

Introduction

As modern polytheism has grown beyond the traditionally small, academic-leaning circles that once made up the bulk of it, it has experienced a fragmenting of its philosophical underpinnings. In the eighties and nineties, for example, there was very little discussion of polytheistic theological philosophy because none was needed. Most polytheists of this era had similar enough backgrounds to share major elements of their theological philosophies. That this is no longer the case is not a bad thing. Having a polytheism that is larger and more diverse invigorates our thinking.

However, this diversification of philosophy has led to a number of problems as well. One is a new vulnerability to a rather hostile philosophical force, one that stands in opposition to it and every other form of religion or spirituality: a pseudoscientific movement that masquerades as an exercise in pure science and logic. It is worth examining the arguments of this movement, and where those arguments fail, in an effort to not only better understand polytheism from a philosophical perspective, but also to prevent some foolish philosophical reactions to this movement impairing modern polytheistic philosophy. Such an analysis should also help modern polytheists establish better dialogue with those who hold different beliefs.

The extreme and hostile position against religion and spirituality taken by this movement, which has sometimes been termed the New Skeptic movement, has provoked two different but equally harmful reactions in the larger pagan community. The first is to reject all science, and cling to superstition instead. The second is to attempt to "prove" polytheistic theological or spiritual beliefs in ridiculous pseudoscientific terms in an attempt to justify them to scientists like Dawkins, one of the most prominent of the New Skeptics. Both are harmful to polytheism in particular and the progress of human understanding in general. Instead of either of these reactions, it would be better to examine traditional polytheistic philosophical beliefs in order to develop a better understanding of them, one that does not reject science and rational thought or embrace ridiculous pseudoscience.

Dawkins and the New Skeptics

Richard Dawkins' work in the field of memetics, which he created, is something that I firmly believe will go down in history as being on par with *On the Origin of Species* as a groundbreaking, important scientific work. There is no denying that he is a brilliant scientist who has done much to advance the cause of science. However, he is also guilty of setting the cause of science and rational discourse back a long way as well. He and the other modern scientists who think like him, the New Skeptics, have invested a lot of effort in peddling some astonishingly unscientific ideas dressed up in scientific trappings, making many of the grossly unscientific errors of which they accuse pseudoscientists and the religious.

The God Delusion is the name of one of Dawkins' seminal works on religion and spirituality. In it, he argues that all of the available empirical evidence, as well as logic, disproves the existence of gods and spiritual forces, and that belief in these things constitutes delusion. These arguments are typical of the New Skeptic movement. They are also predicated on confusing the scientific method with the assumptions that the scientific method is applied to.

The Larger Problem

Their particular brand of pseudoscience is a symptom of a problem that seems to be growing increasingly prevalent in the modern scientific community: a complete misunderstanding of philosophy and how it relates to science.

"Science has grown beyond the need for philosophy," and "Science has disproved philosophy," are two of the more egregious statements made by many scientists today, not just the New Skeptics crowd. This shows a complete failure to understand what philosophy is. It also shows a serious lack of understanding of what the scientific method is.

The Scientific Method

Boiled down to its essentials, all branches of science use variations on the following steps:

1) *Make observations.* Science is based on observing things that happen, and then trying to find explanations as to why things happen that way.

2) *Form a hypothesis.* Once enough observations have been made to find patterns, scientists think up a hypothesis that explains the existence of the observations.

3) *Test the hypothesis.* After the hypothesis has been formed, it needs to be tested. This test usually takes the form of making predictions. If it is a good hypothesis, it should be able to predict that certain things will happen in certain circumstances. This is where experimentation comes in. It is just a matter of setting up those circumstances and seeing if the things the hypothesis predicted actually happen.

4) *Accept, refine, or reject the hypothesis.* Based on the results of the experiment, the hypothesis can either be taken to be proved by the experiment, disproved by it, or in need of modification and retesting.

In short, science is description and explanation. It uses a set of agreed-upon assumptions and the rules of logic to construct the hypothesis that is used to create these descriptions and explanations. There is no way to eliminate making assumptions in science. Without a few basic assumptions, which are often referred to as axioms, there would be no way to do science at all. For example, it is necessary to assume basic things like triangles always being made of three angles that add up to 180 degrees, and that physics on Mars, or on the other side of the world, works the same as it does everywhere else. Without these core axioms, meaningful hypotheses could not be formed. Being necessary assumptions, however, does not magically promote them to the status of facts.

The Role of Philosophy in Science

This is where philosophy comes in. While the scientific method is used to describe and explain things, philosophy frames the questions that can/need to be asked, and sets up the rules for asking them. Philosophy provides a set of guidelines for choosing good basic assumptions. Science cannot do this any more than a locked trunk can be opened with the key inside the trunk. Because science is done with the assistance of these axiomatic assumptions as a foundation, it is completely dependent on them. Science depends on philosophy even though philosophy itself is not scientific.

Monism

Modern science is grounded at its most fundamental level in monism. Monism is the philosophical position that all things in existence can be explained in terms of a single substance or reality. This is just an assumption, but Occam's Razor says that it is a reasonable assumption. After all, a universe in which all things are just variations on a single, fundamental thing is simpler than a universe in which there are many different kinds of things that have no relationship to each other.

Materialism

Materialism is a further philosophical assumption on top of monism. It is a kind of material monism, or the assumption that all things in the universe are made out of the same physical substance. This means that in this philosophy, all things are ultimately physical in nature, including mental phenomena. This is not an unreasonable assumption. Science has come far by figuring out that all matter is made out of the same subatomic particles, for example. The predictive power of this assumption is good. It is sensible to consider this a likely assumption, therefore.

Positivism

Positivism is the final philosophical brick in the foundation of modern science. This is the position that positive knowledge can only result from empirical evidence based on unequivocal observations of natural phenomena. It holds that all authentic knowledge is verifiable objectively. This is not a completely unreasonable assumption to make. It certainly has its advantages. After all, there are many kinds of observations that are subjective, and difficult to verify. This makes it difficult to conclude whether or not statements concerning these observations are true or false. The positivist assumption restricts the scientific view to those things that are objective enough to be easily verifiable, and makes the results from scientific experiments more certain.

However, just because something is difficult or impossible to verify does not mean that it does not exist. Positivism has an enormous built-in limitation. It creates deliberate blind spots in scientific knowledge. As Werner Heisenberg complained, "The positivists have a simple solution: the world must be divided into that which we can say clearly and the rest, which we had better pass over in silence. But can anyone conceive of a more pointless philosophy, seeing that what we can say clearly amounts to next to nothing? If we omitted all that is unclear we would probably be left with completely uninteresting and trivial tautologies."

Materialistic Positivism

Taken all together, then, modern science is based on a philosophy of materialistic positivism.

When answering the question, "What is real?" materialistic positivists will say that because everything that we can observe is made up of physical particles then physical objects must form the primary reality. After all, mental experiences occur in the brain and the brain is made of physical particles. Therefore it seems reasonable to conclude that mental experiences are the creation of the interactions of physical particles.

Philosophy in the Ancient Polytheistic World

Ancient polytheism was not, of course, a monolithic thing, and the beliefs of ancient polytheists were varied and often unrecorded. Still, there are a number of things that can be learned about some kinds of ancient polytheistic philosophy. The ancient Greeks, for example, left behind a lot of philosophical writings.

Dualism was a popular philosophy amongst them. Plato, for example, held that the world was composed of nonphysical archetypal forms and physical shadow-substance, generated by the archetypal forms.

The Pythagorean philosophy is one of numeric monism. The Pythagoreans believed that abstract, mathematical relationships were the fundamental stuff of reality, and defined the ways in which substance and void combined to form the physical world.

Animism was common to many ancient polytheistic religions. The ancient Greeks held that many if not all natural objects had animating spiritual forces such as nymphs and dryads. Ancient heathens had the same concept. Plants, forests, and more had landwights, alfs, and huldrafolk. Dwarfs inhabited the rocks, and the jotuns were the spirits of mountains and other remote, dangerous, desolate places. Animism comes in two philosophical varieties. One is a form of dualism, in which there is a spirit inhabiting every physical form. The other is a form of spiritual monism, which holds that all things, even physical forms, are actually manifestations of spirit.

There are hints of unrecorded ancient polytheistic philosophical beliefs in the records of ordinary, everyday spiritual and religious beliefs. It is interesting to note that the Pythia seems to have been possessed by the god Apollon sometimes, and that Apollodorus speaks of Zeus appearing to a woman in the form of her husband. Such descriptions as these can be found in other kinds of polytheism as well.

Ancient berserkers, for example, are spoken of in two ways at once. *Egil's Saga* says "What people say about shape-changers or those who go into berserk fits," which curiously equates the idea of shape-changing with having a fit. The *Ynglinga Saga* says that berserks "went without mailcoats, and were as frantic as dogs or wolves; they bit their shields and were as strong as bears or boars; they slew men but neither fire nor iron could hurt them. This is known as 'running berserk.'" What these sources do is describe berserkers in two ways at the same time: as shape-changers who turned into ferocious animals when they went berserk, and as human beings who had fits that drove them mad and made them strong.

Now, the Dawkins crowd has a favorite explanation for this sort of thing. They often claim that ancient people were foolish, or stupid, and could not tell the difference between hallucinations/dreams/the imagination and reality. They would say that some ancient people were schizophrenic, or took drugs, or were delusional, and thought they were being possessed by outside spirits. This is an astonishingly arrogant and ignorant assumption. Rather than assuming that almost every single person before the intellectual elite of the modern age appeared was an idiot, it is much more reasonable to suppose that they saw the world differently.

The fact that ancient Greeks could see a person as being both a human and a god at the same time is much the same as the fact that ancient heathens could see berserkers as both shape-changers and people who had fits at the same time. The division of the world of experience into the real, physical part and the false, imaginary part is a product of modern society. It is a philosophical assumption: that of materialistic positivism.

It seems more likely that many ancient polytheists were monistic idealists, philosophically speaking. The best way to understand monistic idealism is to consider the question "What is real?" Materialistic positivists would say that "physical" is the same thing as "real." In other words, the only real objects are physical objects. This would seem to many people to be obvious, but this is not actually the most parsimonious explanation. It fails to take one important observed fact about the world into account.

The only reason that we know that everything in the observable world is made of physical particles is because we have the mental experience of observing them. There is no experiment on the observable world that has ever been conducted or ever will be conducted that does not end with "… and I know this because I saw/heard/touched/smelled/tasted it." In other words, the primary layer of reality as we experience it is mental, not physical. The entire outside world is, at its very foundation a special type of mental experience. Please note that this is not because experiments are badly designed. No experiment, no matter how cleverly set up, can ever change this. Reality as human beings experience it is primarily mental.

Because all that we know of the physical world is a special class of mental experience that is not like other classes of mental experience, all that we can say for sure is that both our experience of the physical world and our experiences of our own private mental worlds are mental in nature, even if they are different from each other. This is literally what the term "monistic idealism" means.

Instead of the real, physical/unreal, mental division of materialistic positivism, ancient polytheistic monistic idealists seem to have divided the world into two kinds of experiences: experiences of the physical world, which are shared with everyone else in the physical world and experiences of the spiritual world, which could be accessed in dreams, or through shamanistic trances, or with the aid of certain entheogens. The experiences of the spiritual world were not shared by everybody else in the physical world. Because this was the underlying philosophical assumption about the world, it did not have to be explained to everybody, or talked about. When somebody spoke of turning into a wolf in battle, everybody knew that he meant that this is what he experienced in the berserker trance. Everybody knew that anybody else looking at him would see him looking as human as he ever did. This did not make them think that he was delusional, or an idiot, however; they just understood that he meant that he experienced the transformation in the spirit world. When somebody spoke of having been impregnated by a god, everybody knew that the father, physically, was a priest or holy man who experienced becoming possessed by the god in the spirit world, but remained his human self in the physical world. Ancient polytheistic religious philosophy was very different from modern scientific philosophy. Still, it is only a philosophical difference, not a factual difference.

The Dawkins Fallacies

The primary fallacy that the Dawkins crowd makes is that of the false dichotomy. Their extremist take on their materialistic positivist philosophy practically forces them to frame everything in terms of a false either-or, black and white choice.

Because Dawkins assumes that all things that are real are physical, he must cast all religious beliefs as making statements about the physical world, even if that was never the intention of the people holding those beliefs. For example, as he argues in *The God Delusion*, if divinity created the world, then natural processes cannot have done so. Then, by showing that there is no evidence of divinity having created the world, and that there is evidence of natural laws having done so, the religious position is disproved, according to his argument. His philosophical assumptions make him disregard all forms of religious belief that do not make demonstrably false statements about the physical world, though. That is what is known as stacking the deck. In reality, his black and white choice is inaccurate in the extreme. Many polytheistic philosophies, such as dualism, animism, and monistic idealism have beliefs that are completely outside his rather simplified picture of the religious world. Many polytheists would say that the gods created the spiritual world, or that the stories of the gods creating the physical world are analogies. It is only a rather small minority of religious positions that would argue that one or more gods actually physically created the world in defiance of scientific law. Dawkins' false dichotomy thus becomes a straw man, as well.

The New Skeptics like to argue that their philosophical assumptions are the most reasonable. Sometimes, they will point out that the fact that neurological advances have shown how the brain creates the elements of spiritual experiences is a strong suggestion that spiritual experiences are nothing but side effects or malfunctionings of the brain.

This, too, is not a rational argument. The error can be demonstrated with a thought experiment about a television sent back in time to the nineteenth century. A scientist of the time could, with a little experimentation and ingenuity, discover that electricity and magnetic fields applied to various parts of the device could make it show pictures. That scientist would conclude, reasonably, that the device created the experience of seeing pictures all by itself, and did not receive mysterious images through some kind of unknown signal originating elsewhere. That scientist would be wrong, and New Skeptics making their arguments about the neurology of visionary experiences are wrong for the same reason. Of course the brain makes the experience of having spiritual experiences. It would do this whether spiritual experiences were generated from the outside or the inside of the brain. The argument from neurology is meaningless. After all, the fact that the brain processes and interprets the experience of eating apple pie by releasing dopamine, restricting the attention to the senses of taste and smell, and causing neurons in the visual cortex to fire in such a way as to create the image of an apple pie does not disprove the objective existence of apple pie.

Similarly, the New Skeptics love to point out that science based on materialistic positivism has such a great track record that it practically amounts to proving the philosophy, scientifically. The more brazen of them even go so far as to claim that science has done away with the need for philosophy, or has "disproved it," somehow. This is impossible. No matter how much success science has, science cannot prove or disprove any philosophy. To think that it can is a form of category confusion.

Then there is the fact that they are vastly overstating the success of modern science. True, it has had great successes. But well over ninety percent of the universe is made of dark matter and dark energy, about which science knows virtually nothing. Science has no idea what the various solutions to the quantum equations that govern all matter and energy actually mean. Theories range from multiple universes to physical determinism to true randomness to consciousness having a privileged place in physics, with no one able to say definitively which if any are true. Science has explained much, but there is far more that remains unexplained, and it is hubris to believe that humankind understands almost everything about the way the universe works.

The New Skeptics also tend to misuse Occam's Razor. Occam's Razor is a rule of thumb that is meant to guide the scientific method. It is often given as "Do not needlessly multiply entities in your hypotheses." More informally, it has been stated as "When you hear hooves think horses, not zebras." They will often claim that the principle of Occam's Razor says that a world with gods and spiritual forces and physical forces is more complicated and therefore less likely than a world with just physical forces, so it therefore argues in favor of materialistic positivism. There are a number of things wrong with this argument. One is that it is based on the unspoken assumption that gods and spiritual forces are physical in some way, and take away from the physical forces by their very existence, as with Dawkins' argument about how if the gods created the world than physics could not have. This does not apply to polytheistic philosophies Even if the gods and the spiritual forces are assumed to have physical reality, then this argument from Occam's Razor is still premature. To draw this conclusion it would be necessary to have a complete understanding of a materialistic physics, as well as one that incorporates the spiritual. Only then can they be compared for complexity. To compare them while knowing nothing about them is just whistling past the graveyard. Then there is the fact that Occam's Razor is just a rule of thumb. It does not hold some transcendent logical status. Often, the real world is more complicated than the simplest explanation. Sometimes, the sound of galloping is being made by zebras. This is another rule of thumb for using the scientific method: Hickam's Dictum.

The Socratic Paradox

In Plato's *Apology*, he records Socrates as saying, of a man he had been conversing with, that "I am wiser than this man, for neither of us appears to know anything great and good; but he fancies he knows something, although he knows nothing; whereas I, as I do not know anything, so I do not fancy I do. In this trifling particular, then, I appear to be wiser than he, because I do not fancy I know what I do not know." From this the so-called Socratic paradox, to know that one knows nothing, has entered Western philosophy. It means that it is important to be as aware of the limits of one's own knowledge as possible, and to not arrogantly claim to know things that one is ignorant of.

The Dawkins crowd is right about one thing. There is a lot of damage being done by certain kinds of religious belief, such as various popular forms of fundamentalism, because of their antagonism toward science and rational thought. However, there are a variety of ways to handle this problem without taking the extreme and unwarranted position that the New Skeptics do. Socrates points the way.

Modern Polytheistic Philosophy and Science

Modern polytheism has so far avoided the problems created by fundamentalism largely because of its philosophy. Modern polytheists tend to see the world with many of the philosophies of the ancient polytheists. A form of Cartesian dualism is popular. Animism is also popular. Monistic idealism is also widespread, if less common than the other two. Each of these philosophies has something in common, however: it accepts, and even embraces, rational thought and the methods of science. Because many modern polytheists do not see significant overlap or competition between the physical and the spiritual, modern polytheistic belief is perfectly consistent with science. Many modern polytheists and atheistic materialists will agree about virtually everything, aside from some largely irrelevant philosophical details.

Modern polytheists do not claim to have a monopoly on truth, as both Christian fundamentalists and the New Skeptics do. Instead, modern polytheistic philosophy tends to embrace Socrates' admonishment, and we acknowledge that there are limits to our knowledge. We can read a cosmologist's account of the Big Bang, and feel that we have a good idea of how the universe came into being. We can then read the *Gylfaginning*'s account of the creation of the world out of the magic void Ginnungagap, with the aid of the gods, and feel that we have learned patterns of understanding the world that can inform our other lives in other ways. By putting ourselves into the frame of mind of the ancients who told those stories, we can see the world through their eyes, and learn important things about our own world because of it. We see the laws of physics as running the material world, while the doings of the gods dominate the spiritual world, which often reflects or parallels the material one in new and enlightening ways.

The Dawkins Problem

The New Skeptics hold a privileged place in the debate on science, religion, and philosophy. Because they claim to "speak for science," and to be free from bias, they have a louder voice, and are paid more attention, than they would be otherwise. This has an effect on the way the larger culture sees these matters, and the effect has been to hold back the progress of human understanding in a number of important ways.

For example, not all internal, subjective, irrational mental experiences are rejected by the New Skeptics. The eureka moment is used, admired by, and even sought after by scientists of all sorts. The sudden flash of inspiration, like being struck by a bolt of lightning, carries valuable information, and a great many of science's most important theories were born in just such a flash. Many scientists have found the answers to difficult problems they worked on in dreams. Of course, scientists are hardly the only ones who benefit from revelatory dreams and eureka moments. Artists, writers, musicians, and more all depend on these things to a significant degree.

The trouble is that they are mostly random, however. They come, or do not, on their own schedule, not when they are desired. Does this have to be the case, though? There is good reason to think that it does not. Many pagan practices, as well as those of Buddhism and certain other religions, are geared toward creating ecstatic experiences that can trigger flashes of revelation. What could modern science become if those practicing it understood such matters as the eureka moment and revelatory dreams well enough to use them as tools instead of hoping for them as gifts? Could the tools of spiritual and religious practices such as these be turned into an effective modern science of the mind that can give greater control over the eureka moment? The Dawkins crowd has effectively shut down all debate or research into such matters, though.

Then there is the matter of intellectual rigor. The majority of human thought occurs at a subconscious level, with the subconscious mind sifting through past experiences and intellectual understandings to come up with relevant ideas. If the mind is filled with unscientific thoughts that are passed off as scientific ones, and positive statements about reality that are not necessarily true, then the mind becomes full of false, clouded thoughts that impair thinking processes, and reduce the likelihood of producing the best results. Adhering strictly to Socrates' advice is more intellectually rigorous, and will produce more rational, truly scientific minds.

Then there are a number of obscure, but interesting lines of scientific inquiry that could result from abandoning the pseudoscientific extremism of the New Skeptics. For example, Dawkins' own theory of memetics suggests that there could very well be something more to the idea of gods than he suspects. After all, if some forms of information are essentially self-propagating, might it not be possible there could exist actual intelligent, memetic organisms that are "embodied" in thousands or even millions of human minds? Each person in a culture-group might form something like a single cell in a much larger, archetypal group mind that has its own will and awareness, that each person is as blind to as each brain cell is blind to the existence of the mind. There are many lines of useful scientific investigation that could be more easily carried out with a less extreme philosophical position than Dawkins advocates.

Conclusion

There is surprisingly little discussion of religious philosophy in modern polytheism. While it might seem to some like this is useless intellectual indulgence, it has some genuine importance. The basic assumptions we make, our fundamental beliefs, shape everything else that follows after. Those who view the gods as Jungian archetypes see the world, and practice their religion, in a very different way than those who believe in the literal existence of the gods. These differences have real world repercussions in the ways that different groups of pagans interact.

Materialistic positivists make a mistake when they try to claim that they know for a fact that everything is really physical. They are making an assumption, a guess, for which there is no evidence, for which there can never be any evidence, and trying to pass it off as a fact. Instead, it is better to observe Socrates' famous dictum. It is better to not pretend to knowledge that one does not possess, instead simply saying "I know that I don't know."

Because many modern polytheists do not know enough to say that one religion is true and the others are false, they do not claim that any religious belief is false. As a consequence of this, many modern polytheists accept all religious beliefs as provisionally true, at least until better evidence one way or another is provided. Therefore, modern polytheists can believe in Odin and the gods of Valhalla, and also believe that Jesus died for their sins. Along with these beliefs they can believe that there is one true god, and Mohammed is his prophet, and that the Buddha was enlightened and that Lao Tzu achieved great comprehension of the Tao. A modern polytheist has no problem believing in the lwa, and the orisha. They can even believe the atheists are correct, and that the flying spaghetti monster is real. Modern polytheistic philosophy is nothing if not adaptive.

Wayland Skallagrimsson has been involved in Northern Tradition religion for decades, and is the author of several books on the subject, including *Heathenry: A Study of Asatru in the Modern World* and *New Edda*. An Odinist, Tribalist, and Adaptive Reconstructionist, he believes in taking the best elements of the old religion and adapting them in a way that makes sense for the modern world but keeps the spirit and principles of the ancient one. His website is www.uppsala online.com. He has taken postgraduate classes in physics, and has had an extensive education in philosophy.

Hearing the Roar of Godzilla:
Looking for the Gods in Pop Culture

VIRGINIA CARPER

Enamored of technology and disassociated from the ancient myths, Pop Culture Pagans prefer creating their own Gods from popular culture. According to their theology, religions (and therefore, Gods) are invented. By examining, The Green Hornet, The Shadow, "Lucky" Luciano, and Godzilla, the article demonstrates how the Gods actually interact with pop culture icons. Modern mythmaking does allow for the Gods to enter the human realm. The issue then becomes for polytheists is how to discern this and the Gods in their modern guises. The issue remains for Pop Culture Pagans is why they should let go of their anthropocentric world view, and seek the Gods.

Pop Culture Pagans feel an intense attachment to popular culture and technology, and none to nature. Since they feel disenchanted with old myths, these Pagans prefer the stories of popular culture. In fact, they identify with various pop culture heroes, that they will often regard them as Gods.

This is problematic for me since people connect with the Gods and Ancestors through nature, myths, and detachment from technology. Can Pop Culture Pagans discover the Gods if they distain the natural world? Since they have rejected the old myths, will they ever know the Gods? The Gods will come into this world when They find some benefit in doing so. Have the Gods entered pop culture? If so, in what way? Finally, will Pop Culture Pagans hear the call of the Gods?

I. THE WORLD ACCORDING TO POP CULTURE PAGANS

Religions are Invented
Various Pop Culture Pagans classify the Gods as archetypes or products of human imagination. Most claim that all religions are invented. Because humans need something to believe in, they create their own Gods. Therefore, popular characters ranging from the Batman to Dr. Who could be Gods.

Investing their emotional energy into fictional characters, many Pop Culture Pagans belong to fandoms, writing stories about their favorite. With their fanfiction, the fans shape the "canon" set up by the author. To me, this reflects the Roman concept of *fanaticus*, belonging to a *fanum*—a shrine. In ancient Rome, *fanatici* were usually devotees of an ecstatic cult. By being *fanatici*, Pop Culture Pagans treat their fictional heroes as Gods, and their beliefs about them as a religion.

Gods Are Created

Pop Culture Pagans have several theories on how Gods are created from fictional characters. The Multiverse Theory[1] and the Law of Finite Senses[2] says that everything exists whether people can prove it or not. Sometimes when creating a story, an author will unknowingly tap into another universe thereby bringing back a God-form. The Law of Personal Universes[3] states that everyone has a singular reality based on their own perceptions. Therefore each person adds their interpretation to the author's God-form, and together form a body of work. This becomes "canon" for the believers of the God-form in this universe.

Pop Culture Pagans see this relationship as an organic system of energy shaping. Pop culture magician Taylor Ellwood says that "Pop Culture reflects the energy and spirit of today's society, rather than one of limited process to yesteryear of something disconnected from one's own reality."[4] Pop culture also shapes a Pop Culture Pagan's ideas about existing entities. Therefore the Norse Gods Loki and Thor become the Marvel Comics Loki and Thor, and are revered in those forms.

Pop Culture Pagans also elevate pop culture idols such as David Bowie to Godhood. Their practice differs from the traditional Polytheistic one of discovering divinity amongst the Mighty Dead. Polytheists have various means of divining to determine the will of the Gods concerning the dead person. In contrast, Pop Culture Pagans believe that the power of human thought is strong enough that paying homage to an idol like Elvis will raise him. Therefore, "hero worship" can confer divinity.

---

[1] *The Multiverse Theory*: The string theory of physics states that: "Our universe is not the only but many universes exist parallel to each other." Pop Culture Pagans interpret this as "There are a myriad of universes in which fictional characters may be Gods." Since a multiverse opens the possibilities for absolutely everything, everything exists.

[2] *Law of Finite Senses*: Because humans have limitations, they can only perceive little outside of their five senses. Simply because someone cannot feel, see, or touch something does not mean that it is not real. This law and other laws of magic comes from the published writings of P.E.I. Bonewits (1949-2010), founder of Ar nDraiocht Fein (ADF).

[3] P.E.I. Bonewits.

[4] Greene, Heather, "A Look at Pop Culture Magick." The Wild Hunt, 19 July 2015. Web.

II. SEEKING THE GODS IN POPULAR CULTURE

The Acheulian Goddess and The Green Hornet

When I first constructed an altar for the Acheulian Goddess, She gave me specific requests of what She wanted for her sacred space. One of her desires was an action figure of The Green Hornet of the 1966 TV show. This confused me since this character was originally an invention of three men for a 1930s radio show.

An ancient Goddess from Paleolithic times, the Acheulian Goddess was first worshipped by *Homo erectus* (the predecessor to modern humans and Neanderthals). Because many generations of the human species have known Her, I wondered why such an ancient Goddess would want a fictional character of the 20th century in her shrine.

To know this Goddess, I have had to side-step a popular notion among Pagans that human society was a matriarchy until it was overthrown by warriors on horseback. I have also had to ignore the pervasive idea that the Acheulian Goddess is only one aspect of the Great Goddess. Today, lost in Goddess worship, She becomes yet another symbol of the fabled past.

To know Her means stripping away modernistic thinking. To see the Acheulian Goddess as *Homo erectus* does requires letting go of the present. As L.P. Hartley noted in his novel *The Go-Between:* "The Past is a foreign country, they do things differently there." To me, She is the Goddess of the Beginnings, the Goddess who appeared in the dreams of *Homo erectus.* To them, She was the Keeper of Mysteries of Life and Death.

Meanwhile, The Green Hornet was created in 1936 by Fran Striker and James Jewell to complement WXYZ's (Detroit) radio program *The Lone Ranger.* Station manager George Trendle requested that The Green Hornet be a continuation of The Lone Ranger. He wanted to carry this character's mission in the Old West into modern times. Therefore, Striker created Britt Reid (The Green Hornet) to be a grandnephew of John Reid (The Lone Ranger). Paralleling The Lone Ranger's Tonto and Silver, this new character had Kato, an Asian sidekick, and Black Beauty, a super-powered car. Britt Reid, who is a newspaper publisher, would pretend to be a mobster to fight crime. Unlike John Reid, Britt would have a public life as himself.

What made The Green Hornet an enduring part of pop culture is his unique character. As a tripartite being, Britt Reid is a crusading publisher, criminal master mind, and a secret warrior for justice. In his triune role, The Green Hornet is devoted to repairing relations amongst people, communities, and authorities. This aspect of The Green Hornet made me think that he is more than simply a fictional character. The triune aspect of divinity shows up in various religions.

Writing for NOW Comics (1989-1990), Ron Fortier devised a family tree

[167]

for the character starting with The Lone Ranger continuing through various generations until the 1990s.[5] Fortier cemented the canon that The Green Hornet was not a single man, but instead a family obligation for the male relatives of the Reid family. Fortier set up that The Green Hornet of the 1930s was the original grandnephew, and that the TV version (1966-67) was that Britt Reid's nephew. NOW Comics continued with the generations into the 21st Century.[6]

In Roman polytheism, families devoted themselves to inter-generational rites of piety to specific Gods. For Romans, *sacra gentilicia* (rites of a clan for their family Gods) were necessary and imperishable. Sometimes a family had a duty to perform public rites (*sacra publica*) on behalf of the Roman people (*sacra pro popula*). When Fortier constructed his family tree, he instituted a web of family obligations for the entire Reid family that went beyond *sacra gentilicia*, and became *sacra publica*. Devoted to the cause of justice in their community, the Reid family became the intermediaries between the people and the authorities.

Through Fortier's actions, The Green Hornet became *sacer*, a thing given to the Gods. He went beyond the nascent obligation set up by the original creators of granduncle and grandnephew. This made the duty of The Green Hornet *res divina*, a divine thing.[7] What occurred was the personification of *pietas*, the maintaining of right relations between people, the Gods, and authorities.

Using divination, I asked the Roman Gods what was The Green Hornet. They said that he was an example of *pietas*, both as an individual and as a family. The Gods gave the thoughtform agency to become a *sacerdos*, a priest.

The request by the Acheulian Goddess for The Green Hornet for her altar meant to me that She claimed him as her own. To Her, he ably demonstrated *sacra publica*. I concluded is that The Green Hornet is probably the *rex sacrorum* (King of Sacred Things) to Her.[8] I believe that the Acheulian Goddess relates to modern humans through what is familiar to Her. Therefore, The Green Hornet acts as the *rex sacrorum*, an intermediary for Her. (Since Roman Polytheists have protocols for integrating non-Roman Gods into their practice, I have chosen to

---

[5] Fortier wanted to connect the various versions of The Green Hornet into a holistic narrative. Desiring to update the character, he worked on retaining the essence of The Green Hornet.

[6] After the demise of NOW Comics, Dynamite Entertainment obtained the rights to the character. In 2010, for the debut of the character at Dynamite Entertainment, Kevin. Smith, noted film-maker and writer, started with the TV version, updated him to the 1980s, and then had his son Britt Reid, Jr. be The Green Hornet for the 21st Century.

[7] Ancient Romans divided the world into two spheres—*res publica* (affairs of the public) and *res divinae* (affairs of the Gods.) In his many writings, Varro theorized that the mythic writings (theology) of poets were *res divinae*.

[8] The office of *rex sacrorum* was established by the Roman Republic to carry out the former Roman king's religious duties.

venerate the Acheulian Goddess in a Roman framework.)

The Green Hornet proves that a longstanding character of pop culture can become more than simply "fictional" without becoming a God as such. Fortier's canon allowed The Green Hornet to be the representation of *pietas*. Afterwards, the Acheulian Goddess chose him to be a part of her veneration.

The Morrigan and The Shadow

Noted Pagan author Morgan Daimler writes that the Irish Goddess The Morrigan is an active force in the world today, appearing in many forms. For me, the voice of The Morrigan comes through the character of The Shadow of popular fiction. I believe that the creator of The Shadow, Walter Gibson, channeled her Voice in writing his stories. Although Gibson created this character in 1930, other writers have continued his legacy. The Shadow remains the Dark Master of Justice much like The Morrigan is the Sovereign Queen.

Often referred to as The Triple Goddess, The Morrigan has three major aspects. She is Morrigu, the Goddess of Battle, Macha, Goddess of Sovereignty, and Badb, the Goddess of Prophecy. As the Goddess of Battle, The Morrigan rouses her warriors for the fight. Shaking her spear, She calls all to war, promising victory for some, but death for many. As the Great Queen, The Morrigan is the personification of sovereignty. In this aspect, She inspires the people to defend their homes and then incites them to go to war as well. As the Goddess of Prophecy, The Morrigan appears as the Washer of the Ford. Often seen washing clothes in a river, She predicts who will die in battle by handling their bloody garments.

Walter Gibson (1897-1985) wrote his many stories in a fugue state. In interviews, he spoke of writing fifteen hours a day for days on end until his fingers bled. Frank Eisgruber, Jr. writes in *Gangland's Doom* that Gibson often based his stories on where he was, what the publisher wanted, and what was happening at the time. However, I think that Gibson actually channeled the Voice of The Morrigan in his stories. Orson Welles in his radio version and various comic book writers over time expanded upon Her Presence in their stories of The Shadow as "the Dark Avenger."

Who is The Shadow? He has a tripartite identity as the human Kent Allard, the stolen identity of Lamont Cranston, and the Dark Instrument of Fate. As Kent Allard, he is the Dark Eagle, an air ace of World War I. Later in Central Asia, Allard was a warlord who vied for supremacy in the opium trade. Sometime during his warlord days, he entered a monastery, and later emerged as The Shadow.

After he fakes his death in Central America, The Shadow goes to New York City. When he arrives, The Shadow steals the identity of Lamont Cranston, a wealthy socialite. He uses Cranston's social position to gain entrance into the city's inner circle of power. After Cranston confronts The Shadow, he is frightened into co-operating with The Shadow's plans.

Since he has a preternatural power over people's destinies, The Shadow refers to himself as the "Weird Avenger of Fate." Gibson first referred to The Shadow with that title, which later became canon for other writers. The Shadow's use of "weird" is in the sense of the "weird witches" of Shakespeare's *Macbeth*.[9] The Shadow knows who has to die, who to kill, who to redeem, and who to make work for him, just as various myths say of The Morrigan.

Gibson discussed his philosophy in writing fiction: "You must treat the character as a discovery rather than your own creation. Treat him not just seriously, but profoundly."[10] Street and Smith, the publisher, had featured The Shadow a year earlier in another pulp fiction story. They assigned Gibson to flesh the character out for a new magazine series. Writing as rapidly as he could, Gibson came up with an uncanny and nebulous figure, who moved mysteriously in and out of people's lives. In a physical sense, The Shadow was a black cloaked man who could fade into the darkness. Gibson always regarded The Shadow as remote and aloof, which gives credence to this character being channeled from outside of himself.

How is The Shadow the same as The Morrigan? Since he possesses a deep core of darkness and moral ambiguity within himself, The Shadow "knows what evil lurks in the hearts of men." Michael Uslen (noted comic book writer and executive producer of Batman/Dark Knight movies) contrasts The Shadow with other pulp fiction characters. He points out, "The Avenger seeks Justice. He tends to define it according to the law. *The Shadow defines Justice the way he himself chooses, making him judge, jury, and executioner. He finds a chasm of difference between 'Justice' and 'the Law.'* (Emphasis mine.) Doc Savage is trying to operate above such ideologies. He is out for the common good of mankind with little regards for countries... and whose justice or whose laws.... *The Shadow kills.* The Avenger does not. Doc avoids it."[11] Glimpsing into the character of The Shadow, The Morrigan emerges.

Because Gibson strove to treat his characters profoundly, he reached into the Mythic realm where the Gods dwell. Using his fugue state, The Morrigan shaped Gibson's writing. By inhabiting The Shadow, The Morrigan speaks to modern people. The divinity that Pop Culture Pagans sense in The Shadow is The Morrigan Herself.

Marduk and Luciano

According to criminal historians, Charles "Lucky" Luciano (1897-1962, Sicilian) had an "other-worldly allure" that made him noteworthy. Arnold

---

[9] The use of *wyrd* ("weird," in this case) is the Anglo-Saxon concept of a person's fate at it overlaps the fates of others.

[10] Will Murray, "Out of the Shadows," *The Shadow*, 61.

[11] "JUSTICE, INC Is Inked for August." Comic Vine. 9 June 2014. Web.

Rothstein (1882-1928), known as "Mr. Big," took Luciano under his tutelage and mentored him. During the Castellammarese War,[12] he belonged to both of the rival gangs at the same time. Long after his deportation from the United States, his peers still recognized him as "The Chairman of the Mob."

What did Luciano do to achieve fan status? By organizing the major criminal gangs of the United States into a national organization, he changed American life. His creation, the National Commission, employed its power to determine elections, circumvent law enforcement, make businesses pay for markets, and force invisible taxes on consumers.

Luciano's aura of glamour (magic) still draws people to him even after his death. Considered to be the archetypal gangster, he is the model for many well-known characters of movies and TV. In his biography of Luciano, Tim Newark say that the closest depiction of Luciano's character and prominence was Michael Corleone of *The Godfather* book and movies.

In exploring Luciano's impact on American culture, crime historian Christian Cipollini notes that people often live vicariously through gangsters. "Good or bad there always going to be fans of Lucky. He may not be a household name...but he has fans," explains David Brooks, who owns The American Gangsters, a T-shirt company.[13] Did this adoration of Luciano make him a God after death?

Information about the status of Luciano after death came from Marduk of Fifty Names, Patron God of Babylon. Since Marduk saw Luciano's rise to power similar to His Own, He made Luciano his servant. As the Servant of Marduk, Luciano has been allowed to hold several *mes*. (*Mes* are the properties or powers of Gods to enable civilization to exist.) The *mes* that are allotted to Luciano are Fear, Terror, Kingship, and Prostitution.

Adopting the creation myth from the Sumerians, the Babylonians rewrote it to include the rulership of Marduk. When Tiamat wages war on Them, Enki and Enlil cede their power to Marduk by granting "Enlil-ship" to Him. Meanwhile, the other Gods confer on Him the power of Anu, another preeminent deity. After that, Marduk defeats Tiamat, and becomes the head of the Gods of Mesopotamia.

In the *Enuma Elish*, the Babylonians acknowledge their predecessors, but they end with Marduk recreating the world. He does this by building the world on the bones of Tiamat. The historical context of this creation myth is that other peoples (including the Sumerians) fought to rule Mesopotamia before the coming of the Babylonians. By ending the constant warfare, the Babylonians

---

[12] The conflict of Guiseppe (Joe) Masseria (1886-1931) and Salvatore Maranzano (1886-1931) was referred to as the "Castellammarese War of 1930-1931," since both bosses were from there.

[13] Christian Cipollini, *Lucky Luciano*, p. 102.

established law and order in the region. Mesopotamia was recreated into a Babylonian construct.

At first glance, the pairing of the activities of American mobsters in the 1920s and 1930s to the Creation Epic of the Babylonians seems absurd. But both involve the overthrow of the old order, a period of disarray, and finally the establishment of the new order. Furthermore, there are subtle similarities. The New York City underworld before Luciano was ruled by two Sicilian bosses—Joe Masseria and Salvatore Maranzano. Like Tiamat and Apsu, these two bosses spawn other bosses, who chafe under their rule. The war between the two finally ends when Luciano kills them both, and recreates the Mob as his own construct.

In both, new groups of peoples move in to replace the original groups. This is implied in the Babylonian epic by the superimposed pantheons within it. In New York's underworld, Rothstein, who is Jewish, is the middle generation of bosses.[14] Like Anu, Rothstein takes the next generation under his wing. He grooms the mixed ethnic group of Luciano, Frank Costello (Calabrian), Meyer Lansky (Russian Jew), and Bugsy Siegel (Ukrainian Jew) to be the future bosses.[15]

Caught between Masseria and Maranzano fighting for supremacy, Luciano decides that the old way of doing things has to end. After Rothstein is murdered, Luciano plots to kill both bosses. As part of his plan, he convinces Maranzano to let Masseria think that he won their war. After assuring Masseria of his "ultimate victory," Luciano murders him. Watching Maranzano, the new "Boss of Bosses" (*Capo di tutti capi*), divide the underworld of New York City into the Five Families,[16] Luciano sees how to organize the other bosses into a cohesive group.

After killing Maranzano, Luciano meets with the crime bosses from all over the United States. He explains that the underworld will be run nationally by a commission of bosses, with the head elected by them. Of course, they choose Luciano, who, like Marduk, establishes a new order. These two stories dissimilar in many ways, Luciano's rise and the Babylonian Creation Epic, nevertheless echo each other.

Luciano's elevation to divinity is the result of many factors. He already

---

[14] Arnold Rothstein had a stranglehold on the drug trade, the rackets, and underworld finance. As a Jew, he made significant inroads in ending power of the ruling Irish gangs. In the 1920s, the power base in the underworld was transitioning from the Irish to the Jews, and finally to the Italians.

[15] Their actual names were: Charles Luciano: Salvatore Lucania, Frank Castello: Francesco Castiglia, Meyer Lansky: Meier Suchowlanski, and Bugsy Siegel: Benjamin Siegel.

[16] The Five Families still govern the underworld in New York City. These are the original families as set-up by Maranzano.

possessed a sense of latent divinity. With his "glamour," he did "mighty deeds" that drew the attention of Marduk. In addition, many humans regarded Luciano as a culture hero. Luciano's semi-divine status is in line with traditional polytheistic practices, since the Gods raised him.

Godzilla[17]

Mention Godzilla, and images of a reptilian monster, stomping around, incinerating entire cities comes to mind. How did this fictional monster[18] become regarded by the Japanese as akin to a *Kami* (God)? Was he created as Pop Culture Pagans believe or was it something else?

In the original 1954 movie, "*Godzilla*," Godzilla is awakened by nuclear testing near his island. The radiation from the atomic bomb mutates the dinosaur into a nearly indestructible monster, who tries to destroy Tokyo with a radioactive ray. The movie, according to articles by the director Ishiro Honda (1911-1993), and special effects master Eiji Tsuburaya (1901-1970), centered on Japan's trauma of World War II. The monster himself symbolized what happened to Hiroshima, Nagasaki, and later Bikini Island. Furthermore, the composer Akira Ifukube (1914-2006) was told by Honda that Godzilla was a child of the atomic bomb.

During the intervening years in pop culture, the depiction of Godzilla changed from being a purely destructive force to becoming both an ally and enemy of humans. Still dangerous, he is helpful in defeating invading monsters, but also destructive in destroying cities. Unpredictable and uncontrollable, Godzilla now stands as the protector of humanity and the agent of destruction. In the process, this fictional monster has become an enduring character, beloved by his fans. Sixty years later after his debut, Godzilla is still popular as ever.

Akira Takarada, who starred in the original movie, explained why people feel empathy for Godzilla. "If Godzilla were truly evil, people wouldn't have loved him so much. We were the ones responsible for triggering Godzilla's violence."[19] Raymond Burr (1917-1993), who starred in the U.S. version of "*Godzilla*" and later "*Godzilla 1985*," said "I think Godzilla is a marvelous human creature...Godzilla came to be because we were using nuclear power badly. I'm sure Godzilla was trying to warn the world."[20]

Allen A. Debus, who examines dinosaurs in popular culture, says that

---

[17] The original Japanese movie and name for Godzilla is *Gojira*, which means "gorilla-whale." I will refer to both as Godzilla.

[18] The Japanese refer to Godzilla as a *Dai Kaiju* (a large mythic creature). English translates this term as "big monster."

[19] Peter Brothers, *Atomic Dreams and The Nuclear Nightmare*. p. 165.

[20] The U.S. version was titled: *Godzilla: King of the Monsters* (1956). Peter Brothers, *Atomic Dreams and The Nuclear Nightmare*. p. 188.

Godzilla is the "Modern Prometheus"—immortal and godlike. Godzilla is nature violated, struggling to purify his world. The film critic for the *San Francisco Chronicle*, G. Allen Johnson wrote, "Godzilla isn't just The Bomb—he's hate and anger, war, the poisoned environment—in short, he is mankind itself, the destruction wrought by the rage with in us."[21] Tomoyuki Tanaka (1910-1997), who produced several of the Godzilla movies, said that Godzilla is the "Nightmare created out of the darkness of the human soul. He is the sacred beast of the apocalypse."[22] In an interview with Mark Schaefer of *Penny Blood* in 2004, Shogo Tomiyama, another producer of Godzilla movies after Honda's death, emphasized that Godzilla was closer to being a *Kami* than simply a movie monster. A "God of Destruction" was how he referred to Godzilla.

In Shintoism, *Kami* are Gods (and Spirits), who live in the Mythic realm, parallel to this one. When the boundary between the Mythic and the human realms are broken (usually through pollution or disrespect), a *Kami* will cross over. Since Godzilla was created by nuclear testing, the ultimate pollution, he comes like a *Kami*, seeking the restoration of his Earth. By interacting with the Mythic realm, his creators (Honda, Tanaka, and Tsuburaya) subconsciously brought Godzilla over into this realm.[23]

III. THE "ENSOULED WORD"

In discussing the spiritual properties of writing, Nonfiction writer Stephen Harrod Buhner says that words are inhabited by a "soul force," a living meaning. When a writer is completely immersed in the imaginal world, this soul force will pass through the writer into the reader. Modern writers such as Robert Bly spoke of meeting the Presences who inhabit the realm beyond this one. Poet Robert Frost (1874-1963) believed that his poetry was a direct living expression of myth, since he facilitated a conversation between his readers and the Sacred.

This occurred with the creators of The Green Hornet, The Shadow, and Godzilla. In each case, their writings were directed by the Gods. When each transcended this realm, the Gods seized them and shaped their thoughts. This is the process of myth making.

What of Luciano, an actual person? Because of his glamour and notoriety,

---

[21] Peter Brothers, *Atomic Dreams and The Nuclear Nightmare*. p. 225.

[22] Allen A. Debus, *Prehistoric Monsters*.

[23] Animal communicator and writer, Dawn Brunke wrote about a polar bear who was dreaming of her, as she was dreaming of him. Investigating further, she realized that the Polar Bear was from the Mythic realm. As the two dreamed together, they crossed worlds. Meanwhile, in *Drawing Down the Spirits*, Kenaz Filan and Raven Kaldera relate the story of Garnet, a Wiccan priestess. She said that her former High Priestess brought forth a trickster, "Sulu," through writing *Star Trek* fanfiction.

he became an object of "hero worship." In his research, Cipollini noted the many myths surrounding Luciano, and concluded that each tale added to his mythos as "The Chairman of the Mob." The stories had overtaken the actual history. Meanwhile, Marduk took note of Luciano, and made him one of his servants.

IV. CONCLUSION

Henry Corbin (1903-1978), French philosopher and theologian, said that people in the West are trained to be agnostics. Western education in the West insists that myths are only superstition, outside the linear and logical (i.e. real) world. Corbin said that the first impulse of Western people is the *agnostic reflex*, which hampers their ability to acknowledge anything outside of the sciences. The objects of imagination, in particular, are dissolved in accord with the demands of a transparent rationality.

Robert Bly decries modern education which encourages everyone to remain in the civilized logical world. American society encourages and rewards flatness. People are forced into the "statistical mentality" where objectivism dwells. He adds that people are taught to "spend their vital energy defending themselves from the godlike furnace that is cooking inside them."

Pop Culture Pagans are wrong about fictional characters being Gods, since most of these characters exist only for media consumption. Sometimes a character will have elements of divinity, if the writer actively entered the Imaginal world and established dialogue between the Gods and the consumer. There are Gods in pop culture but not in the way that Pop Culture Pagans believe.

Living in an anthropocentric world, Pop Culture Pagans sense only echoes of themselves in technology and modern culture. If they let go of their preconceptions, they will understand what postmodernist William Burroughs (1914-1997) said: "In the magical universe, there are no coincidences and there are no accidents."[24] Then they will hear the Roar of Godzilla, and find the Gods.

Works Used

Adkins, Lesley and Roy Adkins, *Dictionary of Roman Religion.* Oxford University Press: New York. 1996.

Ashcroft-Nowicki, Dolores and J.H. Brennan, *Magical Use of Thought Forms.* Llewellyn: Woodbury (MN). 2001.

Black, Jeremy and Anthony Green, *Gods, Demons and Symbols of Ancient Mesopotamia.* University of Texas Press: Austin. 2014.

---

[24] Stephen Buhner, *Ensouling Language*, p. 209.

Blair, Nancy, *Amulets of the Goddess*. Wingbow Press: Oakland (CA). 1993.

Brothers, Peter, *Atomic Dreams and the Nuclear Nightmare: The Making of GODZILLA (1954)*. Self-published: Seattle. 2015.

Brown, Nimue, *Pagan Dreams*. Moon Books: Washington (USA). 2015.

Brunke, Dawn, *Dreaming with Polar Bears*.Bear & Company: Rochester (VT). 2014.

Buhner, Stephen Harrod, *Ensouling Language*. Inner Traditions: Rochester (VT). 2010.

Carlin, Emily, "Questions on Pop Culture Paganism." *Magic Under the Black Sun*. 25 May 2015. Web. http://blacksunmagick.blogspot.com/2015/05/questions-on-pop-culture-paganism.html <accessed 18 February 2016>.

Carmody, Isolde, "Poems of the Morrigan." *Story Archaeology Podcast*. 2013. Web. http://storyarchaeology.com/poems-of-the-morrigan/, <accessed 15 February 2016>.

Cawthorne, Nigel, *Mafia: The History of the Mob*. Arcturus: London. 2012.

Cipollini, Christian, *Lucky Luciano: Mysterious Tales of a Gangland Legend*. Strategic Media: Rock Hill, SC. 2014.

Daimler, Morgan, *The Morrigan*. Moon Books: Washington, U.S. 2014.

Debus, Allen A., *Prehistoric Monsters: The Real and Imagines Creatures of the Past That We Love to Fear*. McFarland & Company: London. 2009.

Eisgruber, Frank, Jr., *Gangland's Doom*. Altus Press: Boston, 2007.

Filan, Kenaz and Raven Kaldera, *Drawing Down the Spirits*. Destiny Books: Rochester (VT). 2009.

Talking to the Spirits. Destiny Books: Rochester (VT). 2013.

Fortier, Ron, "The Outlaw Hero." *The Green Hornet Casefiles*, Ed. Joe Gentile and Win Scott Eckert. Moonstone Books: Calumet City (IL). 2011. 5-12.

Gibson, Walter, "The Shadow Unmasks." *The Shadow*, Ed. Anthony Tollin. Nostalgia Ventures: San Antonio, TX. 2008. Vol. 15, 4-60.

"Godzilla (Character)." *Comic Vine*. Web. http://comicvine.gamespot.com/godzilla/4005-21599/, <accessed 18 February 2016>.

Greene, Heather, "A Look at Pop Culture Magick." *The Wild Hunt*. 19 July 2015. Web. http://wildhunt.org/2015/07/a-look-at-pop-culture-magick.html, <accessed 18 February 2016>.

"The Green Hornet (Character)." *Comic Vine*. Web. http://comicvine.gamespot.com/the-green-hornet/4005-45127/, <accessed 18 February 2016>.

---, "IREI, The Spirituality of the Japanese." Jinja Honcho (Association of Shinto Shrines). 2011. Web. http://www.jinjahoncho.or.jp/en/image/irei.pdf, <accessed 20 May 2016>.Jacobsen, Thorkild, *The Treasures of Darkness*. Yale University Press: New Haven. 1976.

Jinja Honcho (Association of Shinto Shrines). 2011. Web. http://www.jinjahoncho.or.jp/en/index.html, <accessed 20 May 2016>.

Johnson, Buffie, *Lady of the Beasts*. Inner Traditions: Rochester (VT). 1994.

---, "JUSTICE, INC. Is Inked For August." *Comic Vine*. 9 June 2014. Web. http://www.comicvine.com/articles/justice-inc-is-inked-for-august-updated/1100-148955/, <accessed 15 February 2016>.

Kaldera, Raven, *Dealing with Deities*. Asphodel Press: Hubbardston (MA). 2012.

Lai, Rick, *Chronology of Shadows*. Altus Press: Boston. 2007.

Markale, Jean, *The Great Goddess*. Inner Traditions: Rochester (VT). 1997.

Murray, Will, "Out of the Shadows." *The Shadow*, Ed. Anthony Tollin. Nostalgia Ventures: San Antonio, TX. 2008. Vol. 15, 61-63.

"Writing The Shadow." *The Shadow*, Ed. Anthony Tollin. Nostalgia Ventures: San Antonio, TX. 2008. Vol. 15, 126-128.

Newark, Tim, *Boardwalk Gangster: The Real Lucky Luciano*. Thomas Dunne Books: New York. 2010.

O'Grady, Judith, *Pagan Portals: God Speaking*. Moon Books: Winchester (UK). 2013.

Penry, Tylluan, *Sacred Shadows: Ice Age Spirituality*. The Wolfenhowl Epress: U.K. 2013.

"Pop-Culture Paganism Resources." *Polytheist Community Forum*. 4 February 2015. Web. http://polytheistcommunity.boards.net/thread/150/pop-culture-paganism-resources, <accessed 15 February 2016>.

Ravenna, Morpheus, *The Book of the Great Queen*. Concrescent Press: Richmond (CA). 2014.

Reynolds, Jason, "Re-imagining Dragons: Gojira, Kami, and the Kaiju of Unintended Consequence," *Uroboros*. 16 May 2014. Web. https://uroboros73.wordpress.com/2014/05/16/re-imagining-dragons-godzilla-shintoism-and-the-kaiju-of-unintended-consequences/, <accessed 10 March 2016>.

Schaefer, Mark, "Godzilla Stomps into Los Angeles," *Penny Blood*. 2004. Web. http://web.archive.org/web/20050203181104/http://www.pennyblood.com/godzilla2.html, <accessed 10 March 2016>.

Siren, Christopher, "Sumerian Mythology FAQ." 2000. Web. http://home.comcast.net/~chris.s/sumer-faq.html <accessed 5 February 2016 >.

---, "Soul of Japan." Jinja Honcho (Association of Shinto Shrines). 2013. Web. http://www.jinjahoncho.or.jp/en/image/soul-of-japan.pdf, <accessed 20 May 2016>.

Tiara, Creatrix, "The Pop Culture Pagans Who Draw Power from Tumblr." *Motherboard*. 5 June 2015. Web. http://motherboard.vice.com/read/the-pop-culture-pagans-who-draw-power-from-tumblr, <accessed 5 February 2016 >.

Tinker, Fiona, *Pathworking Through Poetry*. Moon Books: Winchester (UK). 2012.

Triarius, L. Vitellius, *Religio Romana Handbook*. Self-published: Charleston (SC). 2014.

Virginia Carper, a Roman Polytheist, lives in the Washington D.C. area with her family. She is a Dedicant (Roman Hearth) of ADF. Majoring in Divination and Minoring in Lore, She is a Level 5 Student at the Grey School of Wizardry. She has published articles in ADF's *Oak Leaves* and *Walking the Worlds*. Her writings can be found at her blog: *Nature: Observations and Meanings* (http://naturemeanings.blogspot.com), and at *Witches and Pagans* (http://witchesandpagans.com/pagan-culture-blogs/animal-wisdom.html).

Made in the USA
Charleston, SC
04 July 2016